"This book will not tak[...] but it dispels the shado[...] a vision of God's good purposes in our suffering that will evoke praise and thanksgiving."

—**James N. Anderson**, Carl W. McMurray Professor of Theology and Philosophy, Reformed Theological Seminary, Charlotte

"Scott Christensen helpfully answers the age-old problem of evil from Scripture. This book is readable, engaging, devotional, and uplifting for any Christian who needs to find hope in God in the midst of the darkness of this world."

—**Scott Aniol**, Executive Vice President and Editor-in-Chief, G3 Ministries; Professor, Pastoral Theology, Grace Bible Theological Seminary

"A wonderful and accessible treatment of the so-called problem of evil. You will find your heart stirred to worship as you see how God glorifies his own name through every single event of history."

—**Grant Castleberry**, Senior Pastor, Capital Community Church, Raleigh, North Carolina; President, Unashamed Truth Ministries

"With clarity, simplicity, and a devotional flair anchored in the Word of God, Christensen's *Defeating Evil* shows us how and why God uses sin and evil for his greater glory. Read it, and I am confident that you will be blessed!"

—**Jack Hughes**, Pastor-Teacher, Anchor Bible Church, Louisville, Kentucky; author, *Expository Preaching with Word Pictures*

"This is a book that confronts you not only with some strong arguments, but also with the Savior, who alone can solve the problem of evil."

—**Mark Jones**, Senior Minister, Faith Vancouver Presbyterian Church (PCA); Research Associate, University of the Free State, Bloemfontein, South Africa

"It is not hyperbolic to say that every Christian needs to read this book and to search the Scriptures to see whether these things are true. I believe wholeheartedly that they are and that every believer can benefit deeply, mind and spirit, from the contents of this book."
—**Chris McKnight**, Lead Pastor, Kerrville Bible Church, Kerrville, Texas

"I don't know of a better unfolding of the ultimate biblical answer to the problem of evil than Scott's excellent, well-written work."
—**John MacArthur**, Pastor-Teacher, Grace Community Church, Sun Valley, California; Chancellor Emeritus, The Master's University and Seminary

"At once captivating and often soaring, the writing draws the reader into biblical and theological profundities. Here you will find gospel medicine and theological balm for the soul."
—**Hans Madueme**, Associate Professor of Theological Studies, Covenant College

"Not only does this book help answer one of the most difficult questions posed to Christianity, but it also serves as a devotional exercise that puts the glory of God on display. I continue to be thankful for Scott Christensen's heavy-lifting ministry to the church."
—**Nate Pickowicz**, Teaching Pastor, Harvest Bible Church, Gilmanton Iron Works, New Hampshire; author, *Better than Life*

"Here we find a combination that is quite rare: the book is biblically grounded, theologically perceptive, and philosophically astute. Explaining evil in the context of the storyline of the Scriptures is particularly helpful."
—**Thomas R. Schreiner**, James Buchanan Harrison Professor of New Testament Interpretation, The Southern Baptist Theological Seminary

"Jesus the Warrior-Savior is truly the answer that unlocks the problem of evil. This truth sings in these pages, lifting our troubled hearts and minds to God."
—**Owen Strachan**, Provost, Grace Bible Theological Seminary; author, *The Warrior Savior*

"*Defeating Evil* is a biblically faithful gaze into the breathtaking majesty of our sovereign God, who does all things in goodness and wisdom. Christensen's masterly handling of Scripture exalts Christ as the ultimate center of God's future triumph and glory. This book humbled me and helped me."
—**Paul Tautges**, Pastor, Cornerstone Community Church, Cleveland, Ohio; author, *Remade*.

"In a day when sound biblical and theological answers to the problem of evil are wanting, this book fills a huge need. I pray that it will have a wide readership so that the church will be grounded in the truth of God's Word and thus have faithful answers to one of the most difficult questions of Christian theology."
—**Stephen J. Wellum**, Professor of Christian Theology, The Southern Baptist Theological Seminary; editor, *Southern Baptist Journal of Theology*

"Scott Christensen offers us a 'greater-glory theodicy'—a rare and compelling trifecta of a biblically profound, philosophically deep, and pastorally uplifting answer to the problem of evil. But best of all, Christensen offers us an answer centered on Christ—God's ultimate solution to evil."
—**Thaddeus Williams**, Professor of Theology, Biola University and Talbot School of Theology; author, *God Reforms Hearts*

"I don't know of a better place to begin an exploration of 'the problem of evil' than this book. It is precise in its articulation of the problem and of the related biblical teaching, it is robustly informed theologically, it is marvelously Christ-gospel-focused, and it is warmly refreshing to the soul."
—**Fred G. Zaspel**, Pastor, Reformed Baptist Church, Franconia, Pennsylvania; Adjunct Professor, Systematic Theology, The Southern Baptist Theological Seminary

DEFEATING

EVIL

DEFEATING EVIL

How God Glorifies Himself
in a Dark World

Scott Christensen

P&R
PUBLISHING
P.O. BOX 817 • PHILLIPSBURG • NEW JERSEY 08865-0817

Library of Congress Cataloging-in-Publication Data

Names: Christensen, Scott, 1965- author. | Christensen, Scott, 1965- What about evil?
Title: Defeating evil : how God glorifies himself in a dark world / Scott Christensen.
Description: Phillipsburg, New Jersey : P&R Publishing, [2024] | Includes bibliographical references and index. | Summary: "Revised, adapted, and condensed for a broader audience, this companion edition of What about Evil? shows how sin, evil, corruption, and death fit into redemptive history and magnify God's glory"-- Provided by publisher.
Identifiers: LCCN 2023046881 | ISBN 9781629959238 (pbk) | ISBN 9781629959290 (ePub)
Subjects: LCSH: Theodicy. | God (Christianity) | Good and evil--Religious aspects--Christianity.
Classification: LCC BT160 .C462 2024 | DDC 231/.8--dc23/eng/20231106
LC record available at https://lccn.loc.gov/2023046881

To my fellow elders:

Chris, Toby, Murray, Thad, Ken, Carson, and Bernie

*Pressing on toward the goal for the prize of
the upward call of God in Christ Jesus*

CONTENTS

FOREWORD

On August 8, 2023 (just two weeks before I wrote this foreword), a wildfire broke out on the island of Maui, Hawaii, and razed the town of Lahaina to rubble. At the time of writing, over a hundred people have been confirmed to have perished in the fire and almost a thousand more remain missing—making the Maui wildfires the deadliest in the United States since 1918. Many people wonder: "Where is God in all this? Why did God allow this to happen? And why does God allow any calamity to happen at all?" We struggle to make sense of pain, suffering, and death, for these are unnatural intrusions that have stormed the postlapsarian human experience because of the curse. Yet it is this very curse that frames the history of redemption and defines the biblical story.

Perhaps you have evangelized someone who asks something like this: "If God exists—and if he is perfectly good and powerful—then why is there evil in the world?" If answered biblically, questions about the problem of evil can be very fruitful by providing immense apologetic value and ultimately leading to doxology. Many Christians are dissatisfied with theodicies—defenses of divine goodness considering the existence of evil—because many of these theodicies are simply unbiblical. Scott Christensen's work *Defeating Evil* is a welcome change to this unfortunate trend.

You hold in your hands a fine work of theodicy. In his other books, *What about Free Will? Reconciling Our Choices with God's Sovereignty* and *What about Evil? A Defense of God's Sovereign Glory*, Christensen has helped the church understand perennial questions about the relationships between divine sovereignty, human suffering, the existence of evil, and the nature of the will. Here, Christensen has carefully simplified, condensed, refined, and abridged (and sometimes expanded!) *What about Evil?* to produce an accessible edition for a more popular audience. Throughout this work, he grapples with thorny questions such as these: "What is the problem of evil, anyway? If God decrees evil, then is he the author of it? And how do we reconcile human freedom and divine sovereignty?"

Christensen begins by scanning the entire field of theodicy, explaining different ways in which the church has responded to the problem of evil. He gives special attention to the two most influential theodicies ever given by the church—the free-will defense and the greater-good defense. He then proves that debates about theodicy are often extensions of the larger Arminian-Calvinist debate: should the center of gravity in our theological systems (including theodicy) settle on human autonomy or on theocentrism? Christensen's solution is thoroughly theocentric (think Calvinist) rather than anthropocentric (think Arminian). For example, within the context of compatibilism (Christensen happens to write an admirable defense of this position), Christensen insightfully rearranges the greater-good theodicy to propose what he calls the *greater-glory theodicy.*

This should be no surprise, of course, for Christensen's treatment of the problem of evil is thoroughly Reformed, and *soli Deo gloria* is the crux of the Reformed worldview. All of life, including evil itself, exists for the glory of God—somehow. And it is that *somehow* that fascinates Christensen and propels his well-articulated work into fertile areas of exploration.

In writing a theodicy of his own, Christensen grounds what he calls his *biblical theodicy* in the work of Jesus Christ, the metanarrative of Scripture (creation, fall, and redemption), and the attributes of God —particularly his holiness, sovereignty, and goodness. Christensen successfully demonstrates that such a biblical theodicy is grounded in both soteriology and Christology and has profound implications for doxology. The reader finds eschatology here too. For example, Christensen explains how the existence of evil is part of the grand story of what God is doing to restore all things forever. He is careful to move from doxology to praxis. In constructing a biblical theodicy, he shows that the Christian's response to evil in this world is a powerful apologetic tool in shining as lights to unbelievers. In this way, Christensen's treatment is practical, evangelistic, and experiential—uniting the head, the heart, and the hands.

I heartily recommend this God-exalting, well-researched, balanced, engaging, and practical volume. This work ultimately leads the reader to glorify Jesus Christ, for he is the Light who shines in the darkness (John 1:5). May Christensen's (shorter) book on the problem of evil lead you, dear reader, to greater depths of knowledge so that the triune God may receive all glory in your life and for all eternity.

Joel R. Beeke
Chancellor, Professor of Systematic Theology and Homiletics
Puritan Reformed Theological Seminary
Pastor, Heritage Reformed Congregation, Grand Rapids, MI

PREFACE

I spent five years researching and writing *What about Evil? A Defense of God's Sovereign Glory* (P&R Publishing, 2020). The book seeks to address the so-called problem of evil, which has proved to be the thorniest issue that the Christian faith has ever faced. The problem is simply stated. If God is supremely good and powerful, then why is there evil in the world? Since the book came out a few years ago, I could not have predicted how important the topic would become, given the rapidly disintegrating culture that we find ourselves living in.

I have been surprised at the wide and favorable response that the book has received. A number of people have shared with me how their lives have been transformed by its contents. That is deeply humbling to me. I had no idea that it would generate this kind of response. All I can do is to give glory to God because God's glory is precisely what I wanted to highlight in this book.

The most common response I have received concerning *What about Evil?* has been this: "When are you going to write the shorter, more reader-friendly version?" Those who have waded through the 544 pages of the big book have acknowledged that it was a chore—though worth the effort, I hope! Although it was not intended as an academic tome, it does contain a lot of foreign terminology and difficult concepts that most readers are unfamiliar with. It is a subject that will certainly tax one's brainpower. And while I encourage *anyone* who is up to the challenge to tackle the bigger book, I also realize the tremendous value of having a smaller, more accessible volume to introduce a wider audience to this important subject.

With that background, I introduce *Defeating Evil*. Much of the basic material is the same as in *What about Evil?*, just in condensed form. I have minimized technical language and simplified concepts. This book contains far fewer footnotes. Other illustrations and subject matter have been added or expanded where appropriate, and I have tried to emphasize more practical concerns. Nonetheless, this is still largely a work of theology and exposition of Scripture because I believe the issue demands that we think theologically and biblically about it. Prayerfully, this will lead to the best practical application.

I have more people than I can count to thank for encouraging me in the writing of this shorter book. I want to thank the members of my Sunday school class at Kerrville Bible Church, who served as taste-testers for the material I present here. I also thank those who have invited me to speak on this subject in numerous podcasts and church conferences. The comments and interactions in all these venues have helped to sharpen my thinking, as I hope is reflected in the present work. I also thank the good folks at P&R Publishing who continue to think I should write books! John Hughes and Dave Almack deserve special thanks for this encouragement. Thanks also go out to James N. Anderson for his thorough review of the manuscript and helpful comments, as well as to Karen Magnuson for her excellent editing skills.

Finally, I thank my wife, Jennifer, and my son, Matthew, for putting up with my long hours of writing; my church family, who is a pure joy to serve; and my Lord Jesus Christ, whose grace brightly shines on me. May he be pleased to use this humble offering to help many see the glory of God in the face of evil.

Soli Deo Gloria

1

ENCOUNTERING THE DARKNESS

Untold evils lurk in the ever-present darkness of our disturbed world, a world that is not what it ought to be, a world that is often cold and inhospitable, where pain and suffering seem to be the rule of the day. Consider the story of Louis Zamperini.[1] Louie was a promising young American track champion who ran in the 1938 Berlin Olympics. But the outbreak of World War II brought unimaginable misery to Louie. Drafted as a bombardier, he inexplicably lost control of his B-24 and crashed into the Pacific Ocean. He managed to survive in shark-infested waters for a record forty-seven days before being captured by the Japanese navy. He was transferred to several POW camps over the course of the next twenty-seven months.

Louie's first experience as a POW was to be shoved into a filthy little wooden shack infested with rats, lice, and the stench of human urine and feces. Beatings were regular, and the food was usually leftover slop full of rat droppings and maggots. Scurvy, dysentery, and beriberi were common killers in the camps. The Japanese strategy for POW treatment during the

---

1. See Laura Hillenbrand, *Unbroken: A World War II Story of Survival, Resilience, and Redemption* (New York: Random House, 2010); Louis Zamperini with David Resin, *Devil at My Heels* (New York: HarperCollins, 2003).

war was to dehumanize their victims, stripping them of every ounce of dignity, to take away their will to live.

In a prison camp named Omori, Louie met his nemesis, Corporal Mutsuhiro Watanabe, the disciplinary officer known as "the Bird." Watanabe was a psychopath of the first order. His menacing black eyes told the story. "Decades after the war, men who had looked into those eyes would be unable to shake the memory of what they saw in them, a wrongness that elicited a twist in the gut, a prickle up the back of the neck."[2] The Bird would beat a man senselessly for hours and then bizarrely come to tears and apologize, hug him, and give him candy, beer, or cigarettes. Then in a moment he'd return to pummeling the poor soul in another fit of rage. "When gripped in the ecstasy of an assault, he wailed and howled, drooling and frothing, sometimes sobbing, tears running down his cheeks."[3]

Seeing Louie's utter determination to survive this kind of hellish treatment, the Bird singled him out for his most malicious attacks. One day Louie's leg was severely injured by a guard. Because he was unable to do the labor of the others in coal and salt mines, the Bird had him clean a pigsty, using no tools. He was consigned to crawl around, wiping excrement from the sty with his bare hands while secretly stuffing his mouth with pig food to keep from starving.

The Bird sometimes enlisted a line of prisoners to punch the faces of their fellow prisoners who were officers as hard as they could. Those who refused were subject to brutal beatings themselves. Louie was pegged for the worst of this kind of treatment. Each of the enlisted men reluctantly hammered him as he repeatedly dropped to the ground and then finally blacked out. When he regained consciousness, the Bird screamed for the men to resume their punches, which lasted several hours into the night. With every new blow, the Bird became increasingly enraptured with glee. Louie's face was swollen like a basketball for days.

The climax of wills between Louie and Watanabe occurred when the Bird punished Louie for supposedly letting a goat die under his care. He

2. Hillenbrand, *Unbroken*, 232.
3. Hillenbrand, 237.

was ordered to pick up a six-foot wooden beam and hold it straight above his head in front of the other prisoners. If he should lower his arms, a guard was instructed to hit him with the butt of his rifle. The Bird sat on the roof of an adjacent building, laughing and mocking Louie as he stood quivering in the baking sun. Louie was undeterred. He looked the Bird straight in the eyes with unflinching hatred.

Louie's arms seared with pain. After ten minutes, they grew numb. He faltered slightly, and the guard jabbed Louie with his gun. He straightened up but started becoming disoriented, his thoughts turning hazy and his consciousness weakening. Nonetheless, he summoned a steely resolve: *He cannot break me.* After some thirty-seven minutes, the Bird was dismayed with Louie's defiance. He jumped off the roof and rushed to his unyielding enemy, giving him a massive blow to the gut. Louie collapsed, the beam striking his head as he fell unconscious.[4]

By now, Japan's defeat was imminent, as the devastating B-29 bombing missions heard and seen overhead made clear. The POWs entertained hope, but they also had every reason to fear that the guards would make good on the military's "kill-all" orders for prisoners if the war were to end. Of the more than thirty-four thousand American POWs held in Japan during World War II, nearly 37 percent (13,000) died, compared to the 1 percent who died while being held by the German Nazis and Italian fascists.[5]

Finally, Louie was liberated, but his ordeal was not over. He could not adjust to civilian life. Flashbacks brought the sounds and sights of war and prison rushing back. The wrong sound or a difficult recollection would elicit panicked outbursts. The Bird followed him, tormenting him almost nightly in his dreams. The line between reality and illusion became blurred. Sudden and unpredictable rage possessed Louie like a demon. He sometimes assaulted innocent bystanders in public places at the slightest provocation. He turned to uncontrolled alcoholic consumption to relieve his terror, but it was useless. He couldn't hold a job. He made shipwreck of everything he tried to do. Even his return to the running track failed.

4. Hillenbrand, 296.
5. Hillenbrand, 315.

Louie then set himself to a singular objective. He would find the Bird and kill him, and all would be set right. But every wasted scheme on this front failed as well. Most of all, he failed his new bride, Cynthia. He treated her as though she were another enemy. She became frightened *for* him and then *by* him. During one nightmare, he found himself in a deadly match with the Bird. He had his neck in a death grip when suddenly he awakened and realized that he was strangling his terrified wife. Sometime later, Cynthia came home to see her drunken husband shaking their newborn baby with the same death grip. She had no choice. She and the baby left him. Louis Zamperini was in worse condition now than he had been in the prison camps.

COMING TO GRIPS WITH THE PROBLEM OF EVIL

The story of Louis Zamperini is one of countless examples throughout history that expose evil in all its feral wickedness. A whole constellation of evils encompassed the life of Zamperini. Not only did he endure morally evil people, but his human vulnerability had to endure all sorts of natural evils. He was a victim of a malfunctioning aircraft. While adrift at sea, he endured an inadequate life raft, ravenous sharks, hunger and thirst, inedible fish and fowl, and unexpected typhoons. In the camps, he experienced scorching heat and bitter cold, muscle atrophy, delirium, repeated multiple contusions, malnutrition, and disease.

Theologians make a distinction between both kinds of evil. *Moral evil* refers to the unrighteous thoughts, words, and actions[6] of all morally responsible creatures—angelic and human—in violation of a holy God's moral commands and principles to whom all stand accountable.[7] These evils cause pain and suffering for others. *Natural evil* refers to adverse conditions in the world that also cause pain and suffering. Such evil can proceed from (1) natural disasters, such as earthquakes, tornadoes,

---

6. See Gen. 6:5; Matt. 5:21–30; 1 John 3:15.
7. See Rom. 1:18–32; 2:14–15; 3:9–20, 23.

wildfires, or tsunamis; (2) accidents and mishaps due to the unfortunate consequences of the laws of nature, such as when someone drowns in a lake because he can't swim or a boulder falls from a cliff and crushes a busload of schoolchildren; (3) sickness and disease, such as pancreatic cancer or COVID-19; (4) physical and mental handicaps, such as paralysis or Down syndrome; and (5) physical toil that inhibits our bodies almost daily.

Natural evil is the result of the fall of Adam and Eve into moral rebellion against God whereby he brought about a perpetual curse on the creation, altering its favorable conditions (Gen. 3:14–19). We live in a broken world where things don't function as they should. The laws of nature do not always work in our favor. Decay and corruption have spoiled the pristine goodness of the original creation. Gone is the order, beauty, and functional perfection of Eden.

Evil in a Fallen World

The collusion of all these heavy chains of pain and suffering can hardly be comprehended. The history of the world is the history of humanity's faltering under the weight of unending systemic moral evils: greed, deceit, exploitation, sexual perversion, rape, racism, terrorism, slavery, murder, war, and genocide. Modern history has no shortage of examples. The Atlantic slave trade captured and sold some fifty million men, women, and children in the fifteenth to nineteenth centuries. In the twentieth century, Adolf Hitler enacted the Final Solution to kill six million Jews. Eighteen million dissenters of Vladimir Lenin's and Joseph Stalin's tyranny suffered in their hellish gulags. Mao Zedong's revolution starved, persecuted, imprisoned, or executed some sixty million innocents. From 1975 to 1979, Cambodia's Khmer Rouge exterminated over two million souls, most of them buried in the mass graves called the Killing Fields. Other harrowing examples could be recounted.

Contemplating the sheer numbers of such atrocities can become numbing, demonstrating our own desensitization to evil. Yet moral evil is not the only problem we face. We are ever threatened to be laid waste as well by a myriad of natural evils: earthquakes cracking the earth beneath our feet, hurricanes assaulting the cities on our shorelines, floods rushing through our docile subdivisions, tornadoes ripping our homes to pieces, and fiery infernos decimating our beloved forestland. Our physical bodies suffer under endless injury, sickness, disease, and threats of worldwide pandemics. Youth and strength give way to old age and an onslaught of incalculable bodily ailments. No sooner do we emerge bright and beautiful from our mother's wombs than we are thrust into a storm-tossed sea of pain that pitches us toward death.

No human being is exempt. We all suffer evil. Our personal tragedies are sometimes unrelenting and unbearable. Life seems unfair. Injustice prevails. True acts of righteousness are rare commodities. Wickedness dominates the menu. The guilty flourish while innocent ones languish. All humanity cries out with Job, "But when I hoped for good, evil came, and when I waited for light, darkness came" (Job 30:26). Just when the future looks bright, evil comes roaring back to shatter our hopes. Even now, we seem to be entering a new and disconcerting age when evil is accelerating at a dizzying pace. This has caused no small amount of consternation, fear, and uncertainty about what lies ahead.

The nefarious thinking behind various Marxist-inspired critical theories has emerged to radicalize the world and marginalize any resistance, castigating those who don't walk lockstep with its tyranny as bigots, racists, privileged upstarts, and truth-deniers who need to conform or be silenced.[8] Its divisive and corrosive effects were first incubated in our universities, and have now infected nearly all our K–12 school curriculums. It is relentlessly pushed by Hollywood and our news media. The poison is injected into all forms of our entertainment, sports, and advertising. The

8. See Voddie T. Baucham Jr., *Fault Lines: The Social Justice Movement and Evangelicalism's Looming Catastrophe* (Washington, DC: Salem Books, 2021); Owen Strachan, *Christianity and Wokeness: How the Social Justice Movement Is Hijacking the Gospel—and the Way to Stop It* (Washington, DC: Salem Books, 2021); Erwin W. Lutzer, *No Reason to Hide: Standing for Christ in a Collapsing Culture* (Eugene, OR: Harvest House, 2022); John MacArthur and Nathan Busenitz, eds., *Right Thinking for a Culture in Chaos: Responding Biblically to Today's Most Urgent Needs* (Eugene, OR: Harvest House, 2023); Carl R. Trueman, *Strange New World: How Thinkers and Activists Redefined Identity and Sparked the Sexual Revolution* (Wheaton, IL: Crossway, 2022).

largest and most influential corporations are colluding with government entities at all levels to utilize this radical ideology to deconstruct all the world's cultural institutions and to reshape education, language, law, economics, entertainment, the arts, and so forth.

This is especially true in the realm of sex and family. The sexual revolution has all but destroyed the family—the fundamental communal institution that God designed for a society to flourish. Our hypersexualized age knows no bounds of perversion with its confusion about so-called gender and sexual identity. Who would have thought that The Walt Disney Company, known for producing family-friendly fare for nearly a century, would redirect its mission to the aggressive sexualization of our children?

Pornography is often a requirement for elementary-school education. Drag shows have become the new entertainment for kids. Genital mutilation is pressed upon young people confused about their gender identity. The purveyors of this abuse have the gall to call it *gender-affirming care*. Pedophilia is the next socially acceptable perversion, calling its perpetrators *MAPs* (Minor-Attracted Persons) to soften its heinousness. Sex trafficking is a multibillion-dollar industry. Unfettered promotion of sex for anyone with anyone or anything is increasingly part of the driving ethos of the age.

The moral landscape of the Western world has completely shifted as we are poised for collapse. We undoubtedly live in a post-Christian world where God has been "de-godded"[9] and set aside as an outdated relic of a childish bygone era. The notion of unchanging, universal, objective morals has been relegated to the trash heap. If you ask the average person on the street how to distinguish between good and evil, most will have no clue. We live in an age of "expressive individualism"[10]—an age reminiscent of the dark days of the judges, when "everyone did what was right in his own eyes" (Judg. 17:6; 21:25).

---

9. See D. A. Carson, *The God Who Is There: Finding Your Place in God's Story* (Grand Rapids: Baker, 2010), 33.

10. Trueman, *Strange New World*, 22–24.

A Corrupted Christianity

Nowadays what usually passes for Christianity, even evangelical Christianity, is nothing more than what Christian Smith calls "moralistic therapeutic deism."[11] This man-centered religion has simply adapted the insipid values of the world to its belief system. Its namby-pamby deity sits aloof and allows us all to set our own course toward happiness so long as we tack a Bible verse to the end of our sentences and try to be nice to others. Its religious creed is "God helps those who help themselves." God is no demanding deity but an easygoing and tolerant buddy, cheering us on from the sidelines so that we can feel good about ourselves while we pursue psychological wholeness and follow our hearts wherever they may lead us. Pay no mind to what the prophets of old declared concerning the deceitfulness of the human heart (Jer. 17:9).

This benign religion and its illusory notion of God obscures a looming problem. We have been programmed by our culture and by our own self-centered and self-deceived nature to put all our focus on the evil that lies outside us, thinking that we are basically good (however we define *good*). But alas, the true God who has revealed himself in his Word does not allow us such a truncated and distorted perspective. We are not merely victims of evil. We are also perpetrators of evil—*all* of us. We are violators of true good—good that is defined and exemplified by God himself, not by us and not by the culture.

Under the divine standard: "None is righteous, no, not one; . . . no one seeks for God. . . . No one does good, not even one" (Rom. 3:10–12). We are selfish glory-seekers, liars and deceivers, lovers of wanton pleasure (2 Tim. 3:1–5). We are willing to kill and steal to get our way (James 4:1–3). This does not bode well for us. Our intractable and inescapable bondage to our own personal sin (John 8:34) deceives us (Rom. 7:11). It generates no true happiness. Rather, it is a path to unrelenting misery.

11. Christian Smith with Melinda Lundquist Denton, *Soul Searching: The Religious and Spiritual Lives of American Teenagers* (New York: Oxford University Press, 2005).

Why, O Lord?

And so we are utterly dismayed by this black world and the hopeless conditions we find ourselves in. Unpleasant questions plague every soul under the sun. We cry out—why!? Why all the lies and deception, the dismantling of truth? Why the ugliness, the marring of what was once beautiful? Why the corruption and waste, the dissolution of what is good? Why all this murder and mayhem, the destruction of life itself? And why are we all helpless and impossibly obstinate accomplices in this cosmic catastrophe? Surely this is not the way that it's supposed to be.

But most of all, we demand—where is God?

We cry out: "Why, O Lord, do you stand far away? Why do you hide yourself in times of trouble?" (Ps. 10:1).

Why couldn't God prevent all this madness from unfolding? Why doesn't he protect us from harm? Why does he allow us to continue unabated down the hellish trail that the devil has blazed for our darkened souls? Does God not love us? The Almighty One has already shown that he has all the requisite powers to stop the wind and stave off the waves with a simple word (Mark 4:39). What about all the other storms that afflict us? Surely his sovereign power could minimize our harm and maximize our safety. Why doesn't he do more to prevent chaos and promote peace? Better yet, why does a supremely good and powerful God permit all this calamity in the first place?

Theologians and philosophers call this the *problem of evil*. It is, no doubt, the most difficult problem that humanity faces. But it is a particularly troublesome matter for genuine and thoughtful Christians, sometimes called the Achilles' heel of the Christian faith. Why is this? Because Christianity alone among all the world's religions and ideologies holds to the belief that God is supremely good, righteous, holy, wise, loving, and powerful—the Creator, Sustainer, and Governor of *all* that exists. His perfections are infinite, unchanging, and unassailable.

No other conception of deity or deities can possibly compare. In fact, the Bible is clear—there is no other God (Isa. 43:10–13). If this is true —and it is—then how can such an unfathomably glorious God permit his wonderfully designed creation and creatures to be decimated by the fall—to descend into this disconcerting darkness?

TRACING THE PROBLEM OF EVIL

Throughout the ages, many unbelievers have refused to acknowledge the God of the Bible directly; nonetheless, they know in their heart of hearts that such a God exists, as Romans 1:18–32 clearly teaches. Furthermore, they have surmised the basic contours of the problem of evil, yet doggedly insist that it proves that God does not exist. And yet, ironically, they intuitively know that if God did not exist, then there would be no problem of evil. Why?

Because we cannot avoid presupposing that a supremely wise God of perfect goodness, righteousness, justice, and truth *alone* sets the standard by which all things that fail to meet this standard must be measured. Without the sun, we'd never know that we lurk beneath the shadows. In other words, without a supremely good God, you cannot say that there is such a thing as evil. And you would have no basis to ask God the question "why?" when evil smacks you hard in the face.

Skeptical philosophers—going back to Epicurus (341–270 B.C.) and, famously, to David Hume (1711–76)—have tried to frame the problem of evil as a logical conflict between the existence of God on the one hand and the presence of evil on the other, as shown in the argument put forth below. Notice, however, that the argument does not target some generic version of God. Only the God of the Bible undergoes the sort of scrutiny that the problem of evil demands. In fact, we all know this as creatures made in his image. We don't have to be skeptics to question how the one true God fares in the face of evil while it tests just how much faith we really have in him.

Here is the argument:

(1) The God of the Bible is all-powerful (omnipotent).
(2) The God of the Bible is all-good (omnibenevolent).
(3) Yet evil exists.
(4) Therefore, the God of the Bible cannot possibly exist.

The argument assumes that statement 3, "evil exists," is not in dispute; and this is true. Rarely does anyone dispute this fact. What is in dispute is either statement 1 or 2. But notice that the argument has some hidden assumptions and can be reworded this way:

(1) The all-powerful (omnipotent) God of the Bible *can* prevent evil.
(2) The all-good (omnibenevolent) God of the Bible *wants* to prevent evil.
(3) Yet evil exists.

This leads to some preliminary conclusions:

(4) Therefore, either God is not all-powerful (he *cannot* prevent evil) or he is not all-good (he does *not want* to prevent evil).

The supposed conflict between these two preliminary conclusions leads to the same conclusion as before:

(5) Therefore, the God of the Bible cannot possibly exist (because the Bible insists that God must be *both* all-powerful and all-good).

Let us examine this argument. Some suppose that statement 1 is false while statement 2 is true. This is what Rabbi Harold Kushner argued in his best-selling book *When Bad Things Happen to Good People*. The famed rabbi wrote, "I can worship a God who hates suffering but cannot eliminate it, more easily than I can worship a God who chooses to make children suffer and die, for whatever exalted reason."[12] People who believe this must find themselves in a miserable quandary, believing in an impotent God who can do nothing more than cry with us when tragedy strikes.

On the other hand, many smug secularists are happy to concede that statement 1 is true while statement 2 is false; this way, they can claim that any God who allows evil when he could easily prevent it must be evil himself. But are these the only two conclusions that one can draw from

12. Harold S. Kushner, *When Bad Things Happen to Good People* (New York: HarperCollins, 1989), 134.

the argument? Christianity does not need to cower in a dark corner when faced with the supposed conundrums here.

When this argument is closely examined, one serious problem is seen with it: statement 2. All orthodox theologians acknowledge that statement 1 is true, and the Bible itself is clear on this matter. God has all the requisite powers to prevent or stop any instance of evil. But it does not necessarily follow that God in his all-encompassing goodness *wants* to prevent or stop every instance of evil, as statement 2 suggests. The fact is, he clearly has not done so, and the Bible is also clear on this. The skeptics think this means that either he is evil or he cannot exist. But is it possible that the God of the Bible can be supremely good, having no possibility of evil in his being, and yet somehow have a sufficiently good and wise reason for allowing evil to exist? The burden of this book is to answer that question in the affirmative.

MORE THAN ONE PROBLEM OF EVIL

There is more than one problem of evil. The mere existence of evil is not a sufficient reason for many people, especially Christians, to question the existence of God. Consider, however, the vast extent of evil or the horrendous nature of some evils. Does this not impugn God? The Holocaust serves as one of countless examples. Maybe one could forgive God if six or even sixty Jews had died at the hands of the demonically inspired Hitler. But what about six hundred? Six thousand? That seems to stretch our patience.

If sixty thousand Jews had died or, God forbid, six hundred thousand, Hitler would still be one of the greatest villains in the history of the human race, and many would demand that God has some explaining to do. Yet that is not what we are dealing with. We are confronted with the fact that nearly all European Jews—six million of them—were wiped off the face of the planet, regarded as vile creatures in the eyes of not only Hitler, but most ordinary, God-believing, hardworking, family-oriented German citizens (and many other ordinary citizens throughout Europe).

Can you see the problem that the Christian faces?

But that is not all. The vast extent of the Holocaust is one thing. Consider the horrendous nature of many of the crimes that were committed by the Nazis. No one has captured the horror of the Holocaust as Elie Wiesel has in his memoir *Night*. Wiesel survived both Auschwitz-Birkenau and Monowitz concentration camps during World War II. When he first arrived at Auschwitz, he watched helplessly as little babies were unloaded from the back of a lorry and nonchalantly tossed into a fire to be reduced to ashes.

> NEVER SHALL I FORGET that night, the first night in camp, which turned my life into one long night seven times sealed.
> Never shall I forget that smoke.
> Never shall I forget the small faces of the children whose bodies I saw transformed into smoke under a silent sky.
> Never shall I forget those flames that consumed my faith forever.
> Never shall I forget the nocturnal silence that deprived me for all eternity of the desire to live.
> Never shall I forget those moments that murdered my God and my soul and turned my dreams to ashes.
> Never shall I forget these things, even were I condemned to live as long as God Himself.
> Never.[13]

We look at such horrendous evil and we say that it is senseless, gratuitous, having no possible good reason to transpire. Why would God allow it? Later Wiesel and multitudes of other prisoners fixed their eyes on two men and a boy who were ordered to the gallows for sabotage in the camp.

> The three condemned prisoners together stepped onto the chairs.
> In unison, the nooses were placed around their necks.

13. Elie Wiesel, *Night*, trans. Marion Wiesel (New York: Hill and Wang, 2006), 34.

"Long live liberty!" shouted the two men.

But the boy was silent.

"Where is merciful God, where is He?" someone behind me was
   asking.

At the signal, the three chairs were tipped over.

Total silence in the camp. On the horizon, the sun was setting. . . .

Then came the march past the victims. The two men were no longer
   alive. Their tongues were hanging out, swollen and bluish. But
   the third rope was still moving: the child, too light, was still
   breathing. . . .

And so he remained for more than half an hour, lingering between
   life and death, writhing before our eyes. And we were forced to
   look at him at close range. He was still alive when I passed him.
   His tongue was still red, his eyes not yet extinguished.

Behind me, I heard the same man asking:

"For God's sake, where is God?"

And from within me, I heard a voice answer:

"Where is He? This is where—hanging here from this gallows . . ."

That night, the soup tasted of corpses.[14]

As Wiesel so poignantly illustrates, it is not just the extent and
horrendous nature of evil that gnaws at us. It is the way in which evil
impacts us directly, personally, powerfully, hauntingly, ripping its deadly
claws through our tender souls and leaving us to cry out to God.

Does he hear us? Is he there?

If you are honest with yourself, you have been in this place too:
When your beautiful baby unexpectedly dies. When your wife declares
that she does not love you anymore and leaves for good. When your
business fails because your partner embezzled all its funds. When the
fire from your faulty furnace lays waste to your uninsured home. When
your church splits in two because your pastor has been exposed as a wolf
in sheep's clothing.

14. Wiesel, 64–65.

How about when your grandchildren have to live with parents who exist in a perpetual delirium while being decimated by methamphetamines? When terminal cancer has canceled all your plans for the future? When your girl comes home from school and declares that she is a boy? When child protective services comes knocking because you disagreed with the school's assessment of your girl's transition?

We have our stories. We have our anger, our bitterness, our depression, our disillusionment. We have our ceaseless sorrow, our unfading wounds. We have our questions for God.

Will he answer us?

SEARCHING FOR A SOLUTION TO THE PROBLEM OF EVIL

Believers have been responding to the problem of evil from the beginning of history. The technical term in theology used by believers to defend the Christian faith with respect to the problem of evil is *theodicy*, a word coined by the eighteenth-century German philosopher Gottfried Leibniz. It combines the Greek words for "God" (*theós*) and "justice" (*dikē*). Consequently, a theodicy is an attempt to put forth a solution that "justifies God" in the face of evil, defending his divine integrity and exonerating him from the charge that he is morally culpable for the evil that permeates his creation. Ultimately, a theodicy tries to show why God has allowed evil to ruin his good creation. While Christians have put forward many different theodicies, they can be consolidated around two basic approaches.

The first and most common theodicy is often called the *free-will defense*. This solution says that evil unfortunately arises as a risk God takes when he grants free will to his moral creatures. There are serious problems with this solution, as we will see in chapter 2. The second basic approach to the problem of evil is often called the *greater-good defense*. This theodicy's solution says that God allows evil only in cases in which that evil is necessary for the emergence of some greater good—a good that could not otherwise emerge unless the evil connected to that good existed.

The theodicy I present in this book is a species of the greater-good defense. It takes the ideas that are crucial to this solution and advances them in very specific and far-reaching ways. Most solutions to the problem of evil are content to provide the most succinct and sufficient way that the Christian faith can avoid the charge that God is culpable for evil. By contrast, a more robust theodicy gives reasons not merely why God is not culpable for evil, but in fact why he has a very clear and definite purpose for it.

In other words, most theodicies are strictly defensive positions, trying to defend God from the fiery darts of the skeptics and all those dismayed with a God who seems too inept to handle all this pain and suffering. This is unfortunate. The God of the Bible is never backed into a corner of the ring, trying to avoid all the punches thrown his way. The Bible is not afraid to expose the full gamut of evil right from its very first pages. Rather, evil, in all its manifestations, is a prominent part of the whole storyline of Scripture, and God is never tainted by his indispensable connection to it.

Evil was no accident.

Yet the Bible does not provide a direct answer to the questions: Why evil? Why the fall? Why all this corruption, pain, and suffering marring the cosmos? Nonetheless, it tells a remarkable story that narrates God's plan for history in which it becomes clear why he not only permits evil, but dare we say, planned for it—all of it—to contribute to his glorious plan. The theodicy that the Bible implicitly unfolds is one in which the incomprehensible magnificence of our God is on full display.

Many Christians suppose that God's purpose in creating human beings is to maximize their happiness. Evil disrupts these plans, and so the solution to the problem of evil is to figure out why God hasn't restored human happiness. But if maximizing human happiness is God's purpose, then let's be honest: he has not done a very good job.

Furthermore, this solution is cringeworthy because it places humanity at the center of God's purposes, as though human happiness were the supreme good of all reality. That is simply not true. God is at the center of all reality. God's purpose in creating humans and the rest of the created order is to put his own glory on display, and to do so supremely. In fact, it could be no other way. If God is truly God, then he must of necessity be at the center. If reality were analogous to our solar system, then he must be the sun and we be the planets orbiting the sun. Only the sun has the mass and gravity to maintain the center and to keep the planets from flying to pieces. Nothing can displace the sun from its central place.

Likewise, we can never imagine a world where God does not occupy the place of singular majesty and glory. Everything that takes place, whether good or evil, must not detract from that glory. Rather, every last vestige of good and evil was purposely designed by God to magnify his glory and to do so supremely. And it is here that a legitimate pursuit of human happiness lies. The first question of the Westminster Shorter Catechism captures this point well: "What is the chief end of man?" The answer: "Man's chief end is to glorify God, and to enjoy him forever." Our joy as human beings is found in one place—the glory of the incomprehensibly magnificent God (Ps. 16:11).

Thus, whatever theodicy the Bible supports must be one in which God is supremely glorified. For that reason, the theodicy I propose is called the *greater-glory theodicy*. The greater goods that God brings out of the darkness must shine a brilliant light on a greater glory resting in himself. Furthermore, he has designed his plan for history to magnify the well-being (happiness) of his adopted children, whom he has chosen to pull out of the darkness and to set before his glorious grace.

In the light of his wonderful countenance we find our greatest good and our greatest joy. Furthermore, what magnifies our own personal well-being is directly tied to the fact that we *had* to be dragged through all the filth and debris of a dirty, broken world, of our souls' being corrupted by evil within as well as victimized by all manner of evil without. The grace of God that penetrates the darkness within and without is what in the end supremely magnifies God's glory and works for our greatest well-being.

THE REST OF ZAMPERINI'S STORY

This is exemplified in the rest of Louis Zamperini's story. Louie's wife filed for divorce after his abuse and violence reached a point of no return.

But shortly afterward, she attended the well-known 1949 Los Angeles Crusade that jump-started the evangelistic career of the young firebrand Billy Graham. Cynthia was converted to Christ the first night she attended and told Louie that she was dropping the divorce.

After days of resisting, Louie finally consented to go with her one night to hear Graham preach. The evangelist was in dead earnest in his gospel appeals. Louie was uncomfortable. But when Graham spoke of divine judgment for those who think they are good, Louie was moved to anger. He thought of himself as a good man. Yet he knew that he was a liar. With every word Graham spoke, Louie's thoughts grew more haunted. He huffed home that night and faced the maniacal Bird once again.

Louie was convinced to see Graham the following night. This time, Graham spoke directly to the problem of evil and why God allows such suffering, and then how he often penetrates the pain with a supernal peace. Louie was transported to a day in 1943 when he was adrift at sea after his B-24 crashed. He entered that place along the equator called the doldrums where the sea mysteriously turns into a motionless sheet of glass. He knew without a doubt that the strange feeling of absolute serenity he felt that day could come only from the hands of an immensely powerful and benevolent God. Louie knew that he should have never survived his ordeal. God's mercy had sustained him every moment.

Then Graham spoke of the saving grace that all must find in Christ. Still, Louie resisted, his head sweating now, throat constricting, the weight on his chest increasing. His rage returned, and he grabbed Cynthia and bolted from the service. But as he rushed outside the tent, it began to rain. He stopped and turned toward Graham. Then he had one final flashback. It was a moment on the life raft when he had made a promise to God: "Lord, bring me back safely from the war and I'll seek you and serve you."[15]

This recollection was the turning point. He soon dropped to his knees and begged God for pardon and trusted Christ. Louie went home that night in a state of serenity that he had never experienced before. God had indeed saved his physical life; now he embraced Christ to save his

---

15. Zamperini and Resin, *Devil at My Heels*, 241.

spiritual life. He threw all his alcohol down the drain along with his anxiety, his anger, and his thoughts of revenge. The Bird came to him no more —neither that night nor any night since. Suddenly, Louie developed an insatiable appetite to know Christ and the Bible.

Louie Zamperini was a new man, and the gratitude he felt for his salvation was incomparable to the misery he had endured for the previous six years. In fact, the contrast between the depths of his misery and the heights of his peace made his experience of God's grace and glory all the more remarkable.

Zamperini's story is one of many that provide us with a glimpse into what God is doing in this broken world. "For God, who said, 'Let light shine out of darkness,' has shone in our hearts to give the light of the knowledge of the glory of God in the face of Jesus Christ" (2 Cor. 4:6). The one whose head is "like white wool, like snow," whose eyes are "like a flame of fire, his feet . . . like burnished bronze, refined in a furnace," and whose voice is "like the roar of many waters" (Rev. 1:14–15)—this One is magnifying his grace and his glory beyond all compare, and this is what is at the heart of the greater-glory theodicy that we will explore.

STUDY QUESTIONS

1. Can you recall some "evil" event that affected your life? How did you respond to it?
2. What is the difference between *moral evil* and *natural evil*?
3. How did evil come about in the world?
4. What do you believe is the greatest evil afflicting our culture today?
5. What is the *problem of evil*? Why is this a unique problem for Christianity?
6. Is the problem of evil more of a problem for God's omnipotence (all-encompassing power) or his omnibenevolence (all-encompassing goodness)? Explain your answer.
7. The author says that there is more than one problem of evil. Aside from the logical problem of evil as expressed by various philosophers

challenging the existence of God, what other two problems does the author discuss?

8. What is a theodicy?
9. Explain the basic difference between the *free-will defense* and the *greater-good defense.*
10. Why must a biblical theodicy be God-centered instead of man-centered?

2

CONFRONTING THE DARKNESS

Throughout the history of Christianity, two opposing approaches to theological reflection on the teaching of the Christian faith have emerged. Each view differs on how to define the attributes of God, how deeply sin has affected fallen man, the nature of saving grace, and how the Christian life can be sustained over the long haul. Predictably, both theological outlooks also come into sharp disagreement when dealing with the problem of evil.

As the history of this theological debate has progressed, each view has been commonly represented in the evangelical and Protestant tradition by two prominent theologians and their respective legacies: the Protestant Reformer John Calvin (1509–64) and his most famous detractor, Jacob Arminius (1560–1609). Subsequently, how biblical Christianity can best confront the darkness of this world has largely been a debate between Calvinism (Reformed theology) and Arminianism.

It is important to consider how each of these two prominent visions of the faith comes to the table with its answers. Arminianism is part of a broader theological perspective known as *free-will theism*.[1] As you might

---

1. Other variations of free-will theism include open theism and Molinism. I assess their specific approaches to the problem of evil in *What about Evil? A Defense of God's Sovereign Glory* (Phillipsburg, NJ: P&R Publishing, 2020), 102–8.

suspect, Arminianism generally adopts the theodicy called the *free-will defense*, whereas Calvinism generally adopts the *greater-good defense*. The free-will defense of Arminianism places human freedom and autonomy at the center of its answer to the problem of evil, whereas Calvinism places the lordship and glory of God at the center. Let us briefly consider the difference between the two theologies.

ARMINIANISM VERSUS CALVINISM

Arminianism distinguishes itself by five basic points.[2] First, humans in their natural state are depraved and do not have free will or the capacity for saving faith and repentance. Yet this is mitigated by the doctrine of *prevenient grace*, which God supplies to all humans so that their free will is recovered. Second, God conditionally elects (predestines) to save those sinners who he foreknew would exercise faith in Christ of their own free will. Third, Christ's death is seen as a universal (unlimited) atonement for all humanity regardless of who believes in Christ for salvation. Salvation is a free gift of divine grace available to all but guaranteed for none. The reception of this gift must be initiated by the sinner's freely exercised faith.

Fourth, because free will has been recovered by prevenient grace, sinners are able to overcome their sinful depravity to choose either to cooperate with God's provisional *saving grace* (in addition to prevenient grace) through saving faith or to resist his saving grace. Fifth, the ongoing grace of God assists the believer throughout his life, but this grace can be neglected so that salvation is lost. In Arminianism, a Christian has a tenuous grasp on the assurance of his salvation because free will can always be used to reject the faith and forfeit all the benefits of salvation. This is one of the risks God takes in granting free will to humans.

---

2. See J. Matthew Pinson, *40 Questions about Arminianism* (Grand Rapids: Kregel Academic, 2022).

The Five Points of Calvinism (TULIP)	The Five Points of Arminianism
Total (Thorough) Depravity Sin has enslaved and corrupted every person. Humans are spiritually dead. They are unable and unwilling to repent and believe apart from God's grace alone.	**Depraved but Free** Sin has infected all people, but their will is freed by prevenient grace. Humans are spiritually sick. With God's gracious help, they are able and may be willing to repent and believe.
Unconditional Election God chose the elect on the basis of his freedom and grace, not for anything seen in sinners.	**Conditional Election** God chose the elect on the basis of their foreseen faith that is freely exercised if they so choose.
Limited (Definite) Atonement Christ's death provides atonement only for the elect, definitively paying the price for their sin and guaranteeing their salvation.	**Universal (Unlimited) Atonement** Christ's death is a provisional atonement for the sins of the whole world, which makes salvation possible for all but guaranteed for none.
Irresistible (Efficacious) Saving Grace Saving grace is irresistible and efficaciously saves the elect. The Holy Spirit regenerates the hearts of the elect, enabling them to repent and believe.	**Resistible (Provisional) Saving Grace** Saving grace is necessary but not sufficient to save sinners. It can be resisted and must be cooperated with by the free will of sinners.
Perseverance of the Saints God's grace preserves the elect and ensures that they will persevere in faith till the end. None of the elect will finally fall away from the faith.	**Uncertain Perseverance of the Saints** God's grace cannot guarantee that believers will not fall away from the faith. Not all will freely cooperate with God's grace to persevere in faith.

Fig. 2.1. Calvinism vs. Arminianism

Conversely, Calvinism is often identified by the five points of Calvinism, traditionally represented by the acronym *TULIP*.[3] They are best called the *doctrines of grace*. These five points were articulated sometime in the nineteenth century, but are generally associated with the conclusions adopted at the Synod of Dort in 1618–19, which rejected the five points (see above) of the Remonstrants, a group of Arminians who gathered to defend their views in 1610.

The *T* in *TULIP* stands for *total depravity*, indicating that humans are in bondage to sin, their souls being thoroughly (but not exhaustively) corrupted by it, and therefore utterly helpless in themselves to escape this bondage. Sinners in this state are unable and unwilling to repent and believe (Rom. 8:7–8). The *U* stands for *unconditional election*, indicating that God freely and graciously elects (predestines) to save a particular people for himself apart from anything they do.

The *L* stands for *limited atonement*, indicating that Christ's death secured an actual, definite, and efficacious atonement only for the elect, which guarantees their salvation. The *I* stands for *irresistible grace*, indicating that God, in his sovereign mercy, draws the elect to Christ for salvation irresistibly through the regenerating power of the Holy Spirit so that they willingly and gladly repent and believe in Christ. The *P* stands for *perseverance of the saints*, indicating that God's continuing grace will preserve the elect so that they will willingly persevere in their salvation until the day of their glorification at the coming of Christ. They will never fall away from their faith.

THE FREE-WILL DEFENSE

Arminians and other free-will theists seek to unravel the problem of evil by asserting that their understanding of free will is vitally important to the solution. But what do they mean by *free will*? They define *free will*

3. For a readable and convincing case for the five points of Calvinism, see Jim Scott Orrick, *Mere Calvinism* (Phillipsburg, NJ: P&R Publishing, 2019).

by two ideas. First, for our choices to be free and morally responsible, they must be made autonomously. In other words, our choices cannot be sufficiently determined by anyone or anything outside our independent freedom to exercise our will. While God seeks to assert his influence on the choices we make, he cannot determine which choices we finally settle on; otherwise, we would be like helpless marionettes dangling on a Grand Puppeteer's strings. Second, whatever choice we make, to be truly free, we must be able to have made any number of alternative choices under exactly the same circumstances.[4]

For example, imagine that you are Doc Holliday living in the Wild West. You're traveling through Kansas, and you come to a fork in the road with a sign indicating that Dodge City is to the left and Wichita is to the right. Nothing can decisively compel you to go one way or the other. You may have reasons for going to Dodge City. Perhaps you are planning to help your friend Wyatt Earp round up the bad guys in that crime-ridden town. But if you have genuine freedom of will, then you have the unfettered ability to disregard such reasons and head to Wichita instead.

Let's suppose that when you reached the fork in the road, you decided to turn west for Dodge City. If through some strange magic you were transported back in time to the same fork in the road under exactly the same circumstances, however, then you could just as easily decide to turn east for Wichita. Given your freedom of contrary choice, nothing could prevent you from the equal ease in making either choice. And as everyone knows, Doc Holliday did whatever he pleased!

How do those who hold to this view of free will think it solves the problem of evil? The *free-will defense* says that this freedom of alternative possibilities is necessary for (1) acting good and righteously, (2) maintaining the value of loving relationships and other virtuous commitments, and (3) establishing moral responsibility for our actions.

---

4. Technically, this view of free will is called *libertarian* free will (*libertarianism*), in contrast with most Calvinistic views of free will, which are known as *compatibilism*. See my book *What about Free Will? Reconciling Our Choices with God's Sovereignty* (Phillipsburg, NJ: P&R Publishing, 2016).

For example, love for God must be freely offered by our autonomous power of will if it is to be genuine and praiseworthy. If God somehow *makes* us love him by his sovereign determination, then such love is not free; it is coerced and therefore not truly love.

In other words, if our love for God is genuine, then we must have the ability to refrain from acting with such love. We must have the equal freedom to hate God if the alternative possibility of loving him carries any weight and moral responsibility. We cannot be blamed for *not* loving God unless we have the ability and freedom *to* love God.

The free-will defense offers these arguments as the solution to the problem of evil. When God grants human beings this kind of moral freedom, however, he is taking a huge risk because there is always the possibility that we will abuse this freedom and choose evil, even sometimes horrific Hitlerian-type evil. But God is willing to take this risk because free will is so highly prized. The benefits outweigh any risks.

The bottom line is this: if we don't have this freedom, then the weight of moral culpability for evil in the world shifts from the creature to the Creator, and that is anathema. Therefore, the free-will defense is designed to exonerate God from being the author of evil.

PROBLEMS WITH THE FREE-WILL DEFENSE

It seems intuitive to most people, even most Christians, that we have this unfettered freedom of will. Every day we are presented with myriad options for choices that seem poised to attract our acts of will in myriad directions. We seem to have a powerful tool at our disposal to shape our lives and the future while God stands alongside us, urging us to make the right choices so that he will be pleased with the outcome.

In fact, we tend to think that God plays nary a role in most things we choose. We seem to be the sole determiners of what we do even when we consider the influence of our upbringing, our education, our friends and family, the culture, or even the Holy Spirit, the Bible, and our pastor or church. But there are serious problems with this view of free will. If it is suspect, then it undermines the free-will defense as a solution to the problem of evil. Let us briefly consider six of its problems.[5]

Free Will Undermines God's Sovereignty

The Bible clearly indicates that God sovereignly orders every event that transpires in his creation, including all human choices, whether good or evil (see chapter 3 for detailed arguments). David boldly declares, "The LORD has established His throne in the heavens, and His sovereignty rules over all" (Ps. 103:19 NASB). The Almighty does not rule over *some* things but rules over *all* things. Nothing we do is independent of God: "In him we live and move and have our being" (Acts 17:28). As the late R. C. Sproul was fond of saying, there is not a "maverick molecule" in all the universe.

Arminianism believes that if God interferes with humans' choices, then their freedom and responsibility are stripped away, even when they act wickedly. Yet Scripture indicates that God often stops evil in its tracks.[6] Most Arminians agree that God has all the requisite powers to intervene in the evil affairs of mankind and that he often does so. But then the question must be raised: why doesn't he intervene in every case of evil?

For example, God warned the magi and Joseph to flee Bethlehem, knowing Herod's evil intentions, yet he did not warn the Bethlehemites themselves of the wicked ruler's plot to murder their little boys (Matt. 2:12–18). God prevents evil in one case and permits it in another. In the latter case, he has sovereignly determined evil to go on uninterrupted by his providential power, as hard a pill as that may be for us to swallow. This inevitably leads to the conclusion that God sovereignly intends all evil to happen that he obviously does not prevent.

Of course, this raises many thorny questions for Calvinism, which we will answer shortly. In either case, the free-will defense cannot escape

5. For a more detailed response to this view of free will, see my books *What about Free Will?* and *What about Evil?*, 84–115.
6. See Gen. 20:6; Ex. 14:21–29; Lev. 10:1–2; 1 Sam. 2:25; Matt. 2:12–15 (cf. v. 20); Acts 9:1–6.

the charge that God is morally culpable for evil. He is like a police officer who stands by while a thug beats an old lady and steals her purse. If the officer is asked why he didn't stop this crime, he can only say, "If I did so, then that would violate the thug's free will." Preserving the thug's free will outweighs preserving the old lady's safety.

Free Will Undermines the Doctrine of Depravity

The Bible does not mince words in describing the moral depravity of mankind. Unregenerate people are corrupted and enslaved in every aspect of their being—the mind, will, and emotions (John 8:34; Eph. 4:17–19). No one is immune from this debilitating condition (Rom. 3:10–18, 23). All humans are born with a hostility toward God. The unregenerate fleshly mind "does not submit to God's law; indeed, it cannot. Those who are in the flesh cannot please God" (8:7–8). Paul is saying that unbelievers are both *unwilling* and *morally unable* to please God. There is no freedom of will enabling the sinner to escape his dreadful condition. This is what is meant by the Calvinist doctrine of *total depravity*.

Only God's *irresistible grace* can break the chains of the bondage of the will and enable the sinful heart to see its desperate condition and entrust itself to Christ. Apart from this wholly effectual grace, there is no good thing within us that would draw us to Christ. Martin Luther said, "If there were enough good in 'free-will' for it to apply itself to good, it would have no need of grace!"[7] Likewise, he asked, "What need is there of the Spirit, or Christ, or God, if 'free-will' can overcome the motions of the mind to evil?"[8] The Arminian doctrine of free will steals all the glory from God and his grace and shifts it to sinners, who suddenly have reason for boasting in their contribution to salvation. This subtly, if unconsciously, sneaks works-righteousness into the back door of the gospel. Yet salvation must be *all* of God and *all* of grace or there is no salvation (Eph. 2:8–9).

7. Martin Luther, *The Bondage of the Will*, trans. J. I. Packer and O. R. Johnston (Old Tappan, NJ: Fleming H. Revell, 1957), 145.
8. Luther, 157.

God Does Not Have Free Will

Arminians regard free will as one of the most valuable traits that a personal and moral being can have. So we would expect God to have this same unfettered power of contrary choice, but he does not. He indeed has freedom to act good, but that freedom requires no possibility for him to risk acting evil. Furthermore, moral responsibility for his actions is not dependent on having contrary choice. No one praises God for his goodness, knowing that he could have equally acted evilly. God is absolute righteousness. He is eternally pure light. There is no darkness in him at all (1 John 1:5), and it is precisely for this impeccable moral righteousness that he is so highly praised.

Furthermore, God is not required to have contrary choice to give an air of genuineness to his good and benevolent actions. For example, God the Father has unhindered and unwavering perfect love for his Son, and he has no freedom to act otherwise (John 17:24). Likewise, Jesus had no possibility of acting against his sinless character during his earthly ministry, yet that did not stop him from willingly, freely, voluntarily loving sinners with a love that is far greater than we could imagine. God's freedom to act is restricted to nothing but good because he is the very fountain of all goodness. So how could God grant to his creatures this supposedly indispensable and highly valuable trait that he himself does not possess?

God Could Design Us to Choose Only Good

Many Arminians believe that God voluntarily limits his sovereign powers to allow our free will to operate unhindered. But why couldn't God simply limit our free will to only good choices, not unlike the limitation that he himself has for making only good choices? Adam and Eve enjoyed perfect love and fellowship with God in the garden of Eden before sin corrupted them. Therefore, it is not clear that unhindered free will (the ability to make *both* good *and* evil choices) is necessary for freedom, love, and moral responsibility.

Furthermore, the Bible teaches that all believers, in their resurrected and glorified state, will have no ability to sin whatsoever (Rom. 8:29; 1 John 3:2); and no serious Christian in history—Arminian or Calvinist—has taught otherwise. Consequently, the greatest place in all of creation and history will contain no hint of the kind of free will that Arminians argue is so valuable in this present world. Nonetheless, the future world will be marked by perfect freedom for the sake of perfect goodness, love, and joy. If the freedom of contrary choice is such a valuable and necessary treasure —indispensable for generating genuine good—then why doesn't heaven have this treasure?

Free Will Cannot Account for Divine Foreknowledge

The orthodox doctrine of divine foreknowledge—which Arminians and Calvinists agree on—states that God knows every event in the past, present, and future exhaustively and infallibly.[9] But if the Arminian brand of free will is true, then even though God knows what every person in history has chosen up until the present, it would be impossible for him to know with absolute certainty any choices made in the future. Why is this? Because free-will thinking says that God in no way determines our choices and that, furthermore, since our choices could go in any number of contrary directions in the same precise circumstances right up to the moment of choosing, then it is not possible for anyone—God included —to know for sure what those choices will be.

For example, how did Jesus know that Peter would deny him exactly three times during his precrucifixion trial (Matt. 26:34)? According to the dictates of free-will thinking, Peter could have changed his mind at the last moment and made a different choice on each occasion. In his autonomous freedom, Peter could as easily have denied Jesus one, two, or ten times. Or not at all. He could have fled from the scene of the trial altogether. If the freedom of contrary choice is true, then it is always possible to fool God.

But the fact is, the future cannot change what God timelessly knows from all eternity. Jesus knew exactly what Peter would do; therefore, it was not possible for Peter to act any other way. This is a deadly blow to the idea

9. See 1 Chron. 28:9; Job 28:24; Pss. 139:1–4; 147:5; Isa. 41:21–23; 42:9; 44:7; 45:21; 46:9–11; 48:3–7; Jer. 1:5 (cf. Heb. 4:13); Acts 2:23; 26:5; Rom. 8:29; 11:2; 1 Peter 1:2, 20; 2 Peter 3:17.

of freedom of contrary choice. The doctrine of God's inexhaustible and infallible foreknowledge means that all events in history are predetermined. The future cannot change. Furthermore, God foreknows the future because he is the very one who foreordained it (Eph. 1:11).[10]

But Arminians protest that this inflexible view of divine sovereignty is nothing more than fatalism and coercion, that Peter had no real choice in what he did. But there is a vast difference between fatalism and divine providence. Fatalism says that "what will be will be," no matter what choices we make. Divine providence says that our freely, voluntarily, willingly made choices are the instruments by which God providentially executes his eternal plans for history and our lives. Divine sovereignty never negates human freedom and responsibility (as properly defined). In Calvinism, the two come together in what is known as *compatibilism* (see chapter 4).[11]

Free Will Allows Gratuitous Evil

Those who espouse freedom of contrary choice have difficulty making sense of so-called gratuitous or senseless evils: various evils that appear to be pointless, having no possible good reason for existing. Again, Arminians do not deny that God has the power to intervene and stop such horrendous evil. Yet only in rare cases do they believe he does so.

Why, for example, didn't God warn the Bethlehemites of Herod's plan to slaughter innocent baby boys after warning the magi and Joseph (Matt. 2:12–19)? What possible good came from this murderous rampage? Why didn't God order a deadly sickness to strike down Herod before the evil ruler issued his deadly order? Did God regard Herod's free will as having more value than those little babies' lives? That seems to be the only answer available to the free-will theist. God passively refuses to intervene for the sake of preserving the free will of wicked perpetrators.

10. The responses to the foreknowledge problem by various free-will theists are complicated. I treat all the major responses, including those of open theists and Molinists, in greater detail in *What about Evil?*, 98–108.

11. For a fuller explanation and defense of compatibilism, see my book *What about Free Will?*

We must conclude that this account of human freedom leads the free-will defense to bankruptcy as a solution to the problem of evil. Upholding human autonomy as the way to deflect charges against God's omnipotence and perfect goodness ends up becoming a burden too great for Arminianism and all free-will theists to bear. The free-will defense proves to be an impossible escape hatch for a God who must throw his hands up when the world doesn't quite go his way. This theodicy provides no true solace to the beleaguered soul haunted by darkness within and without. We must recover a more lucid vision: that of a God for whom evil is no match in this wretched world, a God of such magnificence that all things without exception bow before his supreme lordship.

THE GREATER-GOOD DEFENSE

This leads us to the *greater-good defense*, which locates evil not in the unintended results of free-will choices' having gone bad, but rather in God's particular intentions for the course of all things, whether good or evil. In this regard, nothing escapes his plans and purposes for history, which is why the greater-good defense is generally associated with the meticulous brand of divine sovereignty that Calvinism espouses.

This view states that if there is any evil in this world, then it could come about only because God has purposed it for some good and wise reason. The early church father Augustine said, "For God judged it better to bring good out of evil than not to permit any evil to exist."[12] Scripture is replete with indications of God's good purposes for pain, evil, and suffering, especially for the believer.[13]

Furthermore, it's not as if evil happens and then God reshuffles things so that he can salvage some good from it. Every instance of evil has already

---

12. Augustine, *Enchiridion [Handbook] on Faith, Hope and Love*, 8.27, http://www.ccel.org/ccel/augustine/enchiridion.

13. See Gen. 50:20; John 16:33; Acts 2:22–24; 4:27–28; 14:22; Rom. 8:28; 2 Cor. 4:17; James 1:2–4; 1 Peter 1:6–7.

been fitted within the scope of his predetermined plans for history. Now, if there were the possibility of the existence of some evil for which God had no good and wise purpose, then we all would have cause for great concern. Thankfully, it is not possible to imagine that an all-powerful, all-good, and all-wise God would ever have less than sufficiently good and wise reasons for evil to enter his pristine creation. If God cannot get the necessary goods he intends from the various evils that permeate this world, then we can be sure that those evils would never have come about in the first place.

Greg Welty has insightfully demonstrated that a theodicy worth its salt must meet two criteria.[14] Only the greater-good defense appears poised to meet these criteria. Furthermore, one common objection to the greater-good defense is that good ends cannot justify evil means. The fulfillment of these criteria answers that objection.

The first criterion states that whatever good God brings about as a result of evil must be a unique sort of good that could not have otherwise come about unless it was dependent on some evil. For example, consider the unique goodness of compassion. George Müller could have never provided exemplary care for over ten thousand orphans in his lifetime unless there existed a crisis of British children in abject poverty that cried out for such compassion.[15] Müller simply emulated the tender compassion of Jesus that has made our dear Lord the most beloved figure in history. "When he saw the crowds, he had compassion for them, because they were harassed and helpless, like sheep without a shepherd" (Matt. 9:36).

The second criterion states that the good that comes about in connection to some evil must be weighty and important enough to justify the existence of the evil that the good is dependent on. For example, Welty notes, "Imagine if someone asserted that unless the Holocaust happened, the inventor of his

14. Greg Welty, *Why Is There Evil in the World (and So Much of It)?*, (Fearn, Scotland: Christian Focus, 2018), 43–46.

15. See Roger Steer, *George Müller: Delighted in God* (Fearn, Scotland: Christian Focus, 2006).

favorite flavor of ice cream would not have existed (and he tells some crazy story that allegedly links the two things)."[16] We have no reason to expect that God is going to pursue trivial goods out of some weighty and horrendous evil. The good that God gets from evil must be significantly greater than the evil itself—thus the name: greater-good defense.

CAN WE KNOW WHAT GREATER GOOD GOD IS ACCOMPLISHING?

This leads to one of the perplexing and often disconcerting facts about the greater-good defense. We do not always know what greater good God intends to bring about in connection to evil or how to ascertain whether the good is worth bearing the evil that it is connected to. Now, some greater goods are self-evident. For example, we know that the evil of Jesus' crucifixion brought about the extraordinary good of salvation for countless multitudes. We know that God's saving grace could never come about unless there are sinful wretches to whom God decided to extend this weightier grace. This is why forgiven sinners sing out joyfully:

> Marvelous grace of our loving Lord,
> Grace that exceeds our sin and our guilt. . . .
>
> Grace, grace, God's grace,
> Grace that is greater than all our sin.[17]

In other cases, the good that emerges from some evil needs to be explained to us. For example, consider the Old Testament patriarch Joseph, who was sold into slavery by his brothers who hated him. This eventually resulted in a lengthy prison sentence when Joseph was falsely accused of attempted rape. Yet God used these events to exalt Joseph to the position

---

16. Welty, *Why Is There Evil?*, 45.
17. Julia H. Johnson, "Marvelous Grace of Our Loving Lord" (1910).

of prime minister of Egypt, and his wisdom mitigated the effects of a vast regional famine.

At the climax of the story (which can be read in Genesis 37–50), Joseph's brothers are reunited to him. They are afraid for their lives, but Joseph reassures them: "Do not fear, for am I in the place of God? As for you, you meant evil against me, but God meant it for good, to bring it about that many people should be kept alive, as they are today" (Gen. 50:19–20). The evil actions of Joseph's brothers were instrumental in God's good purposes.

In most cases of evil, however, the goods that God brings about from them are neither self-evident nor easily explained to us. But this does not mean that the goods are nonexistent. Let me illustrate the point. Like most little boys, I hated to eat my spinach. It tasted terrible. I could see no good in eating it. But what I couldn't tell from the slimy green stuff was that it is loaded with vitamins A, B, C, E, and K; with the minerals potassium, magnesium, copper, zinc, and manganese; and with a variety of antioxidants—all stuff that is not discernible to the sight, taste, or smell but is extremely good for one's health. The fact is, we may never discern, in this life or even the next, all the manifold goods that God brings about from even the most appalling evils.

Nonetheless, what we need most is to cling to the assurance of God's inscrutable wisdom. In our puny and corrupted minds, we do not have the knowledge and wisdom to declare that some evil could never have any possible good reason for transpiring. We may think that it would have been the wisest course of action for God to warn the Bethlehemites of Herod's evil plans to murder their baby boys or to prevent his evil altogether (Matt. 2:13–18). But we simply cannot plumb the depths of God's infinite and perfect wisdom (Isa. 55:8–9). "Who has measured the Spirit of the LORD, or what man shows him his counsel? Whom did he consult, and who made him understand? Who taught him the path of justice, and taught him knowledge, and showed him the way of understanding?" (Isa. 40:13–14; cf. Rom. 11:33–36).

The most serious objection to the greater-good defense is that no matter how you cut it, God cannot be exonerated from being the author of evil. This is an important matter, and we will address it in more detail later (see chapter 4). But in the meantime, simply note that there is a certain paradox in saying that an unimpeachably good God has nothing but good purposes for evil. His *sovereign will* often ordains that which his *moral will* detests.

Yet this is not the only paradox of the Christian faith, several of which are crucial to Christian orthodoxy. A paradox is an apparent contradiction, but not a real contradiction. For example, the Bible is quite clear that God is one God and there is no other, yet he subsists in three distinct persons: Father, Son, and Holy Spirit. Likewise, God the Son is one person within the triune Godhead, yet he has both a fully divine and fully human nature. God predestines sinners to salvation, and yet they will not be saved unless they willingly repent and believe.

WHEN TRAGEDY HITS HOME

When the rubber hits the road, how do these opposing theological views handle real-life tragedy? Let us consider two respected theologians and how each interprets the way in which God works amid tragedy. Ben Witherington, an Arminian, and Fred Zaspel, a Calvinist, each lost his precious daughter to a premature death.

Witherington's daughter Christy died of a pulmonary embolism in 2012 when she was only thirty-two years old. Responding to this tragedy, Witherington states: "God did not do this to my child. . . . God does not terminate sweet lives."[18] We cannot help but sympathize with Witherington's sentiments. In the darkness of grief, most Christians, regardless of their theological persuasion, have a hard time believing that God had a role in taking their dear loved ones away from them. But Witherington is clear: "One primary reason I am not a Calvinist is I do not believe in God's detailed control of all events."[19]

---

18. Ben Witherington, "When a Daughter Dies," *Christianity Today*, April 2012, 37.
19. Witherington, 37.

He considers the situation of Job, who lost all ten of his sons and daughters. A devastating tornado ripped through the home of the oldest son while he and his siblings were enjoying a meal together (Job 1:18–19). Witherington doesn't find Job's response helpful. The grieving father laments: "The LORD gave, and the LORD has taken away; blessed be the name of the LORD" (v. 21). Witherington is convinced that "this is not good theology."[20] He believes that Job hovers near blasphemy. Instead, Witherington believes that the devil, not God, took his daughter Christy's life. The devil certainly had a role in Job's suffering, but it was a subordinate role.

The fact is, Witherington has failed to consider the context of Job's assertion. In the very next verse, the divinely inspired narrator offers instructive commentary on Job's claim that God "has taken away" his children: "In all this Job did not sin or charge God with wrong" (Job 1:22). Job is correct to assign *sovereign responsibility* to God for this calamity, but he has not charged God with *moral responsibility*. There is an important difference here. God is the one who ultimately took Job's children away, but in doing so he committed no wrong. Why? Because he had unimpeachably good and wise intentions for this calamity that outweighed the pain and suffering it caused Job.

In contrast, consider the response of Zaspel regarding his twenty-nine-year-old daughter Gina, who died after battling debilitating illness for twelve years. Gina died about a year after Witherington's daughter Christy died.

> Through the years of her suffering we reminded ourselves often that the God who in grace had rescued her in Christ from sin loves her even more than we do. And so we trust his providence. He is too wise ever to make a mistake, and too good ever to do us wrong. And we acknowledge that just as he was free and sovereign in giving Gina to us 29 years ago, so now he is free and sovereign—and good and just—in taking her. He has not wronged us. Indeed, not only

20. Witherington, 37.

do we affirm this great truth—we rest in it. This God is himself our Father, a Father who knows what is best for his children and faithfully directs our lives accordingly. Moreover, he is the Father who in love one day gave up his own Son to bear our curse in order to redeem us to himself. Yes, there are many "Why?" questions that we cannot answer, but we lack no proof of God's love or his goodness. And we bless him today with deeper passion than ever.[21]

Note the stark differences between Witherington's and Zaspel's views of God. Witherington assumes that the Calvinist God cannot possibly be good. Rather, he supposes that a God who is completely sovereign over evil must thereby be "almighty and malevolent."[22] Nothing could be further from the truth, as Zaspel in his grief makes clear. Both Arminians and Calvinists are zealous to defend the all-encompassing goodness of God in the face of evil. But only one of these theological outlooks—Calvinism—is faithful to uphold the biblical testimony to God's goodness expressed, not despite evil, but *in* and *through* occurrences of evil. Again, it is part of the burden of this book to demonstrate this truth.

The book of Job is written to vindicate God's meticulously sovereign and mysterious ways when evil seems to undo us. In the eyes of God, Job was an extraordinarily wise and righteous man (Job 1:8; 2:3). Job knew that if something or someone other than God dictated and directed what evil came against him and against the divine plan, then we would have trouble on our hands. It would indicate that some nefarious entity far more powerful than God was thwarting his designs. If this were true, it would give us ample reason for fear. But the book of Job shows us that powers such as the devil have no hold on God. Satan is merely a pawn

---

21. Fred Zaspel, "Reflections on the Loss of Our Daughter," Credo, November 14, 2013, https://credomag.com/2013/11/reflections-on-the-loss-of-our-daughter-fred-zaspel/.

22. Witherington, "When a Daughter Dies," 37.

in the divine stratagems for history.[23] As Luther quipped, the devil is "God's devil."[24]

This means that we can rest easy on our pillows at night only in the knowledge that God is in full control, directing every detailed course of history and our lives, whether good *or* evil. This fact does not eliminate our pain when tragedy strikes, nor does it answer all our questions about the mysterious ways of God. Job, among all people, was aware of this (see Job 42:1–6). Nonetheless, his words are instructive: "Though he slay me, I will hope in him" (13:15). If God is not in control of all calamity and ill-fortune, then to whom can we turn for solace when the darkness tries to claim our souls? "My flesh and my heart may fail, but God is the strength of my heart and my portion forever" (Ps. 73:26).

Furthermore, not even the greater-good defense is poised to answer the most important question—what overarching plan could God have that justifies a world that has been sullied by so much pain and suffering? We must acknowledge that the Bible nowhere gives us a tidy little answer to why there is evil in the first place. No chapter and verse spells it out: "And the Lord God saith, 'This is the reason that evil hath entered the world . . .'"

Nonetheless, as we continue this journey, we will see that a very clear theodicy (an answer to the problem of evil) emerges from its pages. This theodicy is a pointed variation of the greater-good defense that I have called the *greater-glory theodicy*. In the remaining pages, we will lay the groundwork for this theodicy and then present it in all its *glory*!

---

23. The Bible often indicates that God uses evil spirits as his instruments to incite evil, but *always* for his good and wise purposes. See Judg. 9:23; 1 Sam. 16:14; 19:9; 1 Kings 22:2–23; 2 Chron. 18:19–22; 2 Thess. 2:11. See also chapters 3 and 4.

24. Martin Luther, *Lectures on Galatians, 1535: Chapters 1–4*, vol. 26 of *Luther's Works*, ed. Jaroslav Pelikan and Walter A. Hansen, trans. Jaroslav Pelikan (St. Louis: Concordia, 1963), 190.

STUDY QUESTIONS

1. What is the basic difference between Calvinism and Arminianism?
2. What are the two basic ideas behind the Arminian definition of *free will*?
3. How do Arminians believe their view of free will solves the problem of evil?
4. How does the story of God's warning to the magi and Joseph in Matthew 2:12–18 present a problem for the free-will defense?
5. Does God have the kind of free will that Arminianism subscribes to? Why or why not?
6. Why is the doctrine of divine foreknowledge a problem for the free-will defense?
7. According to Greg Welty, what two criteria must a theodicy meet?
8. In what situations will God stop or prevent evil from occurring?
9. How should we respond when we don't know what purpose God has in permitting some evil?
10. Consider the tragic stories of Ben Witherington and Fred Zaspel. How would you assess each of the responses to their tragedies?

3

THE GRAND AUTHOR OF HISTORY

Before we can understand the biblical answer to the problem of evil and what I call the *greater-glory theodicy*, we must start with what is foundational —the most fundamental thing.

We must start with the state of things when there was no passage of time. No clocks to mark each second, each minute, each hour. No years, decades, or centuries piling up. No past. No present. No future.

There were no boundaries defining any geometric location we can think of. No up. No down. No latitude or longitude. No north, south, east, or west. No massive or minuscule volumes of space that could be measured in any way.

There was no material stuff, no mass or substance. No protons or neutrons forming atomic nuclei. No electrons circling that basic unit of all matter. No hydrogen, uranium, platinum, carbon, or any of the other known elements. No Saharan sand. No Amazon River water. No Rocky Mountain air. No molecular structures whatsoever. No sun, no moon, no planets. No starry host stretched across an endless cosmos.

There were no motions to be found. No velocity or acceleration of objects. No energy acting on matter. No gravity holding the earth to the sun. No electromagnetism producing the northern lights. No strong or weak nuclear forces working invisibly at the subatomic level.

There were no living things. No flora or fauna. No Bermuda grass, lilac bushes, or spruce trees. No amoebas. No carpenter ants. No long-whiskered catfish or ruby-throated hummingbirds. No arctic foxes or African elephants. Humankind was missing. No men, women, or children. There was no breathing. No blood flowing. No muscles twitching or synapses firing. No seeing, hearing, tasting, smelling, or touching. There was nothing and no one of the sort to be found anywhere.

Yet before the advent of time, space, matter, energy, and the vast array of living things, there was *something*—because if there was *nothing*, then there would still be nothing. To be more precise, there had to be *Someone* —and we know who.

"In the beginning, God . . ."

The eternal triune God is fundamental. He is foundational. He alone is necessary. Furthermore, he is before all things and the Creator of all things —things that he had no need of creating. Nonetheless, he was pleased to make it all. The God of the universe governs all things and holds them together. He is the Author of life and the determiner of death. And herein lies a truth that we must never miss. If we fail to understand who God is, then we can never understand the matrix of all that he has created. We can never understand good and evil, ourselves, or anything at all. Everything is dependent on him.

Most of all, we lowly creatures uniquely created in his image are especially dependent on him. What is fundamental to us is how we relate to this God. John Calvin rightly said, "True and sound wisdom consists of two parts: the knowledge of God and of ourselves."[1] To clarify, he points out, "It is certain that man never achieves a clear knowledge of himself unless he has first looked upon God's face, and then descends from contemplating him to scrutinize himself."[2]

Therefore, the one thing that a biblical theodicy (an answer to the problem of evil) must never do is compromise the Bible's testimony

1. John Calvin, *Institutes of the Christian Religion*, ed. John T. McNeill, trans. Ford Lewis Battles, Library of Christian Classics 20–21 (Philadelphia: Westminster, 1960), 1.1.1.1.
2. Calvin, 1.1.1.2.

to God's maximal greatness, especially at the expense of propping up some pretended autonomy that we possess as his creatures. Orthodox theism says that God is a perfect being in a category all by himself. It is not possible to imagine a greater being than God. "He is an immeasurable and unbounded ocean of being; the absolute being who alone has being in himself."[3]

Consequently, he is the ground of all other things that come into existence out of nothing by the word of his power (Col. 1:16–17; Heb. 11:3). He is eternally and unchangeably nothing less than all power, all goodness, and infinite wisdom—those specific divine attributes that come under scrutiny when the afflicted are groping in the darkness, searching for answers to the conundrums of evil. But God is far more, and we must begin our journey by considering how big and glorious this God truly is.

THE HOLY ONE

Human beings are naturally self-absorbed and view themselves more highly than reality warrants. The hubris of this thinking is exemplified by the Greek philosopher Protagoras (485–415 B.C.), who said, "Man is the measure of all things." Nothing much has changed over the last twenty-five hundred years. Unfortunately, our depraved condition is perpetually tuned to this default setting, distorting the view not only of ourselves but of God. Humans tend to deify themselves while humanizing the essence of God. The difference between us and the Almighty does not appear to be so very great. He thinks like us. He acts like us. And he relates to the world in the same way that we do.

Yet nothing could be further from the truth.

God paints a picture of himself in his divinely inspired Word that shatters all illusions we may have about him. One of the stark features of God is that he is singularly *holy*. The prophet Isaiah learned something

---

3. Herman Bavinck, *Reformed Dogmatics*, ed. John Bolt, trans. John Vriend, 4 vols. (Grand Rapids: Baker Academic, 2003–8), 2:123.

of this frightful notion in a vision in which he encountered a special and visible manifestation of God's presence called a *theophany*. He saw Yahweh seated on a throne in the heavenly temple, "high and lifted up" (Isa. 6:1). The wings of seraphim covered the One seated there so that the prophet could not see his face. The seraphim called to one another, addressing Yahweh as holy. They did not say that he was holy just once or even twice. This would have been enough to cause Isaiah to tremble with unimaginable fear. Instead, they called out three times:

> Holy, holy, holy is the LORD of hosts;
> the whole earth is full of his glory! (Isa. 6:3)

No other attribute of God is given this threefold emphasis in Scripture, indicating how much we need to pay attention to it. What is divine holiness? One aspect concerns the supreme righteousness of God. When God calls his people to "be holy, for I am holy" (Lev. 11:44, 45), he means for them to separate themselves from unrighteousness and to pursue the perfect righteousness that marks their Lord's moral character. In this regard, God supernaturally grants those whom he has redeemed the capacity for moving in the direction of this kind of holiness. Without his gracious renewal of our spoiled condition, we could never become holy. Thus, such holiness is called a *communicable* attribute of God because he "communicates" or shares such attributes with us as his image-bearing creatures.

But there is another dimension to holiness that concerns us. The Bible often speaks of God as holy in the sense that he is wholly *other*. He is uniquely separate and distinct from all else. "To whom then will you compare me, that I should be like him? says the Holy One" (Isa. 40:25). The answer is clear—no one. We can never possess this kind of holiness. It is an *incommunicable* attribute of God. He does not share it with us. It is a holiness that theologians call divine *transcendence*.

When we think of the notion of transcendence, we think of something beyond the pale of our mundane existence—eating crackers, driving to the laundromat, shouting at the neighbor's incessantly barking dog to shut up.

When you stop and take the time to gaze at the Milky Way or get lost in a sunset where the sky is all ablaze in red and orange and vermilion hues, you may find yourself transported to an otherworldly place of wonder where all of a sudden the things of this earth fade into nonimportance. You are more self-aware in these moments as your existence seems to be absorbed into something big—too big to comprehend. But somehow it is deeply serene and satisfying, yet scary at the same time. The awe of it feels as though there is a larger purpose to reality, and even though you appear insignificant, yet somehow you know that being a small part of this larger-than-life reality is where your purpose lies.

Ultimately, transcendence points us to the incomprehensible wonder and vastness of God. The Almighty One is far above us. The uncreated One is not confined to the plane of his creation. He is not bound by space and time. He is an eternal spirit (John 4:24), "from everlasting to everlasting" (Ps. 90:2), without beginning or end (Rev. 1:8). As Boethius (A.D. 480–524) said, God's timeless eternality is the "whole, simultaneous, and perfect possession of unending life."[4] He is all-absorbing reality standing behind our feelings of insignificance, and we intuitively know that such an exalted One deserves our full attention and worship.

The life of the triune Holy One is completely independent, self-existent, self-sufficient, and self-satisfied in the glory of his own eternal blessedness, having no needs whatsoever. The Dutch theologian Herman Bavinck observes: "The distance between God and us is the gulf between the Infinite and the finite, between eternity and time, between being and becoming, between the All and the nothing. However little we know of God, even the faintest notion implies that he is a being who is infinitely exalted above every creature."[5]

> Can you find out the deep things of God?
> Can you find out the limit of the Almighty?

4. Quoted and translated by Gavin Ortlund, *Theological Retrieval for Evangelicals: Why We Need Our Past to Have a Future* (Wheaton, IL: Crossway, 2019), 93.
5. Bavinck, *Reformed Dogmatics*, 2:30.

> It is higher than heaven—what can you do?
>   Deeper than Sheol—what can you know?
> Its measure is longer than the earth
>   and broader than the sea. (Job 11:7–9)

On another level, the supremely righteous and transcendent dimensions of divine holiness wreck our fragile human selves. Isaiah encountered this comprehensive holiness, and it undid him (Isa. 6:5).

These stupendous realities also confronted Moses when God made himself known to him in another *theophany*, which occurred via the burning bush that Moses encountered in the Sinai wilderness (Ex. 3:1–4). God spoke audibly from the bush to the man he had appointed to lead his people out of Egyptian slavery, saying, "Do not come near; take your sandals off your feet, for the place on which you are standing is holy ground" (v. 5). Why did God say this to Moses?

He wanted to signify that there was an unbridgeable barrier between himself and this lowly creature. Not only was Moses tainted by sin and unable to enter the righteous realm of a holy God, but he also could not come face to face with the one who "dwells in unapproachable light" (1 Tim. 6:16). God's ineffable glory separates him from all that he has made. The burning bush was but a faint representation of the exaltedness of Yahweh—the great and mysterious "I AM" (Ex. 3:14). There exists a profound Creator-creature distinction whereby the holy domain of the Creator cannot be penetrated by mortal creatures.

Yet we long to gaze into his holiness.

Later, when Moses wanted to see the unveiled essence of the divine glory, he was denied access. Yahweh said to him, "You cannot see my face, for man shall not see me and live" (Ex. 33:20). Human beings, in our finite and tainted condition, would utterly disintegrate if we were to see God as he is in himself. Nonetheless, Yahweh gave Moses a glimpse of his glory that no other mortal has ever experienced.

But this glory did not overtake him directly. It came from God's backside, so to speak, while he hid Moses in the cleft of a rock (Ex. 33:22–23) up on Horeb, "the mountain of God" (3:1). As God spoke to

Moses, a minuscule dose of his ineffable glory caused a holy afterglow to shine forth from Moses' face. When the Israelites encountered him, they were frightened by his appearance (34:29–30). Subsequently, Moses was compelled to shield his face with a veil every time he finished speaking with Yahweh (vv. 34–35).

This explains why we have difficulty even comprehending God. Our words crumble to the ground whenever we try to explain what he is truly like. The Bible must use language we can understand to afford us some glimpse into God's nature. He is often described with humanlike features because we have no categories for the Godness of his true nature. This doesn't mean that God is *absolutely* transcendent such that we may know *nothing* about him. Rather, it simply means that "his greatness is unsearchable" (Ps. 145:3).

Calvin remarks that God gently condescends and comes near to us from his lofty position and speaks to us with baby talk.[6] The Bible is all baby talk—coming from the Spirit of the Creator down to the creature (see 1 Cor. 2:6–16). Consequently, we can possess a knowledge of God that is undeniably abundant, allowing us to enter into a full and satisfying relationship with him; nonetheless, it is never exhaustive or exacting. We will never escape the mystery of our wonderful God. But this is why we sing:

> Immortal, invisible, God only wise,
> In light inaccessible hid from our eyes,
> Most blessed, most glorious, the Ancient of Days,
> Almighty, victorious, thy great name we praise.[7]

What does all this mean for us and making sense of the problem of evil?

It means that we do not get to set the terms for the issues at stake. We cannot be the rightful judges of how God has ordered the universe and how he interacts with it. The mysteries surrounding God's deep connections

---

6. Calvin, *Institutes*, 1.1.13.1.
7. Walter Chalmers Smith, "Immortal, Invisible, God Only Wise" (1867).

to the unfolding of the world drama will never be fully understood. We can only partially grasp how he weaves himself and his secret designs into the particulars of history's ebbs and flows, its highs and lows, its strange turns and surprising outcomes, and indeed, all its good and evil. When we try to explore the outer reaches of the divine stratosphere, we enter the murky domain of his inscrutable ways: "For my thoughts are not your thoughts, neither are your ways my ways, declares the LORD. For as the heavens are higher than the earth, so are my ways higher than your ways and my thoughts than your thoughts" (Isa. 55:8–9).

Therefore, we cannot treat God as though he were like us. He is not a creature. We are in an entirely different category from God. He is not bound by our severely limited existence and perceptions of reality as he has defined it. He is infinite; we are finite. He is timeless; we are *in* time. He is outside space; we are confined to it. He is necessary and independent; we are contingent and wholly dependent on him for everything (Acts 17:28). He is the wellspring of all knowledge and wisdom (Col. 2:3); we lack any understanding or wisdom apart from him. "He upholds the universe by the word of his power" (Heb. 1:3). This means that he is the prime initiator of all movement, energy, and action; we are the mere conduits and instruments of his actions. He is the authoritative King; we are the submissive servants. He is the Author of the story; we are simply the actors. He is the Potter; we are but clay in his hands. The vessels do not get to question the Potter and ask why he made us as he did (Rom. 9:19–21).

Without understanding this magnificent vision of God and our humble place before him, we can have no real answer to the problem of evil.

THE SOVEREIGN ONE

Another crucial issue concerning the nature of God that needs to be clear before we can make sense of pain, suffering, and evil is the precise nature of his sovereignty over creation and history. Calvinism is known for emphasizing the Bible's testimony regarding the *absolute* and *meticulous* sovereignty of God over all things, and many chafe against this notion. But that is understandable, given our tendency to cling to a pretended autonomy.

It is important, however, not to isolate this attribute of God from his transcendent holiness, as explained above.[8] Rather, God's sovereignty rightly flows from his eternal self-existence, his independence from all else, his incomprehensibility, and his status as the sole Creator and Sustainer of the universe. He is the unfathomable Lord of all. Ironically, it is from this vantage point that we can make better sense of the doctrine of divine sovereignty.

It was in this lowly place that the once-proud king Nebuchadnezzar stood. He was the greatest ruler of his era, and he was not afraid to boast, pretentiously speaking of "the glory of my majesty" (Dan. 4:30). But God humbled him for seven years when he turned mad, crawling on the ground and eating grass like an animal (vv. 31–33). After he had been sufficiently educated in self-abasement, God gave his reason back to him, and suddenly Nebuchadnezzar gained remarkable clarity about his true identity and especially that of God:

> At the end of the days I, Nebuchadnezzar, lifted my eyes to heaven, and my reason returned to me, and I blessed the Most High, and praised and honored him who lives forever,
>
> for his dominion is an everlasting dominion,
>   and his kingdom endures from generation to generation;
> all the inhabitants of the earth are accounted as nothing,
>   and he does according to his will among the host of heaven
>   and among the inhabitants of the earth;
> and none can stay his hand
>   or say to him, "What have you done?" (Dan. 4:34–35)

8. Truth be told, none of God's attributes can be isolated from the others. Theologians call this the *simplicity* of God. God is not composed of parts and pieces and put together like a jigsaw puzzle. He is a singular unity. Therefore, all his attributes must be seen as a whole in the fullness of their perfections. His essence as God is never less than altogether perfectly holy, righteous, just, loving, sovereign, knowledgeable, wise, and so on.

Nebuchadnezzar unabashedly embraces a comprehensive and unfettered view of divine sovereignty here. But notice that he also intuitively recognizes that this fact leads people to question how God orders the affairs of the world as they look at what transpires, self-confidently thinking to themselves, "What have you done?" This is especially true when things go awry—when dark clouds come billowing in, obscuring the light and ruining the day. But there is something else in Nebuchadnezzar's timeless words. The questioning of God demonstrates that his ways are not our ways (Isa. 55:8–9). Thus, Nebuchadnezzar situates God's meticulous sovereignty within the framework of his holy and incomprehensible transcendence. And this is where other portions of Scripture locate divine sovereignty as well. Let us consider this doctrine in more detail.

God's Comprehensive Sovereignty

David provides one of the clearest declarations of the comprehensive nature of God's sovereignty in Scripture: "The LORD has established His throne in the heavens, and His sovereignty rules over all" (Ps. 103:19 NASB). Historically, God's sovereignty has been understood to have three components: (1) his eternal decree, (2) his ongoing providence, and (3) his omnipotence (all-encompassing power). Let us consider each component.

God's Eternal Decree

God established his eternal plan, or decree, for history from before the foundation of the world. The Westminster Confession of Faith provides a good definition: "God, from all eternity, did, by the most wise and holy counsel of his own will, freely, and unchangeably ordain whatsoever comes to pass."[9] Since God ordains everything "from all eternity" (see Eph. 3:11), it is "unchangeably" fixed: "The counsel of the LORD stands forever, the plans of His heart from generation to generation" (Ps. 33:11 NASB). The psalmist here not only says that God's decree is eternal in the same timeless sense as Ephesians 3:11 indicates, but also states that the decree

9. Westminster Confession of Faith 3.1 (on "God's Eternal Decree").

encompasses the passage of time from one age ("generation") to the next within the context of creation itself.

Isaiah declares: "For the LORD of hosts has purposed, and who will annul it? His hand is stretched out, and who will turn it back?" (Isa. 14:27). No plan of God's can fail (Hab. 2:3), and nothing escapes those plans. In Ephesians 1, Paul insists that everything that transpires ("comes to pass") in heaven and earth (Eph. 1:10) is set "according to the purpose of him who works all things according to the counsel of his will" (v. 11).

Furthermore, the Westminster Confession says that God's plans proceed from his "most wise and holy counsel." God would never order a universe that did not proceed from his all-encompassing wisdom and righteousness; otherwise, we would have reason to impugn his character. Every last detail has been carefully worked out. He did not need to consult anyone (Isa. 40:13–14). All that he planned he did "freely" out of his own sovereign pleasure. The psalmist proclaims, "Our God is in the heavens; he does all that he pleases" (Ps. 115:3).

God's Providence

God is not only the architect of history's plan, but also the executor of that plan, ensuring that everything proceeds exactly as he drew it up. God is always active in the world, sustaining every thought, every movement, and every action in the part and in the whole (Col. 1:17; Heb. 1:3). He did not set the world in motion, turning it on as though it were the Energizer Bunny, and then sit back to see what would happen. The Heidelberg Catechism defines divine providence as "the almighty and ever present power of God by which God upholds, as with his hand, heaven and earth and all creatures, and so rules them that leaf and blade, rain and drought, fruitful and lean years, food and drink, health and sickness, prosperity and poverty—all things, in fact, come to us not by chance but by his fatherly hand."[10]

God's providential actions govern times and seasons (Acts 14:17) and whole epochs (Dan. 2:21; Acts 1:7), encompassing all the nations

---

10. Heidelberg Catechism, Lord's Day 10: Q&A 27.

(Isa. 40:15; Acts 14:16), determining the places where people will live (Acts 17:26) and which leaders will rule the world (Dan. 2:21). He determines life and death, who will be rich or poor, and whether one will succeed and another fail (1 Sam. 2:6–7). God is in the little things too. He feeds the birds and cares for the lilies of the field (Matt. 6:26, 28–30). Not a single sparrow falls to the ground apart from him (Matt. 10:29). His hand causes lightning to strike its precise mark (Job 36:32). When coins are tossed and dice are thrown, he produces the results (Prov. 16:33). Nothing happens by chance (1 Kings 22:28, 34). Chance and luck are illusions in God's universe.

God's Omnipotence

God's plan for the unfolding of all things and his actions that providentially ensure that his plan will succeed would mean nothing if he did not possess the power necessary to make it all happen. Thus, an important component of God's comprehensive sovereignty is his possession of all power—his omnipotence: "O Lord, God of our fathers, are you not God in heaven? You rule over all the kingdoms of the nations. In your hand are power and might, so that none is able to withstand you" (2 Chron. 20:6; cf. Isa. 40:21–26).

God's power is limited only by what does not contradict his other attributes. For example, God is a logical God; therefore, he does nothing that defies logic, such as making married bachelors or square circles. Because God is wholly righteous, he has no power to sin or act unjustly. When understood within the totality of all of God's attributes, his power is so immense that it is beyond our capacity to fathom. After describing God's actions both in the heavens and on the earth, Job declares: "These are just the beginning of all that he does, merely a whisper of his power. Who, then, can comprehend the thunder of his power?" (Job 26:14 NLT).

God's Sovereignty over Evil

Most Christians have no problem accepting God's sovereignty when it comes to all the good we see in the world and in our lives. But we start to get sideways when we speak of God's sovereignty over evil.

Like Professor Witherington (see end of chapter 2), many Christians want to distance God from having his hand mixed up in evil, as though this would somehow taint him or make him morally blameworthy for its existence. But God's revelation of himself in Scripture is not concerned to picture him as tiptoeing around this unpleasantness. God expresses no fear that his connection to all the evil that transpires in his creation is going to corrupt him. Rather, the Bible places his sovereignty over evil in the context of his holy and otherworldly transcendence such that we cannot think of his relationship to evil in the same way in which we lowly creatures relate to it.

Isaiah chapters 40 through 48 constitute one of God's clearest and most striking testimonies to his sovereignty as the Creator, Possessor, Sustainer, and Lord of the universe.[11] Yahweh, in this divine monologue, looks to his exiled and beleaguered people in the future in order to declare to them his sovereign greatness over every event that transpires in their lives—and indeed, all of history. God's sovereignty in these remarkable chapters is placed within the context of his all-consuming transcendence, which becomes mind-boggling when we try to grasp its enormousness.

One pointed passage peers down the portals of every natural and moral evil. When declaring the future to the great Medo-Persian king Cyrus, whom God calls "his anointed" (Isa. 45:1), Yahweh proclaims:

> I am the LORD, and there is no other,
> > besides me there is no God;
> > I equip you, though you do not know me,
> that people may know, from the rising of the sun
> > and from the west, that there is none besides me;
> > I am the LORD, and there is no other.
> I form light and create darkness;
> > I make well-being and create calamity;
> > I am the LORD, who does all these things. (Isa. 45:5–7)

---

11. See especially Isa. 40:13–17, 28–31; 42:8–9; 43:11–13; 44:6–8, 18, 24–28; 46:9–11; 48:3, 11–16.

God sets himself apart from all other so-called gods—indeed, from every other creature. God is saying: "I am unique. I am utterly other. I alone am supreme. I exist in a class all by myself." This is meant to give us pause. We cannot think of him in the way that we think of anyone else or any other thing. He is not like us, so we must stop making such comparisons.

It is in this context that God makes a stunning claim about his sovereignty over both good *and* evil in Isaiah 45:7. Notice how "light" is contrasted with "darkness" and "well-being" is contrasted with "calamity." This is a Hebrew literary device called a *merism*. A merism compares and contrasts two extremes as a way of saying that everything in between those extremes is to be included. This meristic feature is further emphasized by another Hebrew literary device—repetition. Twice God speaks of his control over the gamut of these disparate forces in the world.

Now, the shocking thing to note is the term "calamity." This is the standard Hebrew term for "evil" (*ra'*). But this is not the only significant word in this verse. Two times a unique word for "create" (*bara'*) is used in connection to "darkness" and "calamity" (evil). This particular Hebrew word is reserved in the Old Testament for God alone (see Gen. 1:1; Isa. 42:5; 43:1), and Isaiah's Hebrew readers would know this. Notice that the term is used not when speaking of "light" or "well-being" but in connection with "darkness" and "calamity." God seems to be emphasizing his sovereign control over evil in particular.

The use of the word does not mean that God created evil in the same sense that he created everything else, which could only be "very good" in the initial creation (Gen. 1:31). Rather, it indicates that God is ultimately the source of evil, whether natural or moral—but not in the sense that it emanated from his being, which is impossible because of his unbridled and unassailable goodness (1 John 1:5). Instead, it comes from him in the sense that he decreed its existence before the foundation of the world (Eph. 1:9–11). He figured it into his plans for history before the first scene of history unfolded.

The book of Lamentations has the same exalted view of God as Lord over evil that we see in the book of Isaiah: "Who has spoken and it came to pass, unless the Lord has commanded it? Is it not from the mouth of the Most High that good and bad come?" (Lam. 3:37–38). Just as Isaiah 45:7 attributes the emergence of good and evil to the transcendent God of the universe, so also Jeremiah says that "good and bad" issue forth "from the mouth of the Most High" (Lam. 3:38). In fact, the term "bad" in Lamentations 3:38 is yet again the standard Hebrew term for "evil" (*ra'*).

But lest we become dejected that God stands behind all our ill-fortune, a few verses earlier Jeremiah qualifies this truth: "But, though he cause grief, he will have compassion according to the abundance of his steadfast love; for he does not afflict from his heart or grieve the children of men" (Lam. 3:32–33). Yes, God determines all the bad stuff that leads to the "grief" humans suffer, but his intention is not to "afflict" us simply for the sake of affliction. A good God never purposes evil for evil's sake. Of necessity, it must have a purpose that transcends our limited vision—a purpose always designed for a greater good (see vv. 19–26).

Job stands in the same line of thinking that we see in Isaiah and Jeremiah. Job did not acknowledge Satan as the primary agent who took his children away (Job 1:6–19). He knew nothing of Satan's involvement. Instead, he attributed this act to God, but did so without blaming God, something that the inspired narrator of Job's calamity clearly indicates (vv. 21–22). And just when you'd think that the man could not bear a further ounce of suffering, God instigates a second wave of calamity through his pawn the devil (2:3–6).

All things considered, Job bears the weight of his pain magnificently, but his wife does not. She says to him: "Do you still hold fast your integrity? Curse God and die" (Job 2:9). She doesn't say, "Curse Satan and die." No matter who we think is responsible for evil, deep in our hearts humans turn to God when calamity strikes because we know that he is ultimately in control.

Job is a model of wisdom. He responds: "You speak as one of the foolish women would speak. Shall we receive good from God, and shall we not receive evil?" (Job 2:10). Job uses the same Hebrew term for "evil" that Isaiah and Jeremiah do. This is no impertinence on Job's part. Again, the inspired author of the book tells us, "In all this Job did not sin with his lips" (v. 10). God ultimately caused all this evil, but that is no indication that he is morally responsible for it, a matter that we will take up in the next chapter.

God as Transcendent Author of All

When we consider that God is the utterly unique, holy, incomprehensible, transcendent, and all-encompassing Lord over his creation, then an illuminating analogy emerges, helping us better understand his sovereign providence. God's providence does not operate like a chain reaction, setting off events in time and space like an elaborate maze of dominoes laid out on a massive gymnasium floor and then set in motion by the guy who tips over the first domino.

Nor is God like a grandmaster chess player, simultaneously outmaneuvering a host of opponents to achieve his victorious goals. The Almighty does not operate on the fly, acting and reacting to his creation and creatures as though they were operating independently of him. He is not trying to anticipate this move or that move, hoping that things line up in his favor. This would put God on our plane. He is altogether on a different plane.

God is more like a Shakespeare writing *Macbeth*, a Steinbeck penning *The Grapes of Wrath*, or a Dickens plotting *A Tale of Two Cities*. He is a grand and transcendent Author of a storyline that has been perfectly scripted to encompass every epoch, every event, every nation, every people and tongue, along with their every thought, word, and deed all the way down to the minutest detail.

In fact, the works of every lesser human storyteller unconsciously mimic the grand Storyteller himself. Furthermore, the plotline of history is merely an extension of the narrative arc that we find in divine Scripture, starting in Genesis and ending in Revelation. Thus declares the psalmist: "Let all the earth fear the LORD; let all the inhabitants of the world stand in awe of Him. For He spoke, and it was done; He commanded, and it stood fast" (Ps. 33:8–9 NASB).

THE GOOD ONE

Two particular attributes of God come under assault when skeptics wrangle over the problem of evil. The first attribute we have already canvassed—his sovereign power, which encompasses his eternal plan and the execution of that plan by his ongoing providence. The second attribute is God's goodness. If God were all-powerful but he wasn't all-good, then we would have reason to fear.

The Arminian Jerry Walls says, "The Calvinist must sacrifice a clear notion of God's goodness for the sake of maintaining his view of God's sovereign decrees."[12] Nothing could be further from the truth. What assures us that God's omnipotence and all-encompassing sovereignty are worthy of our full trust and unfailing praise is precisely the truth that God is also nothing less than perfectly and absolutely good. God's sovereignty and goodness must never be isolated from one another. They always act in perfect tandem.

The Belgic Confession states that God is "the overflowing fountain of all good."[13] David declares, "Oh, taste and see that the LORD is good! Blessed is the man who takes refuge in him!" (Ps. 34:8). God's goodness relates to his benevolence, all that is designed for the benefit of his creation. He is the source of all natural, moral, and spiritual good. "The LORD is good to all, and his mercy is over all that he has made" (145:9). God is identified with the very essence of love (1 John 4:8), kindness (Ps. 145:17), and faithfulness (36:5). He is eternally merciful and gracious (Lam. 3:22). The good God is long-suffering, is steadfastly loyal, and forgives ill-deserving sinners (Ex. 34:6–7). Nothing can interfere with his "abundant goodness" (Ps. 145:7).

To say that God is good is also another way to say that he is holy —holy in the sense of perfect righteousness and moral purity. "God is light, and in him is no darkness at all" (1 John 1:5). God "dwells in

---

12. Jerry Walls, "The Free Will Defense, Calvinism, Wesley, and the Goodness of God," *Christian Scholar's Review* 13, no. 1 (1983): 29.

13. Belgic Confession, art. 1.

unapproachable light" (1 Tim. 6:16), meaning not only that he stands far above his creation in glorious majesty, but that he is a God of white-hot righteousness. It is not remotely possible that God could have an evil thought or intention, let alone speak an evil word or perform an evil action. Habakkuk says of his Lord, "You . . . are of purer eyes than to see evil and cannot look at wrong" (Hab. 1:13). David is even more emphatic: "For you are not a God who delights in wickedness; evil may not dwell with you" (Ps. 5:4). The presence of evil is entirely foreign to the nature of God. Every form of wickedness is repugnant to his being (Prov. 6:16–19).

God's righteous goodness also speaks of his justice. He is called "the Rock, his work is perfect, for all his ways are justice. A God of faithfulness and without iniquity, just and upright is he" (Deut. 32:4). He rewards righteousness equitably and punishes all wickedness impartially (Ex. 34:7; 1 Sam. 26:23; Rev. 20:12–13). In God's sovereign designs, righteousness will never ultimately fail, nor will evil ultimately triumph. All wrongs will be righted. His just verdicts will prevail. Rebellion against his holy goodness is folly.

Every Jack the Ripper, Josef Mengele, and Jeffrey Dahmer will tremble before God's bar of unyielding justice. "It is a fearful thing to fall into the hands of the living God" (Heb. 10:31; see also the oracle of doom in Isa. 13:6–13). Every soul must face one of two destinies. Some will be redeemed by God's unexpected grace (Rom. 3:24) whereby the "fullness of joy" emanating from God's goodness is granted to them forever (Ps. 16:11). But all those who are unrepentant will "suffer the punishment of eternal destruction, away from the presence of the Lord and from the glory of his might" (2 Thess. 1:9).

When all is said, the believer's hope is grounded in these two realities: an *all-sovereign* God in which nothing escapes his plans and an *all-good* God in which everything, no matter how good or bad, serves these same supremely good plans. Few people understand this better than Joni Eareckson Tada. She was paralyzed from the neck down in a diving accident in 1967. Although a Christian at the time, Joni fought anger, depression, suicidal thoughts, and doubts about her faith. Amid the ironic and intense pain that comes with paralysis, a divine hope began to penetrate and sustain her inner being.[14]

After forty years of successfully cultivating spiritual contentment, however, new levels of excruciating pain assaulted Joni. Her struggle was not done. In 2010 Joni wrote of these renewed battles:

> Pain is a bruising of a blessing; but it *is* a blessing nevertheless. It's a strange, dark companion, but a companion—if only because it has passed through God's inspecting hand. It's an unwelcome guest, but still a guest. I know that it drives me to a nearer, more intimate place of fellowship with Jesus, and so I take pain as though I were taking the left hand of God.... These afflictions of mine—*this very season of multiplied pain*—is the background against which God has commanded me to show forth his praise.... God bids me that I not only seek to accept it, but to *embrace* it, knowing full well that somewhere way down deep—in a secret place I have yet to see— lies my highest good.[15]

Joni has grasped the twin truths of our Lord's sovereignty and goodness. God is sovereign over our pain, not always allowing it to be removed from us, even ramping it up at times. But God is also good, never allowing our pain to go to waste. The apostle Paul astutely instructs us, "And we know that for those who love God all things work together for good, for those who are called according to his purpose" (Rom. 8:28). God is not causing *some* things to work for good. He is not causing only *good* things to work for good. He is causing *all* things, whether good or bad, to work for his redeemed children and their abundant good. This fact is a fundamental truth that a biblical theodicy must embrace if it is to be worthy of consideration.

---

14. See Joni Eareckson Tada, *Joni: An Unforgettable Story* (Grand Rapids: Zondervan, 2001).

15. Joni Eareckson Tada, *A Place of Healing: Wrestling with the Mysteries of Suffering, Pain, and God's Sovereignty* (Colorado Springs: David C. Cook, 2010), 34–35.

STUDY QUESTIONS

1. According to John Calvin, what are the two most important kinds of knowledge?
2. What are the two ways that the Bible speaks of the holiness of God?
3. How do you see yourself in light of God's incomprehensible transcendence and greatness?
4. What does Calvin mean when he says that God speaks to us with baby talk?
5. Why is it important to understand God's transcendent greatness when trying to make sense of the problem of evil?
6. What are the three components to God's sovereignty? How are they distinguished from one another?
7. How does Isaiah 45:5–7 emphasize God's comprehensive sovereignty? Compare this passage to Job 2:10 and Lamentations 3:32–33. How do these passages affect the way in which you view God's sovereignty?
8. What is the value of comparing God to a grand author of epic stories?
9. According to the author, what two realities is the believer's hope grounded in? How does this help you face adversity?
10. How does Joni Eareckson Tada view the pain of her paralysis? What can we learn from her example?

4

WHO IS TO BLAME?

John Bunyan (1628–88) was known as the Tinker of Bedford, a poor metalworking peasant eking out an existence forty miles north of London. He lived a life of wanton pleasure in his early days, claiming that he "had but few equals ... both for cursing, swearing, lying, and blaspheming the holy name of God."[1] But for some years he began wrestling with God, with doubts, depressions, and unyielding convictions of his vileness, even feeling possessed of the devil. Then the truth of the gospel began to dawn upon him. Bunyan moved forward into the light of Christ with fits and starts. Slowly the testimony of the four Gospels and the preaching of his pastor, John Gifford, were indelibly pressed upon him until finally his chains fell by the wayside and he gained sufficient evidence of his salvation "with many golden seals thereon, all hanging in [his] sight."[2]

But Bunyan took no leave of his trials. Shortly after his conversion, his dear wife died and left him to care for four small children. Then his beloved pastor, Mr. Gifford, died as well. While Bunyan was suffering under these tragedies, God called him into the pastorate. Soon, hundreds began

1. John Bunyan, *Grace Abounding to the Chief of Sinners* (Westwood, NJ: Barbour, 1988), 18.

2. Bunyan, 75.

to flock to hear his plainspoken preaching, and many were converted. Bunyan became the most well known of the English Puritans—pastors and theologians who were deeply committed to the biblical truth recovered by the Protestant Reformation. Furthermore, the Puritans sought to purify the corrupt and theologically deficient Church of England. In their opposition, so-called Nonconformists such as Bunyan refused to abide by the official state church's tyrannical demands, forcing its narrow and lifeless form of worship on preachers of the gospel.

For this Bunyan was arrested in 1660, refused the right of a proper trial, and sent to jail, where he languished for over twelve years. The magistrates slandered him and unjustly accused him of all manner of religious ill-deeds. If he agreed to meet their demands to abandon his biblical convictions, then he would be released immediately. Such tantalizing temptations did not wreck his resolve. He knew that if he was released, he would not conform but go on preaching the glories of Christ as before. Yet inside those dank prison walls, the Bedford pastor encountered that old companion called Despair once again, haunting many of his days.

But the worst of it was the aching of his heart to care for his family, especially his oldest child, Mary, who had been born blind. He relates that the pain of this yearning was like "pulling flesh from the bones." When he thought of deteriorating in his wretched cell, and perhaps dying, his mind contemplated

> the many hardships, miseries, and wants that my poor family was like to meet with, should I be taken from them, especially my poor blind child, who lay nearer my heart than all besides: Oh! the thoughts of the hardship I thought my poor blind one might go under, would break my heart to pieces.
>
> Poor child! thought I, what sorrow art thou like to have for thy portion in this world! Thou must be beaten, must beg, suffer hunger, cold, nakedness, and a thousand calamities, though I cannot now endure the wind should blow upon thee.[3]

3. Bunyan, 174.

The pull between Bunyan's family and remaining faithful to his biblical convictions was far harder than most could imagine. It felt as though honoring God was to drive a stake through the heart of his beloved family.

How could God have placed him in this position?

THE PROBLEM OF MORAL RESPONSIBILITY

This points us to one of the vexing questions that we must grapple with: When facing life in a depraved and fallen world, where do we cast blame? Where does moral responsibility lie? Who is to blame for Bunyan's unjust imprisonment? Of course, it is easy to point to a corrupt state church or wicked magistrates who did its bidding. But where was God? If he has the sovereign power to prevent such injustice and he doesn't, should he not bear ultimate culpability?

Who is to blame for the blindness of Bunyan's daughter? Was this an irrevocable consequence of his former life of reckless sin? Perhaps she had been born with pitch-black vision as a form of precondemnation for her own sin. We may scoff, but this is not the first time that such notions have been contemplated (see John 9:1–2). Wouldn't blindness unjustly predispose this unfortunate little victim to cultivate a lifetime of bitterness? She never had a chance to see the world fairly as the rest do. Some would say that her birth defect was an accident of nature and that no one was at fault. But this is a cop-out. Humans instinctively know that God holds the power of sight. He declared to Moses: "Who has made man's mouth? Who makes him mute, or deaf, or seeing, or blind? Is it not I, the LORD?" (Ex. 4:11).

If, as the Bible declares, God is meticulously sovereign in every detail of time, space, history, and the whole scope of actions taken by every human he creates, then how can he escape being charged with all the evil that unfolds in his creation—both moral and natural? This is the first and most fundamental charge that a theodicy must answer before it can even canvass possible reasons that God may have for all the evil that afflicts our world. Neither the Arminian nor the Calvinist is immune from answering this question.

We have already seen, however, that the free-will defense of Arminianism has failed to answer the charge. This view of God can be likened to a policeman standing on the corner while allowing thugs to assault old ladies. The custodian of law and order declares: "I don't endorse the thuggery of thugs, but they have been granted free will to stop themselves and act civilly if they want to. They can never act civilly if I'm always interfering with their free will." All he can do is shake his head and say, "Sorry, but the possible assault of old ladies is simply a risk I must take for respecting the precious gift of free will." If this held true for God, even those least concerned for justice would be left to stand frozen and flabbergasted, eyebrows raised in disbelief.

But many suppose that the Calvinist conception of God faces an even more sinister problem. Because such a God exercises more direct power than the law-officer God, he is likened to a mob boss—a divine Vito Corleone of Mario Puzo's *The Godfather* fame. In this case, God is not passively watching as crimes unfold, as does the noninterfering policeman, but in fact, he sits on high, ordering thugs to assault the old ladies, and the thugs apparently have no choice in the matter.

If this analogy of the Calvinist understanding of God were true, then could it solve the quandary of God's moral responsibility any better? No, it could not. But that is because the illustration doesn't capture the true God. As we have already noted, we cannot think of God's relationship to evil in the same way we think of human beings' relationship to evil. This illustration tries to humanize God, and that is simply not possible. Let us examine this point further.

IS GOD THE AUTHOR OF EVIL?

We made the case in the previous chapter that a model for understanding how God providentially works in the world is to consider him as the transcendent Author who crafts the unfolding plotline of history into a grand epic. This model of God-as-Author is reflected in someone such as J. R. R. Tolkien's crafting the story of Middle-earth in his books *The Hobbit*, *The Lord of the Rings* trilogy, and *The Silmarillion*.

The Reformed and evangelical tradition, however, has consistently denied that God is "the author of sin."[4] Thus, we must be careful in delineating what we mean by the God-as-Author metaphor. What Calvinists mean when they say that God cannot be "the author of sin" is no different from what any other theologian means by the phrase. God cannot be justifiably *blamed* for sin or evil. He is not the *doer* of evil. He does not infuse an evil will or implant evil thoughts into creaturely minds.

James 1:13 tells us, "Let no one say when he is tempted, 'I am being tempted by God,' for God cannot be tempted with evil, and he himself tempts no one." Because God is wholly and perfectly good and righteous and just, he cannot entertain even the slightest evil thought or intention. There is no remote possibility that evil can toy with the mind of God, tantalizing him to consider evil thoughts and intentions. Evil is confined to the creaturely plane of existence; therefore, it cannot touch him. And this means that God cannot tempt others with evil. That would be anathema. That would make him a creature, not the Creator—and one who would be no better than Satan. Thus, it is in this sense that God cannot be the author of evil.

But because God is incomparably holy and transcendent, residing independently on a wholly different plane from his creation or creatures, and because he is supremely in control of all things, then we must be able to say that God is the author of evil in an entirely different sense. God has an asymmetrical relationship to good and evil.[5] Since he is the fountain of all goodness as the all-encompassing good God, then all good in the world directly proceeds from him.

For the same reason, God cannot be the *direct* cause of evil. Nonetheless, he ordains all evil to exist as the one who stands outside history as its Author, ensuring that every detail of the story of history unfolds as he wrote it in eternity past. Thus, God is the "ultimate cause of everything" without being the direct cause of evil.[6] Only those creatures who do evil can be said to be the

---

4. See, for example, Westminster Confession of Faith 3.1 and 5.4.

5. Paul Helm, *The Providence of God* (Downers Grove, IL: InterVarsity Press, 1994), 190–91.

6. John M. Frame, *The Doctrine of God* (Phillipsburg, NJ: P&R Publishing, 2002), 321–22.

direct (or immediate) cause of their evil thoughts and actions, even as God must be the mysterious and *remote* (indirect) cause of those same actions.

Tolkien is not the direct cause of the evil actions of Sauron in *The Lord of the Rings*. No one blames Tolkien as the author of the book for the actions of Sauron.[7] Yet no one believes that Sauron would act wickedly without Tolkien's determining that he would do so as the one who created the character and wrote his actions into the fictional story of Middle-earth. And this leads to another important point in the God-as-Author metaphor.

Tolkien not only creates the fictional world of Middle-earth, but also frames the moral worldview that guides the story of Middle-earth. It just so happens that Tolkien stands squarely in the tradition of the Judeo-Christian worldview that has shaped much of Christendom and the West. Thus, the moral worldview of Middle-earth is such that Sauron's actions are clearly regarded as evil, violating all the principles of moral goodness. The moral presuppositions of the author, Tolkien, regarding good and evil lead us to despise the evil actions of Sauron and to praise, for example, the good actions of Frodo, the principal hero of Tolkien's story.

In the real world, since God is the source of all that is good and right and beautiful and true, this means that anything that is evil and wrong and ugly and false can be rightfully judged by this divine standard and thereby despised and rejected. Evil can be evil only if there is a perfect standard of goodness and righteousness by which to make that evaluation. God *is* that standard. And anything that deviates from his perfect righteousness is, by definition, poisoned by evil.

Furthermore, when considering Tolkien's story of Middle-earth, what makes it so compelling is the fact that its villains are especially despicable and its heroes especially virtuous. Framing the plotline with this steep contrast is no accident, as I will explain in detail in chapter 5. We would never find Tolkien's story so compelling without stark lines drawn between good and evil, and then seeing evil ultimately defeated by good.

---

7. *Sauron* means "abominable" in Tolkien's invented Elvish language in his Middle-earth mythology. See Robert Foster, *The Complete Guide to Middle-earth* (New York: Ballantine Books, 1978).

Likewise, we would never see Christ's defeat of evil as so compelling without despicable villains such as Satan and the utter sinfulness of the enemy of our souls called *sin*. Evil *must* be part of the storyline if we are ever to appreciate the triumph of good in the end. And for this reason, we don't so much praise the protagonists in stories such as those of Tolkien, Dickens, and Dostoevsky as much as we praise the authors themselves. This is why such storytellers show us the worth of the greater-good defense whereby there are certain unique goods in this fallen world that can come about only via their dependence on some evil, and those goods end up gloriously outweighing the evil that they are dependent on. We must cling to this point because it hints at where a more detailed biblical theodicy will lead us in the pages ahead.

MORAL RESPONSIBILITY IN SCRIPTURE

So where does Scripture locate moral responsibility? There are two criteria in the Bible's answer to this question.

The Knowledge of Good and Evil

First, as human beings, we possess an innate knowledge of good and evil. The apostle Paul establishes the truth that all humans are morally accountable before God in Romans 1–2. God gave the Israelites his moral law enshrined in the Ten Commandments, but most people throughout history have never heard of the Ten Commandments. No matter—God has already written the substance of these fundamental moral laws on the heart of every human being, according to Romans 2:14–15, where Paul explains that the human conscience bears witness to moral right and wrong.

In fact, Romans 1 demonstrates that all human beings suppress the truth that God has revealed concerning himself through their rebellious commitment to unrighteousness (Rom. 1:18–20). Paul goes on to say, "For although they knew God, they did not honor him as God or give thanks to him, but they became futile in their thinking, and their foolish hearts were darkened" (v. 21). Humans tend toward the vilest behaviors unless God restrains them (vv. 24–31). They engage in such vile deeds with full knowledge that they are abandoning the God who watches their every move (v. 28). Paul asserts, "Though they know God's righteous decree that those who practice such things deserve to die, they not only do them but give approval to those who practice them" (v. 32).

Thus, we are without excuse (Rom. 1:20). No one will stand before God in judgment and complain: "God, I never knew you! I never knew that you demanded my obedience to your moral laws!" All who fail to turn to Christ for sweet forgiveness of their sins will be crushed under the weight of their own guilt, knowing full well that it demands their eternal punishment at the hands of the eternal Judge.

The dire prospect of such an end prompts the urgent call to the gospel. The Puritan Richard Baxter (1615–91) pleads with sinners: "Shall the living God send so earnest a message to his creatures, and should they not obey? Hearken then all you that live after the flesh; the Lord that gave thee thy breath and being, hath sent a message to thee from heaven, and this is his message, 'Turn ye, turn ye, why will ye die? [Ezek. 33:11].'"[8]

The Intentions of the Heart

Second, moral responsibility is most crucially tied to the intentions of one's heart. The heart is mission control central of the human soul: "Keep your heart with all vigilance, for from it flow the springs of life" (Prov. 4:23). Jesus says, "For where your treasure is, there your heart will be also" (Matt. 6:21). The heart forms the fundamental desires that determine the choices we make. "Treasure" here is a way of speaking of where the affections of our hearts lie. Jesus declares, "The good person out of his good treasure brings forth good, and the evil person out of his evil treasure brings forth evil" (12:35). A few verses earlier, Jesus also compares the heart (i.e., our fundamental spiritual nature) to trees that are known by the sort of fruit they produce (v. 33). Thus, a sinful heart (nature) is like a poisonous tree producing poisonous desires producing poisonous fruit.

---

8. Quoted in Joel R. Beeke and Mark Jones, *A Puritan Theology: Doctrine for Life* (Grand Rapids: Reformation Heritage Books, 2012), 508.

Unfortunately, the default disposition of every person is marked by an evil nature. Jesus minces no words: "For out of the heart come evil thoughts, murder, adultery, sexual immorality, theft, false witness, slander" (Matt. 15:19). We do not evolve into sinners because some of us fall into unfortunate patterns of sinful behavior. Jesus indicates that we all sin because at the core of our being we are already sinners, having inherited a sin nature from our primordial father, Adam (Rom. 5:12). Thus, a corrupted heart must undergo radical surgery at the hands of the divine Physician before it is capable of producing good fruit. This indicates the need of spiritual and supernatural regeneration (John 3:3–8; cf. Ezek. 36:26).

Jesus' teaching reflects the Old Testament. This is especially true in Jeremiah 17. The prophet said that Judah's sin—and by extension, the sin of all people—"is written with a pen of iron; with a point of diamond it is engraved on the tablet of their heart" (Jer. 17:1). He goes on to lament, "The heart is deceitful above all things, and desperately sick; who can understand it?" (v. 9). Sin is indelibly engraved on our supremely deceitful, desperate, and sick hearts. Their potential for wickedness is beyond comprehension.

Therefore, when God evaluates our moral culpability, he zeroes in on the heart, the nucleus of our moral faculties. "I the LORD search the heart and test the mind, to give every man according to his ways, according to the fruit of his deeds" (Jer. 17:10). This means that God evaluates our morally responsible actions by considering the intentions, the motives, the fundamental desires and affections of the heart that drive our thoughts, words, and actions.

We may seek to justify our corrupted actions, but God knows the true source: "All the ways of a man are clean in his own sight, but the LORD weighs the motives" (Prov. 16:2 NASB).[9] The catastrophic judgment of the ancient world via the global flood was based on the fact that "the LORD saw that the wickedness of man was great in the earth, and that every intention of the thoughts of his heart was only evil continually" (Gen. 6:5). Likewise, when Paul speaks of the final judgment, he informs us that the Lord "will bring to light the things now hidden in darkness and will disclose the purposes of the heart. Then each one will receive his commendation from

9. See also Prov. 17:3; 21:2; 24:12.

God" (1 Cor. 4:5). Moral culpability finds its roots not in the ability to act other than we could have, as the free-will theist says, but in the internal machinations of our hearts and whether they are intent on good or evil.

GOD'S SUPREMELY GOOD INTENTIONS

The Bible's testimony that moral responsibility is crucially tied to one's internal motivations, desires, purposes, and intentions has important implications for whether God can be held responsible for the evil that he ordains to take place in his sovereign plans. God has motivations, desires, purposes, and intentions as well, but they can in no sense be regarded as evil.[10] Furthermore, the intentions of God for the broad sweep of history are tied to his uniqueness as the transcendent and sovereign Lord of the universe.

God declares through the prophet Isaiah:

Remember the former things long past,
For I am God, and there is no other;
I am God, and there is no one like Me,
Declaring the end from the beginning,
And from ancient times things which have not been done,
Saying, "My purpose will be established,
And I will accomplish all My good pleasure";
Calling a bird of prey from the east,
The man of My purpose from a far country.
Truly I have spoken; truly I will bring it to pass.
I have planned it, surely I will do it. (Isa. 46:9–11 NASB)

The term "good pleasure" (*hepes*) in Isaiah 46:10 means "to will something in which one finds delight or pleasure."[11] This must be

---

10. Passages that speak this way of God include Gen. 6:6; Ps. 33:11; Jer. 23:20; 30:24; cf. 2 Kings 17:20; Isa. 44:28; 55:11; 63:4; Jer. 15:1; 31:20; Hos. 10:10.

11. Willem A. VanGemeren, ed., *New International Dictionary of Old Testament*

understood in light of Psalm 5:4, which uses the same Hebrew terminology: "For You are not a God who takes pleasure in wickedness; no evil dwells with You" (NASB). The utter holiness, goodness, righteousness, and justice of God make it impossible for him to take delight in wickedness for the sake of wickedness. If God can take no pleasure in wickedness, then we can be assured that whatever the Lord of the universe brings to pass must have some transcendently good intention standing behind it.

No better example of this can be found than God's "good pleasure" in bringing to pass the greatest injustice that the world has ever known. Isaiah shocks us when he says that it "pleased" Yahweh "to crush" the messianic Servant (i.e., the Son of God), "putting Him to grief" (Isa. 53:10 NASB).[12] How could this be true? Could God take pleasure in seeing —even ensuring without fail—that his innocent Son would be murdered? Is this not preposterous? Blasphemous?

No. Not at all.

Not if we grasp the wonder of what is going on here. God's good pleasure here is not a *sinister* pleasure, like that of a serial killer stalking innocent women. God could never take pleasure in evil for the sake of evil, in other words, because of evil *intentions*. Making such a statement would truly be blasphemous. Rather, his pleasure stems from the unsearchable riches of *good* that necessarily came from the *evil* perpetrated on his Son. Those abundantly good riches are found in the wondrous work of the Son's atoning death for the sake of redemption! Can you see the greater-good theodicy woven into the answer to this conundrum?

Here is a point that we must not lose sight of: The transcendent Author of history can never have evil intentions for the evil that he providentially ensures will take place. A paradox is at work here—a seeming contradiction that is no contradiction at all, just a mystery. God is pleased to ordain that which he otherwise vehemently hates. In his transcendent holiness and

---

Theology & Exegesis (Grand Rapids: Zondervan, 1997), 2:231–34. It could also be translated "good purpose, good plan, good intention."

12. "Pleased" is related to the same Hebrew term translated "good pleasure" in Isaiah 46:10.

wisdom, he exercises his *sovereign will* in the death of his beloved Son even as it comes at the hands of those who violate his *moral will* (Acts 2:23; cf. 4:27–28). God's sovereign will is that which he ordains to come to pass, whether good or evil.[13] His moral will always relates to what he has established and commanded as good, righteous, just, and true because all these things proceed from his good, righteous, just, and true nature.[14]

God alone reserves the right to sovereignly will that which otherwise violates his moral will. But remember, God ordains evil *only if* he can gain some unique and weighty good from it that could come no other way. As strange and mysterious as it seems, the ultimate outcome from any given occurrence of evil is better than if the evil had never happened in the first place. This truth carries particular comfort for believers, many of whom suffer a lifetime of untold physical and heart-wounding pain while others seem to live lives of uncharted ease. The Puritan John Flavel (1627–91) writes, "O how many have been coached to hell in the chariots of earthly pleasures, while others have been whipped to heaven by the rod of affliction."[15]

BIBLICAL COMPATIBILISM AND MORAL RESPONSIBILITY

Another way to view how moral responsibility is assigned in Scripture is to understand how the Bible often views the intentions and actions of human beings as they coincide with those of God. Calvinism has endorsed a view of human freedom and responsibility that is in stark contrast to the view of free will endorsed by Arminianism. It wholeheartedly embraces a

13. Passages indicating God's sovereign will include Pss. 33:8–11; 103:19; Prov. 21:1; Isa. 14:24, 27; 46:10; Jer. 50:45; Lam. 3:37–38; Dan. 4:17; Acts 2:23; 4:27–28; Rom. 1:10; 9:19; 1 Cor. 1:1; Eph. 1:5, 9, 11; Phil. 2:13; Col. 1:19; James 1:18; 1 Peter 3:17; Rev. 4:11.

14. Passages indicating God's moral will include Ezra 10:11; Ps. 103:21; Isa. 65:12; Ezek. 18:23; Matt. 7:21; John 7:17; Acts 17:30; Rom. 12:2; Eph. 6:6; 1 Thess. 4:3; 5:18; Heb. 10:36; 1 Peter 4:2; 1 John 2:17.

15. Quoted in Brian H. Cosby, *Suffering and Sovereignty: John Flavel and the Puritans on Afflictive Providence* (Grand Rapids: Reformation Heritage Books, 2012), 28.

dual explanation for all the choices that humans make. God, by his sovereign will, ordains all our choices and ensures that we will make them. Yet this does not mitigate the fact that, distinct but not independent from God's sovereign will, we willingly and freely make the choices that he has already ordained.

Explaining Compatibilism

This is known as *compatibilism,* the idea that God's meticulous sovereignty is compatible with human freedom and responsibility.[16] God is the *remote* but *primary* (ultimate) cause of all human actions as the transcendent Author of those actions. Conversely, we are the *immediate* but *secondary* cause of all our actions. Examples from Scripture could be multiplied, but statements from the book of Proverbs will suffice: "The heart of man plans his way, but the LORD establishes his steps" (Prov. 16:9). "Many are the plans in the mind of a man, but it is the purpose of the LORD that will stand" (19:21). "The king's heart is a stream of water in the hand of the LORD; he turns it wherever he will" (21:1).

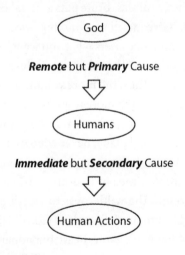

Fig. 4.1. Biblical Compatibilism

16. For a detailed defense of this position, see my book *What about Free Will? Reconciling Our Choices with God's Sovereignty* (Phillipsburg, NJ: P&R Publishing, 2016).

There is some mystery in how this "double agency" works in reality. Rarely are humans, even Christians, aware that God is standing behind their actions. We freely act with no sense that an invisible hand has planned our actions and providentially ensures that they take place according to that plan. From the human perspective, we always do what we *most want* to do based on the *strongest motive[s]* in our hearts acting on our will. And all this is done because God designed it so. Yet God's providence is not coercive. He never causes people to act against their will. To be sure, there are often coercive forces in the human-earthly-temporal plane of our actions working against our will.

For example, other people can exercise physical or psychological power over us. Circumstances can be out of our control and force us down paths that we do not want to take. Ignorance of facts, outside deceptions working on our minds, or other factors can serve to unwittingly direct our actions and violate our primary intentions, producing competing or conflicting intentions that we would not otherwise have had.

For example, when a ruthless brute puts a .45 caliber handgun to your head and demands, "Give me all your money!" you may not *want* to do so, but the coercive influence alters what you want in that instance—to save your life, not your cash. These kinds of influences generally lessen our moral responsibility. Thus, the more voluntarily or willingly we act, free from external coercion, the more responsible we are for our actions.

Nonetheless, God, as the primary initiator of what takes place in the human-earthly-temporal plane, never coerces us to act in ways that we ultimately do not intend. For example, God is said to have hardened Pharaoh's heart multiple times in Exodus 4–14 so that he refused to let God's people go into the wilderness to worship God and flee the Egyptian ruler's wicked tyranny.[17] Somehow God did this without directly implanting ill-intentions in Pharaoh's heart, but nonetheless ensured that he would indeed have a hardened heart.

Pharaoh is never described as having resisted God's invisible hand of providence. Rather, his "stubborn" will was in full—but

17. See Ex. 4:21; 7:3; 9:12; 10:1, 20, 27; 11:10; 14:4, 8.

unknowing—compliance with the sovereign will of God (Ex. 7:13–14), which is why we read that he hardened his own heart as many times as we read that God did so.[18] He acted voluntarily without divine coercion. Thus, he maintained full responsibility for his actions (9:34) even as they necessarily aligned with God's sovereign will. Exodus 10:27 clearly shows the compatibility of divine and human components in Pharaoh's actions. God willingly "hardened Pharaoh's heart" as part of his sovereign intentions, yet Pharaoh simultaneously "was not willing" to let God's people go (NASB).

Now, the important thing to note is that when it comes to fundamental spiritual and moral actions, there are two kinds of people. As Jesus puts it, there are good trees and bad trees. Good trees produce good fruit and bad trees produce bad fruit (Matt. 7:16–20). In other words, there are regenerate people (good trees) who have been born anew by the Spirit (Titus 3:4–6), and these produce good fruit (Eph. 2:10). And there are unregenerate people (bad trees) who have not been born unto new life, and all the fruit they produce is bad. In other words, it is fruit tainted by corrupted hearts that produce corrupted intentions that produce corrupted actions.

Thus, their wills are in bondage to sin, and they can act no other way, nor do they *want* to act in any contrary way, as Paul indicates in Romans 8:7. Their wills are not *able* or *willing* to choose the good—that which is truly righteous and God-glorifying (Rom. 3:23). In order for a bad tree to escape the enslavement of producing bad fruit (John 8:34), it must be set free of its corruption by the work of the Son of God (John 8:36). The bad tree must be made into a good tree (Matt. 12:33). It must be "born again" or it "cannot see" (so as to understand) or "enter" (with a believing heart) "the kingdom of God" (John 3:3, 5).

Good and Evil Intentions

Compatibilism also makes sense of how the evil intentions of human actors can coincide with the good intentions of God, helping us to see how moral responsibility is assigned. There is no clearer example of this ironic tension than in the story of Joseph and his brothers (see especially Gen. 37,

---

18. See Ex. 7:13, 22; 8:15, 19, 32; 9:7, 34, 35.

42–45, 50). Joseph was Jacob's favored son, and the boy was not afraid to flaunt this fact. Consequently, his brothers hated the little braggart, so they sold him into Egyptian slavery.

After years of suffering unjust imprisonment for a false accusation of attempted rape, God exalted Joseph to prime minister of Egypt, second only to Pharaoh. God supplied him the wisdom to avert disaster from a seven-year famine that the embattled patriarch prophesied by interpreting the dreams of Pharaoh. Then, after years of separation, God orchestrated the reunion of the estranged brothers. Of course, when they realized who Joseph was, they began to tremble in their sandals, knowing that he now had the power to dispose of them just as they had done to him years earlier.

But Joseph was a changed man. He said, "And now do not be distressed or angry with yourselves because you sold me here, for God sent me before you to preserve life" (Gen. 45:5). Joseph did not deny that his brothers were culpable for selling him into slavery, but he saw the bigger picture. He acknowledged that it was God who "sent me" long before the thought ever entered his brothers' minds. Why? "To preserve life."

He clarifies: "God sent me before you to preserve for you a remnant on earth, and to keep alive for you many survivors" (Gen. 45:7). In the broad scheme of redemptive history, God was using this whole ordeal, and the choices of everyone involved, to preserve his long-standing covenant with Abraham (12:1–3): to create and preserve a great nation out of which would come a great messianic Savior—the Son of God—by whom the gospel of life would come to all the nations of the earth (Gal. 3:8).

What Joseph's brothers did and how it coincided with what God was doing is given the greatest clarity in Genesis 50. Again, they stood fearful before the one whom God had made "ruler over all the land of Egypt" (Gen. 45:8). They said, "It may be that Joseph will hate us and pay us back for all the evil that we did to him" (50:15). Note that they rightfully blamed themselves for their evil, not the God who orchestrated it. They sought Joseph's forgiveness, and this brought their brother to tears (v. 17). Through all his trials, God had transformed the conceited and ignorant teenager into a humble and wise man of God. As they bowed before Joseph (v. 18), he responded, "Do not fear, for am I in the place of God?" (v. 19).

Then Joseph makes one of the most remarkable statements in Scripture indicating God's unique and transcendent relationship to evil: "As for you, you meant evil against me, but God meant it for good, to bring it about that many people should be kept alive, as they are today" (Gen. 50:20). Notice two important truths here. First, Joseph rightly assigns moral responsibility to one's motives—what one "meant" by what one does. Second, the same evil action has two different motives because there are dual agents standing behind the action—one human and one divine. The human motive for evil is evil. But the divine motive for the same act of evil is good. It could be no other way. God can never entertain a motive for evil that is not supremely good and wise.

Think again about the life of John Bunyan. He endured grief over the untimely loss of his wife and his beloved pastor. He suffered inordinate degrees of mistreatment by church authorities and evil magistrates. Like Joseph, he suffered unjustly for years in a prison cell, where he had tortured thoughts about the well-being of his blind daughter. Just as Satan intended evil for Job (see Job 1–2), he had ill-intentions for the Tinker of Bedford as well.

But not God.

The all-benevolent One used Bunyan's afflictions to call him to ministry and to preach to hundreds upon hundreds of lost souls who were converted to Christ. But it was in the depths of his darkest afflictions in prison that God pursued his greatest designs for the suffering Puritan. It is there that Bunyan wrote perhaps the greatest book outside the Bible itself—*Pilgrim's Progress*. This timeless allegory of the Christian life and all its challenges, obstacles, afflictions, and difficulties has been a source of hope and encouragement for countless believers for nearly 350 years.

What evil men, dastardly demons, and the devil himself mean for evil, God always means for good. When an Egyptian ruler hardened his heart, intending to oppress and enslave God's people, Yahweh hardened that same heart, intending to show him that there is no one like the God of Israel—indeed, the whole universe (Ex. 9:14). God intended to show the proud ruler his unmatched power so that his name would be "proclaimed in all the earth" (v. 16). Indeed, even to this day, the story of how Egypt was devastated by unprecedented plagues and the Israelites were delivered through the parting of the Red Sea by the hand of the Almighty has not been forgotten. Cecil B. DeMille will long be forgotten before the story he brought to the silver screen will be—the 1923 film and 1956 remake of *The Ten Commandments*.

When Isaiah 10 records that a pompous Assyrian king (Isa. 10:12) sought "in his heart to destroy, and to cut off nations" (v. 7), little did he know that he was simply a "rod" of God's just "anger" and "fury" (v. 5) against the "godless nation" that his people (Israel and Judah) had become (v. 6). The self-absorbed king had no intentions of being an instrument of righteous judgment (v. 7) because no righteousness resided in his "arrogant heart" (v. 12). Instead, he boasted in his own "strength," "wisdom," and "understanding" (v. 13), never realizing that the "axe" cannot "boast over him [Yahweh] who hews with it" (v. 15). God remains just and righteous as the wielder of evil men, even as those men are held accountable for their evil actions (vv. 16–19).

In the same way, the godless Jews of Jerusalem had the Lord of glory "crucified and killed by lawless men" even though he was ultimately "delivered up according to the definite plan and foreknowledge of God" (Acts 2:23). As we saw before, this plan was in accordance with God's "good pleasure" (Isa. 53:10 NASB). "Herod and Pontius Pilate, along with the Gentiles and the peoples of Israel," were all culpable for the death of God's "holy servant Jesus." And yet they did only what God's invisible "hand" and "plan had predestined to take place" (Acts 4:27–28). They meant for evil what God could mean only for good.

In fact, that good was the greatest good of all because it is part of the greatest story of all. We turn to that story next.

STUDY QUESTIONS

1. Have you ever had your moral or biblical convictions challenged such that maintaining them would require great sacrifice? How did you manage this situation?

2. Have you ever been angry with God? Have you been tempted to blame him for some injustice or troublesome trial in your life? How did you resolve this matter?

3. How does James 1:13 help exonerate God from being morally responsible for evil?

4. How does the analogy of J. R. R. Tolkien's writing evil into the storyline of his trilogy *The Lord of the Rings* help us understand God's relationship to evil?

5. How do Romans 1:18–32 and 2:12–13 help us understand how human beings are morally culpable for their actions?

6. Where does the Bible locate moral responsibility? In other words, on what basis will God judge human beings' moral actions?

7. Based on where the Bible locates moral responsibility, how can God be exonerated from the evil that he has decreed will take place in the world? How is the death of Christ a prime example of this point (see Acts 2:22–23; 4:27–28)?

8. What is *compatibilism*? How does it help us make sense of the choices we make in light of God's sovereignty?

9. How do we explain the numerous instances of Pharaoh's hardened heart in Exodus 3–14? Who was responsible for the hardening—God or Pharaoh? What difference does it make?

10. How does compatibilism in the story of Joseph and his brothers (see especially Genesis 50:20) help us understand moral responsibility when people make evil choices?

5

TELL ME THE OLD, OLD STORY

When my sons were young boys, they would often beg me to tell them scary stories. As evening drew near and the sky grew dark, we'd venture on top of the king-sized bed in our master bedroom, turn off the lights, pull the sheets over our heads for protection, and turn on a flashlight. They would all draw tight to me as I proceeded to craft a frightful tale. Of course, I would quiet my voice, deliberately adopting a slow pace and a throaty, unsettling tone.

The story usually started out with a small boy (so that my audience could identify) walking cautiously through a dark forest. The woods were alive with strange sounds and fleeting but unnatural movements. Hidden peril was all around. In the course of the journey, our courageous little hero would encounter minor threats that were easily dispatched, giving my listeners a sense of false security.

Nonetheless, the boys' excitable fear and anticipation would build. When it reached a fever pitch, some menacing and unfamiliar creature (we lived in the mountains of Colorado, where such things were real) would suddenly spring out of nowhere with great ferocity, at which point I would roar loudly to incite pandemonium. Presently, their mother would enter the room to question the ensuing chaos: "What in the world are you guys doing?!" Then they'd clamor, "Daddy, tell us another one!"

Children love stories. We all love tales of romance, drama, adventure, suspense, and excitement.

Why is that?

Because God uniquely made us as no other creature on earth—we humans are endowed with the precious gift of language. We were designed to employ sophisticated systems of words to communicate to one another the full sweep of our thoughts, ideas, and fertile imaginations. And storytelling is the highest art of language. Elie Wiesel said, "God made man because he loves stories."[1]

God is a speaking God. He is the master of language, and he is the master Storyteller who scripts the whole history of the world as a grand epic. Therefore, it only makes sense that his image-bearing creatures mimic the storytelling God of creation. We must tell stories. It doesn't matter if they are true or fictitious. The best retelling of history imitates fiction, and the best fiction sounds like it came right out of history.

Flannery O'Connor observes, "A people is known, not by its statements or its statistics, but by the stories it tells."[2] Whole civilizations are characterized by their historical and mythic narratives. For example, America has its founding historical narrative in the American Revolution (1775–83), replete with its heroes (e.g., George Washington) and villains (King George III). Others have their mythic tales. The Greeks had Homer's *Iliad* and *Odyssey* (eighth century B.C.), the Romans had Virgil's *Aeneid* (29–19 B.C.), and the Anglo-Saxons had *Beowulf* (A.D. 1000).

The historical narratives of a nation are often crafted with enough embellishments and pure fictions to achieve the same outsized status as these mythic tales. What is important is that the stories we tell and retell ourselves help forge our identity. They say things that ring true to our experience of being human while anchoring us to a set of inviolable and cherished values.

Now, what does all this have to do with the problem of evil?

The Bible does not give explicit propositional answers to the broad problem of evil. Instead, God inspired its authors to tell us the story about

1. Elie Wiesel, preface to *The Gates of the Forest*, trans. Frances Frenaye (New York: Holt, Rinehart and Winston, 1966).
2. Flannery O'Connor, *Mystery and Manners: Occasional Prose* (New York: Farrar, Straus & Giroux, 1969), 192.

what he is doing in the world. It gives us a framework for understanding the larger all-encompassing story that God is writing for all of history in which he establishes a purposeful place for every actor and every event across time, whether good or evil. Because the infallible God is the ultimate Author of the biblical storyline, then we know that it is no myth. It is wholly true in every sense of the word. At key points throughout the plot, Scripture explains the significance of the story and what it means for human beings. Those who believe the story are transformed by its giving *true* and lasting meaning to their lives, something that all lesser stories are incapable of doing.

Yet strangely enough, all good storytelling outside the epic narrative that God tells in the Bible imitates the pattern of that story. The truth contained in the *One True Story* of the Bible is missing from all lesser stories; nonetheless, they point to the deep-seated longing that all creatures have for redemption, rescue, restoration—a bold plan of salvation.

Why is this?

Because we are all subjects of a fallen world where all our stories at one level are deeply flawed and want for something far better. Nonetheless, our faulted tales help us to express this longing through the seeking of a good ending—the "happily-ever-after." Exploring the connection between these realities is a crucial starting place as we begin to unveil a more specific biblical theodicy. As you might imagine, that theodicy is embedded in the grand narrative of Scripture, which helps us make sense of the crisis of evil in the world and its ultimate redemption. The Bible outlines a sweeping rescue plan centered on an utterly unprecedented Redeemer—the Son of the living God.

THE UNIVERSAL PATTERN IN STORYTELLING

In trying to understand the human impulse to narrate all of life, literary critics have discovered that the art of telling a good story, whether it be fiction or history, tends to follow a universal pattern. Every well-crafted story highlights a poignant *conflict* that grabs the attention of the audience and then proceeds to map out a compelling *resolution* to that conflict in the unfolding plot. This *conflict-resolution* pattern is sometimes called the *monomyth* or "the one story."[3]

Without this universal conflict-resolution motif, the audience gets bored. We don't like our stories to be straight, flat, smooth lines: tedious and trivial. There need to be twists and turns. The plot needs to plunge into the abyss and rise back up, ascending toward the stratosphere. The way forward needs to confront insurmountable obstacles. The plot needs a crisis that threatens to end or undermine something valuable and worth fighting for. It should put the audience on the edge of their seats, wondering what, if any, hope of resolution is possible.

The greater the conflict, the more compelling the resolution becomes. We need warriors who achieve victories in unwinnable wars, peasants who rise impossibly out of abject poverty, and nerdy scientists who make unprecedented discoveries that save the world. To garner our praise, these characters need to face villains that are fearsome, despicable, and virtually unstoppable—a Goliath, Sauron, Darth Vader, or Thanos.

Furthermore, we need our heroes to be courageous and virtuous, especially when the conflict they face is so overwhelming that our certainty that they will remain strong is tested. We love it when our heroes emerge as superheroes, more unstoppable than the villains—a Samson, Hercules, Superman, or Captain America. But we seem to love the ordinary and unlikely heroes even more, those that rise as consummate underdogs and succeed against all odds—a David, Jane Eyre, Frodo Baggins, or Peter Parker.

J. R. R. Tolkien coined the term *eucatastrophe* to capture the goal of good storytelling.[4] Strangely, it means "good catastrophe," which indicates that well-crafted stories maintain a paradoxical tension. He explains that a eucatastrophe is "the sudden happy turn in a story" just when things seem hopeless. In the most gripping stories, once the bad (or sad) downward trajectory of the plot reverses course, surging toward the good, then it

3. See Leland Ryken, *Triumphs of the Imagination: Literature in Christian Perspective* (Downers Grove, IL: InterVarsity Press, 1979), 77–81.

4. J. R. R. Tolkien, "On Fairy-Stories," in *The Monsters and the Critics and Other Essays*, ed. Christopher Tolkien (London: George Allen & Unwin, 1983), 155–56.

"pierces you with a joy that brings tears."[5] If a good ending can bring you to happy tears, then you know that the tale was worth telling. Anyone who is familiar with films such as *Old Yeller* (1957), *Life Is Beautiful* (1997), or *Toy Story 3* (2010) knows what Tolkien is talking about. In either case, Tolkien says, stories that begin and end in joy serve the highest function of storytelling.[6]

The ideal plot is U-shaped.[7] Good—the way that things *ought* to be—is followed by a descension into catastrophe—how things go wrong—which is followed by an ascension—restoring things back to a state of good. The darker the catastrophe, the brighter the restoration. We are most moved by plotlines in which "the darkest hour is just before dawn."[8] For two excruciating days, Jesus' tomb was cold and dark and surrounded by hopelessness until those first rays of Sunday-morning light peered above the horizon and the stone that concealed the tomb began to rattle. At that point, we know that the story is going to end well.

Comedy (not the laughing sort) represents stories that end well. *Tragedy* (think of the Shakespearean sort) represents stories that do not end so well. For example, Samson (see Judges 13–16) represents the classic tragic hero, the one we are cheering on, but who doesn't quite triumph as we had hoped because of some fatal flaw in his character. Samson ignores his vows to God (Judg. 16:17) and foolishly falls for the empty seductress Delilah—the villain of the story. Subsequently, he loses his supernatural physical strength that God supplied him to overcome Israel's enemies, the Philistines. In a final act of desperation, he pleads with God to restore his strength one last time while he is brought out of his prison cell to amuse the lords of Philistia. God hears his cry. Samson exerts this last gasp of power to literally take the house down, killing more Philistines in his death "than those whom he had killed during his life" (v. 30).

5. "Letter 89," in *The Letters of J. R. R. Tolkien*, ed. Humphrey Carpenter (New York: Houghton Mifflin Harcourt, 2000), 101.

6. Tolkien, "On Fairy-Stories," 156.

7. Ryken, *Triumphs of the Imagination*, 80.

8. Laura Ingalls Wilder, *On the Banks of Plum Creek* (New York: HarperCollins, 1971), 228.

Stories of the tragic variety are unpleasant but serve a useful purpose. They have a cathartic effect, uncovering the deeper yearning we have for happy resolutions that often escape us in real life. Tragedy points us back to the ideal plot of comedy. Furthermore, when both tragedy and comedy are embedded with a genuine (God-ordained) moral order highlighting the way that things *ought* to be (comedy), even, and *especially*, when they are not that way (tragedy), it serves the audience well, reinforcing how important proper moral order is for shaping our lives and providing them with divinely sanctioned meaning.

UNIVERSAL PLOT STRUCTURE

In 1863, the German novelist and playwright Gustav Freytag studied the plot structure of Greek and Shakespearean tragedies and published his findings in a book entitled *The Technique of Drama*. Ever since then, novelists, screenwriters, and playwrights have adopted Freytag's simple manner of summarizing the plot structure of good storytelling. It is known as *Freytag's Pyramid*. The basic pattern is near-universal, however, long predating Freytag. Aristotle pointed out the same things in Greek tragedies in his work *Poetics* (c. 335 B.C.). Here is how it works:

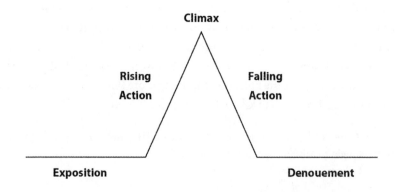

Fig. 5.1. Freytag's Pyramid

Exposition. The story is set up, introducing the characters and themes that lead to the emerging conflict. A well-crafted story develops the characters so that the audience is engaged, endeared to its heroes and appalled by its villains.

Rising action. As the conflict builds, the plot thickens. Aristotle called this the "entanglement" or the tying of a knot. The principal hero faces an uncertain future as the audience anxiously cheers him on.

Climax. The story progresses to the critical moment of crisis when the conflict reaches its apex and there appears to be no reasonable way to resolve it. The audience is most deeply engaged here, feeling the strain of the story's tension. The climax marks the turning point of the plot. In the case of a comedy, it goes from bad to good, and in a tragedy from bad to worse.

Falling action. The conflict moves toward the resolution, whether satisfying (comedy) or unsatisfying (tragedy). Aristotle called it the "reversal" when the knot of the conflict starts to be loosened. Often there is a plot twist, or the hero experiences an *epiphany*, some previously hidden truth or earth-shattering revelation, that leads to the resolution of the conflict or sheds light on matters as they truly are—for better or worse.

Denouement. The final unraveling of the action takes place, when the conflict is fully resolved—the knot finally untied. In the case of a comedy, all is made well; the happily-ever-after begins. In a tragedy, it is the final catastrophe that unfolds, but always with a moral lesson to be learned.

Most novels, movies, and television dramas, even sitcoms, follow this basic plot structure. Consider the 1946 Frank Capra classic film *It's a Wonderful Life* (warning: spoiler alert!). The (1) *exposition* (back story) of the film shows George Bailey (Jimmy Stewart) as Bedford Falls' greatest citizen, always helping others in their distress. This leads to the (2) *rising action.* George has aspirations for greatness. He wants to "shake the dust off this crummy little town" and explore inspiring options in some exotic locale. Instead, he is compelled to take over the family business, "the broken-down" Building & Loan. If he doesn't, it will be gobbled up by the cutthroat businessman Mr. Potter (Lionel Barrymore), "the richest and meanest man in the county." The conflict and the villain are set in place. Things look up when George gets married and has a family. The Building &

Loan is successfully helping struggling residents buy their own homes so that they don't have to grovel at the feet of Potter.

But George's bigger dreams remain unrealized. Potter dogs his every move and tempts him to compromise his moral scruples. Then his absent-minded partner, Uncle Billy, misplaces eight thousand dollars to keep the Building & Loan solvent—ironically, in the hands of Potter, who cherishes this opportunity to crush George Bailey for good. George fears being charged with fraud and ventures out into a snowy night in suicidal desperation. The (3) *climax* comes as he contemplates jumping off a bridge into icy waters below. But in answer to a despondent prayer, his guardian angel, Clarence, materializes at the bridge and jumps off first, knowing that George will save him (ignore Capra's wacky theology!). Yet this is really Clarence's move to save George.

The plot reaches its turning point.

George tells Clarence that everyone in his life would be better off if he had never been born. Suddenly, the angelic helper has an *epiphany* that will resolve the conflict. Through some heavenly magic, Clarence shows George what Bedford Falls would look like without his existence. As the (4) *falling action* unfolds, there is an eerie sequence of encounters in which no one knows who George is. He soon realizes that in his absence, Bedford Falls turns into a hellscape named after his nemesis—a town called Pottersville where everyone suffers a dreadful existence. This shocking reality reaches its full impact when George's own wife doesn't recognize him but runs away, shrieking in fear. Now he understands.

In an act of reverse desperation, he returns to the bridge where he saved Clarence and prays for his real life to be restored. "I want to live again! Please, God, let me live again!" The prayer is answered as the alternative reality dissipates and George is resurrected as a new and better man. Pottersville becomes Bedford Falls once again. The (5) *denouement* of the plot takes place when he gets back home, and everyone has rallied together to pay his eight-thousand-dollar bank debt. George Bailey finally discovers that his life's dream was not in some lucrative and exciting region of the world but had been in the homely Bedford Falls all along. The town didn't need him as much as he needed the town.

STORYTELLING, REDEMPTION, AND NATURAL REVELATION

Stories come in endless shapes and sizes, but at the heart of the best storytelling resides a single universal theme. Brian Godawa comments that all "storytelling is about *redemption*—the recovery of something lost or the attainment of something needed. . . . Stories are finally, centrally, crucially, primarily, *mostly* about redemption."[9]

For example, *It's a Wonderful Life* is about the redemption of George Bailey. He was consumed with being somebody that he was not, thinking his life was a failure. He faced a crisis of confidence disguised as the looming demise of the Building & Loan. He needed this crisis in order to see his life the way that it *ought* to be. We suppose that he merely needed Clarence to show him the way. But without his evil nemesis—the "sick in the soul" Mr. Potter—he would have never had his false illusions shattered, forcing him to reexamine the wonderful life that he thought he could never have in Bedford Falls.

The theme of redemption is threaded through most novels and screenplays while utilizing a plot structure that resembles the conflict-resolution motif worked out in Freytag's Pyramid. The conflict of ideal stories drives the movement of the plot toward redemption—the recovery of a state of goodness. In fact, Freytag's Pyramid could be inverted to reflect the mood conveyed in the actual U-shaped movement of the plot. Often, the climax represents the point in the story when the conflict is strongest. In other words, hope is at its lowest and we await redemption—the upward return to that happy state. Yet arriving at that final state is marked with a deeper appreciation precisely because it was achieved by descending into the fiery bowels of a conflict that appeared inescapable. Who doesn't cherish life more dearly after narrowly escaping death? It takes being delivered from the lion's jaws to inject renewed vitality and purpose into one's existence.

9. Brian Godawa, *Hollywood Worldviews: Watching Films with Wisdom & Discernment,* updated and expanded ed. (Downers Grove, IL: InterVarsity Press, 2009), 21.

These near-universal features of good storytelling bewilder literary critics, defying explanation . . . unless you have a Christian worldview. All such U-shaped storylines indistinctly mirror the grand narrative of Scripture: creation, fall, and redemption. Jerram Barrs notes: "All great art contains elements of the true story: the story of the good creation, the fallen world, and the longing for redemption."[10] How do we make sense of these universal patterns and themes?

Natural (general) revelation indicates that God has embedded certain truths within creation and within the imaginative impulses of his image-bearing creatures who seek meaning for their disordered lives, often through devising meaningful stories. John Calvin observes that all human beings have a sense of the divine (*sensus divinitatis*) that points them to truths that could be revealed only by God.[11] Paul says: "What can be known about God is plain" to all human beings, "because God has shown it to them. For his invisible attributes, namely, his eternal power and divine nature, have been clearly perceived, ever since the creation of the world, in the things that have been made" (Rom. 1:19–20). Of course, inherent sin unfortunately suppresses and distorts this truth flowing from God's self-revelation in creation (vv. 18, 21–23).

Consequently, unbelievers have a faint, though severely fractured, apprehension of certain truths. Even though the unbeliever has a fundamentally flawed worldview, however, no unbeliever is steeped in sheer falsehood, as Romans 1 and 2 make clear. Unbelievers pick up bits and pieces of truth here and there; unfortunately, they are unable to put them together in a cohesive system of redemptive, saving truth. Paul declares, "The god of this world has blinded the minds of the unbelievers, to keep them from seeing the light of the gospel of the glory of Christ, who is the image of God" (2 Cor. 4:4). The light of the gospel

10. Jerram Barrs, *Echoes of Eden: Reflections on Christianity, Literature, and the Arts* (Wheaton, IL: Crossway, 2013), 67.

11. John Calvin, *Institutes of the Christian Religion*, ed. John T. McNeill, trans. Ford Lewis Battles, Library of Christian Classics 20–21 (Philadelphia: Westminster, 1960), 1.3.1.

of salvation shines forth with untold glory, yet it is all blackness to the unbelieving masses.

There is no light for those that stumble in the dark apart from the work of regeneration and the Holy Spirit's illumination of the special revelation that God has given us in Scripture (1 Cor. 2:1–16). Therefore, only believers can have an unsullied view of divine truth, especially the truth of the gospel contained in the unfolding story of redemption. Nonetheless, unbelieving worldviews have at least *some* perception of "the original state of reality (creation), what went wrong with that original state (Fall) and [the longing] to recover or return to that original state (redemption)."[12] We tell redemptive stories because we know that there is something wrong with this world and we want to make it right. And this in itself is an apologetic for the truth of the paradigmatic storyline of Scripture.

THE STRUCTURE OF THE BIBLICAL STORYLINE

The whole of Scripture is God-breathed (2 Tim. 3:16) and preserved by the divine Author; therefore, its chronicles of the historical and factual plan of redemption are *incapable* of error (infallible) and consequently *devoid* of error (inerrant). Not only is the Bible true in every sense of the word, but its influence is unprecedented and unmatched by anything else in the history of literature and storytelling. It is the *One True Story*. Understanding its narrative flow is the starting place for making sense of good and evil and establishing a biblically and theologically coherent theodicy (explanation for evil). Furthermore, once one comes to understand the full and penetrating sweep of this grand narrative, nothing else comes close to resonating with the aching for redemption buried in the human heart.

How is this story framed?

Throughout the successive acts of its narrative, the Bible "has a unifying plot conflict consisting of the great spiritual struggle between

12. Godawa, *Hollywood Worldviews*, 22.

good and evil. Virtually every event that we read about in the Bible shows some movement, whether slight or momentous, toward God or away from him, toward good or evil. The world of the Bible is claimed by God and counterclaimed by evil."[13] Yet it is critical for us to acknowledge that this is no duel between equal but opposite cosmic powers. God alone serves as the transcendent Author of these two trajectories such that *good*—flowing from the very goodness of God—will necessarily triumph over *evil*.

The main theme of the Bible is how God's glory is supremely magnified in sending his beloved Son, Jesus Christ, who rescues a world overtaken by evil. The unfolding story *is* the Bible's theodicy. Every lie, every murder, every theft, every act of malice and violent oppression forms part of the crisis—not just in the biblical plotline but in how this crisis has swept through all of history. The conflict is cruel, crushing us all in horrific ways.

Yet the size and weight of this conflict cannot compare to the resolution, nor to the hero who resolves it. Christ far exceeds the crushing weight of the curse, the darkness, the devil, and the sin that inhabits the souls of damnable sinners. Thus, instead of blaming the Author for introducing the crisis, he is praised for writing a story whereby evil, pain, suffering, and death are swallowed up in victory (1 Cor. 15:54), all "to the praise of his glorious grace" (Eph. 1:6).

The human authors of the Bible never had Freytag's Pyramid in mind when they wrote the scenes of the story. Nonetheless, it serves as a useful literary tool to think about how the grand narrative of Scripture unfolds.[14] Let us see how it helps frame the story.

---

13. Leland Ryken, *Words of Delight: A Literary Introduction to the Bible* (Grand Rapids: Baker, 1992), 31.

14. The larger U-shaped narrative of the whole Bible and its plot structure is also seen in smaller narratives. For example, in the Old Testament, consider the story of Abraham and Isaac, Joseph, Samson, Ruth, David, Nehemiah, Esther, Daniel, and Jonah, to name a few. In the New Testament, consider the birth of Jesus, Peter's denial and restoration, Paul's conversion, and the larger passion narratives in the four Gospels. See also Jesus' parables: the good Samaritan (Luke 10), the prodigal son (Luke 15), the rich man and Lazarus (Luke 16), and the persistent widow (Luke 18). For how these stories work, see Ryken, *Words of Delight*.

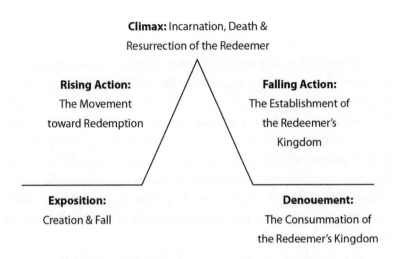

Fig. 5.2. The Biblical Storyline

Exposition: Creation and Fall

The Creation

The historical drama of redemption begins with creation. Genesis 1:1 sets up the *exposition* of the story: "In the beginning, God created the heavens and the earth." The Bible begins with God. His existence is the fundamental precondition of all reality. He simply decides to speak, and the entire universe in the fullness of its incomprehensible wonder emerges out of nothing. Note the clear dissimilarity between God as Creator and that which he created. Everything is wholly dependent on the one who requires nothing outside himself to exist. He is self-sufficient in himself, but all-sufficient for his creatures (Acts 17:25). And he is no idle god of deism, but the living, active, sustaining Lord of all.

The earth is a microscopic speck compared to the rest of the cosmos, but already Genesis 1:1 alludes to the central place it has in the story. According to Genesis 1, this otherwise piddling planet will be the primary stage for God to display the riches of his glory. Then the lens of the narrative narrowly focuses on one special object of God's creation called *adam*, the Hebrew word for "man." God created both "male and female," uniquely in his own image (vv. 26–27). No other creatures possess such dignity (Ps. 8:4–5). God is *the* center of the story, but man is central to his unfolding plan. He is a supporting character, designed to live in perfect harmony and fellowship with his Creator, serving and honoring him in the establishment of a holy kingdom on earth (Gen. 1:28).

The whole of creation was pronounced to be "very good" (Gen. 1:31). It was a place of sheer beauty, without blemish—the way that things *ought* to be. It could be no other way, having proceeded from the perfect goodness of the Creator (Ps. 100:5). Here in Eden, his creatures could bask in the beauty and wonder of the Almighty, experiencing the "fullness of joy" with "pleasures forevermore" flowing from the palm of his hand (16:11). There was no trouble in this paradise. No worries. No dissatisfaction. No sin or death. All was as it should be.

But it would not last. Soon the glory of paradise would dissipate.

The Fall

The conflict of the story quickly emerges in Genesis 3. Disrupting the bright warmth of the garden, dark, billowy storm clouds descend on the tranquil scene. The order, beauty, and harmony of Genesis 1 and 2 are swept aside. The devil, who disguises himself as a "crafty" serpent (Gen. 3:1; cf. Rev. 20:2), slithers into the garden, positioning himself as the main villain of the story. Just as the Bible portrays God without a hint of evil, it portrays Satan without a hint of goodness. He is the consummate liar of liars (John 8:44), maligning God, seeking to usurp his authority and to turn humanity against him. Satan jump-started this career in Eden.

God invited Adam and Eve to enjoy the fruit of the trees of the garden. But as a test, he commanded them to avoid "the tree of the knowledge of good and evil," lest they die (Gen. 2:17). The serpent tempted the woman to defy her God and her husband and partake of the forbidden fruit (3:1–5). Her heart was captured. Furthermore, Adam abandoned his wife and acquiesced to her corrupted desires (v. 6). In one dastardly moment, Satan subverted the whole order of the creation, derailing humanity's task of glorifying God. The couple placed God's goodness and wisdom on trial and found it wanting. Instead, they trusted to themselves, in defiance of his command.

They failed the test.

The fruit held false promises. They would be like just like God (Gen. 3:5). As they ate, "the eyes of both were opened" (v. 7). But what wonders came into view? None. No power, pleasure, or freedom. No feeling-like-God euphoria. Instead, the unnatural burden of ugliness and nakedness, of shame and disillusion fell upon their unsuspecting souls. Instead of power, they acquired vulnerability and helplessness. Instead of pleasure, they felt searing pain. Instead of freedom, chains of bondage became their lot. Instead of becoming like the Creator, they took on a new and unbearable weight of frail creatureliness. *Shalom* ("peace") was replaced by fear, restlessness, and anxiety. Wounded by the guilt of their disobedience, they hid themselves from God (v. 8). Instead of experiencing harmony and fellowship with him, they found themselves exposed before his holy justice.

No sooner had the fruit touched their lips than paradise was lost.

The conflict of the ages is set in stone, marked by divine curses on the man, his wife, and their progeny (Gen. 3:16–20). The material creation also comes under a curse, and the stench of death now permeates its landscape. Death is not merely physical and spiritual. Ultimately, "death is alienation from the life of God."[15] And that alienation extends to every level of existence. Adam and Eve are alienated not only from God but from one another (v. 16) and from the creation itself. Before the fall, the creation was idyllic—a domesticated wonderland. After the fall, it became a thorny wilderness, resisting every effort to tame it (vv. 17–19). Furthermore, "the whole world" now "lies in the power of the evil one" (1 John 5:19), and no mortal can break the chains by which he binds humanity.

Rising Action: The Movement toward Redemption

The *rising action* of the story is a movement toward redemption. But it stutters and stumbles along the way. We see two trajectories. One arc foreshadows divine redemption—God's solution to the conflict. The other arc chronicles the failure of humans to redeem themselves, exemplified by the plight of Israel in the Old Testament. But it is first expressed when

15. James M. Hamilton Jr., *God's Glory in Salvation through Judgment: A Biblical Theology* (Wheaton, IL: Crossway, 2010), 78.

Adam and Eve fashion crude coverings from fig leaves to hide the shame of their sin and nakedness (Gen. 3:7).

This proves insufficient. Every attempt of fallen human beings to rectify our sin-racked brokenness runs headlong into bankruptcy. Instead, God graciously meets Adam and Eve's failure by supplying them with adequate "garments of skins" (Gen. 3:21). This introduces atoning blood sacrifices for the first time, prefiguring what is necessary for redemption.

Genesis 3:15 provides another glimpse at where the redemptive trajectory must move. This primordial prophecy indicates that the divine Author had already conceived a plot for the resolution of the conflict. Speaking to the serpent, God says, "I will put enmity between you and the woman, and between your offspring and her offspring; he shall bruise your head, and you shall bruise his heel." The "offspring" (literally, "seed") of the serpent refers to those throughout history who oppose the divine trajectory of redemption (John 8:44).

The offspring of the woman (Eve) ultimately refers to a single "seed" (the Messiah) whose heel the serpent will crush. The serpent will wound him, but he will recover—that is, he will die but rise again. By contrast, the Messiah will "crush to pieces" the head of the serpent.[16] Both crushings are *fatal*, but only one is *final*.[17] Ironically, the crushing of the Messiah results in utter defeat for Satan, sin, death, and the full spectrum of moral and natural evil.

In the meantime, the postfall failures of mankind continue to plunge as sin and alienation lead to the first murder (Gen. 4:1–8) and then worldwide anarchy: "The Lord saw that the wickedness of man was great in the earth, and that every intention of the thoughts of his heart was only evil continually" (6:5). The Judge unleashes his wrath on all mankind through a global flood while graciously sparing Noah (v. 8) so that he might preserve the "seed of the woman."

---

16. Walter C. Kaiser Jr., *Toward an Old Testament Theology* (Grand Rapids: Zondervan, 1978), 36.

17. William Varner, "The Seed and Schaeffer," in *What Happened in the Garden: The Reality and Ramifications of the Creation and Fall of Man*, ed. Abner Chou (Grand Rapids: Kregel Academic, 2016), 166.

God then establishes the "seed" (descendants) of Abraham—the nation of Israel—through a set of far-reaching promises that God will maintain (Gen. 12:1–3; 15:1–21). The Israelites will be God's vehicle for redemption, which is prefigured by their four hundred years of bondage to the Egyptians and subsequent miraculous deliverance that displays God's mighty redemptive power (Ex. 9:16). God brings the Israelites to their promised land, but like Adam and Eve, they fail to obey the stipulations of his law given through Moses, bringing on themselves nothing but curses (Deut. 28). But God knows that his people have to fail so that he can highlight the truth that salvation always comes by looking to him alone.[18]

Throughout Israel's successive history, her kings and her people repeatedly fail. Yet through all her defections, and occasional bright moments, God is advancing his plan. He provides ever-expanding glimpses of the coming messianic Redeemer through covenant promises and prophecies, through types and shadows in the sacrificial worship of the temple, and through events and people who prefigure his heroic work.

Climax: Incarnation, Death, and Resurrection of the Redeemer

When all seems lost, when hope is like a morning mist that burns off in the heat of the emerging day, a bright and mysterious star appears on the horizon (Matt. 2:1–2). It signals that the *rising action* of the story was moving to the *climax*. The messianic hero was born, but to everyone's surprise, he was no ordinary hero. The divine Author himself dons the robes of humanity and enters directly into the plot (John 1:1, 14).

The incarnated God is the center of the story. Jesus Christ alone is capable of addressing history's great entanglement, of untying the impossibly tight knot that Adam and his descendants tied. Jesus came as the second Adam, demonstrating perfect obedience to his Father (John 4:34) and achieving what neither Adam nor anyone else could (1 Cor. 15:22, 45).

But there is another unexpected twist in the plot.

The Messiah was not the conventional warrior that the Jews had expected, wreaking righteous havoc on their Roman oppressors. Their greatest enemy

---

18. See Ps. 62:1; Isa. 45:22, 25; 55:6–7; cf. Gal. 3:24.

was not outside them but deeply rooted within. No ordinary means of power can defeat the principal conflict of history—the evil residing in the human heart. That conflict requires an unconventional hero—one who has been born for a singularly important purpose: to die. In 1 Corinthians 1, Paul says that the Messiah's heroic death on a bloodstained cross was regarded as utter foolishness (1 Cor. 1:18). It all seemed shocking—scandalous.

Strangely, sin and evil are vanquished by God's weakness, not his mighty power (1 Cor. 1:25). The cross bears all the weight of the conflict. In this one excruciating moment of the hero's complete vulnerability, when the audience (i.e., his disciples) is expecting his defeat, ironically, the greatest and most enigmatic heroics in history are at work, subverting all the malevolent streams of the curse. Satan is convinced that he has defeated Christ, crushing his heel (Gen. 3:15). Yet he is blinded to his own crushing defeat (Heb. 2:14; 1 John 3:8). No one could fathom a cursed Messiah's dying the ignoble and humiliating death of crucifixion (Gal. 3:13). It brings his followers down to the Slough of Despond.

But they are even more unprepared for what would come next.

The intervening hours between 3 o'clock on a cold, dark Friday afternoon and the emerging dawn that we now call the *Lord's Day* are characterized by the longest and eeriest silence the world has ever witnessed. Yes, victory is achieved on a bloodstained chunk of wood, but that victory could be realized only when, three days hence, before decay sets in, the bloody graveclothes of the God-man are left behind on the shelf of an empty tomb. When several forlorn women arrive at his burial site, the whole story swings around in a grand reversal as the angel declares to them, "He is not here, for he has risen" (Matt. 28:6).

Could neither Seal nor Stone secure,
Nor Men, nor Devils make it sure?
The Seal is broke, the Stone cast by,
And all the Pow'rs of Darkness fly.[19]

19. Charles Wesley, "Hymn I," in *Hymns for Our Lord's Resurrection* (London: W. Strahan, 1746), 2.

The Son of God does not come into this world merely to die. He comes to reverse the curse, and that requires his resurrection. C. S. Lewis captures this stupendous reality: "The Christian story is precisely the story of one grand miracle, the Christian assertion being that what is beyond all space and time, what is uncreated, eternal, came into nature, into human nature, descended into His own universe, and rose again, bringing nature up with Him. It is precisely one great miracle. If you take that away there is nothing specifically Christian left."[20] Christ descends into the abyss of seeming defeat, and then rises up from the chaos to establish a kingdom over which sin, Satan, and death have no power.

Falling Action: The Establishment of the Redeemer's Kingdom

The *falling action* of the plot is marked by the Son's ascension into heaven and exaltation at the right hand of his Father. Jesus says, "I will build my church, and the gates of hell shall not prevail against it" (Matt. 16:18). He instructs his followers—the founding members of his church—to go into all the world and proclaim the gospel (28:18–20), the message that God in his grace reconciles to himself the sons of Adam through the work achieved by the Son of God (2 Cor. 5:17–21). The long-term impact of Jesus' death and resurrection is incalculable. What started as 120 persons in a crowded room hidden in the backstreets of Jerusalem (Acts 1:15) has enveloped the whole world. It enables sinners to repent of their sin and to entrust themselves to Christ for eternal pardon, for everlasting life.

Because of their union with Christ, believers have the power and privilege of crushing that wily old serpent under their feet (Rom. 16:20). But Satan and his evil minions are not easily deterred. The progress of redemption is marked with battles against lingering evils within and without. There is ongoing war with the inner corruption of the flesh, the lure of this godless world, and the sinister schemes of the devil (Eph. 2:1–3; 4:17–27; 6:10–17). But Christ will not fail the church. He will conform all its members to himself (Rom. 8:29). Nor will he fail to magnify the glory

---

20. C. S. Lewis, "The Grand Miracle," in *God in the Dock*, ed. Walter Hooper (Grand Rapids: Eerdmans, 1970), 80.

of the Father until his kingdom includes "ransomed people for God from every tribe and language and people and nation" (Rev. 5:9).

Denouement: The Consummation of the Redeemer's Kingdom

The *denouement* of the story is revealed at the consummation of the Redeemer's kingdom when he returns in sun-shattering glory to earth to establish his righteous rule forever: "Then comes the end, when he delivers the kingdom to God the Father after destroying every rule and every authority and power" (1 Cor. 15:24). All the knots of the conflict will be fully loosened and the crisis of evil completely resolved. All the followers of Christ will shed their broken and battered bodies, trading them in for newly resurrected bodies fit for life in a newly restored paradise. All human and satanic opposition will come to its end, each enemy of Christ being banished forever in "the lake that burns with fire and sulfur, which is the second death" (Rev. 21:8).

Furthermore, the rest of creation that was "subjected to futility" by God as a result of the Edenic curse will experience its own material death and redemptive resurrection (Rom. 8:20–21; 2 Peter 3:10–12). Paradise will be restored. A "new heavens and a new earth" will emerge out of the ashes of the old creation (2 Peter 3:13). The new Jerusalem (a restored Eden) will come down and fill the whole earth with its glory—a glory emanating from the throne of God that sits at its center (Rev. 22:1). "Nothing unclean will ever enter it, nor anyone who does what is detestable or false, but only those who are written in the Lamb's book of life" (21:27). God's redeemed creatures will bask in his presence forevermore without fear of the kingdom's order, beauty, or harmony being disrupted again.

The new creation will far outshine the old. Why? Because the crisis of evil means that there is something extremely valuable that is worth fighting for, and that fight does not come easy. It would be nigh impossible had not the transcendent Author himself taken on human flesh and descended into the plotline. Only the God-man has the requisite divine and human natures necessary to achieve redemption and to pay the unimaginable price to restore the irrepressibly tattered and tainted world. The Son of God willingly and joyfully embraces this rescue mission (Heb. 12:2), showering ill-deserving rebels with the riches of God's glorious grace (Eph. 1:7–8).

When the redeemed of God stop and soberly reflect on the nether regions of darkness to which the conflict of the ages has dragged us fallen creatures, only then can the surprising glory of our redemption begin to emerge. Humanity has infected itself with this festering poison of evil and has no will or power to suppress it, let alone reverse it. But when we gaze upon the divine hero who is dragged even deeper through the conflict, who succumbs to the deadly curse of it all, and who then rises up victorious— then we can see where glory is *supremely* magnified.

"God freely chose to create a world with a more difficult and more beautiful story, in which there is both Adam and Christ, sin and redemption, Good Friday and Easter Sunday."[21] Christ puts the weight of the weary world on his shoulders and ushers it into the one and only true happily-ever-after. This is the One True Story. It is the Old, Old Story that we must constantly tell ourselves. None other can compare.

Yet we cannot be content to merely *tell* the story. We must *explain* the story more fully. We need a clear theodicy put in propositions. We need a theology of it. We need an argument for it. We need a thoroughgoing exposition of the truth that drives the plot of this grandest of stories, and that is what we turn to now.

STUDY QUESTIONS

1. As you were growing up, what was one of your favorite stories— perhaps a novel, a movie, or a real-life adventure? What made the story so compelling to you?
2. What pattern does every good story need to be compelling?
3. What are the five movements in the plot structure of Freytag's Pyramid? Explain each of them.

---

21. Phillip Cary, "A Classic View," in *God and the Problem of Evil: Five Views*, ed. Chad Meister and James K. Dew Jr. (Downers Grove, IL: InterVarsity Press, 2017), 35.

4. The author illustrates how Freytag's Pyramid works in the well-known film *It's a Wonderful Life*. Can you think of other films (or stories) in which this plot structure is apparent?

5. What theme is nearly universal in all good stories? Where does this idea come from?

6. How does Genesis 1–3 set up the rest of the Bible's storyline?

7. How does Genesis 3:15 help us see where the story of the Bible is going?

8. How does Christ defeat evil, and what makes the way he does this so surprising and unusual?

9. How does the story of the Bible end?

10. How does the whole scope of the biblical storyline help us frame the rest of history? How does it help you frame your own life?

6

THE GREATER-GLORY THEODICY

The epic poem *Paradise Lost* (1667) written by John Milton (1608–74) contains a brilliant passage delving into the very heart of the problem of evil. How can we justify God's allowing, and dare we say purposing, mankind to fall into sin? Milton answers this question by imagining a conversation between Michael the archangel and Adam:

> "With glory and power to judge both quick and dead,
> To judge th' unfaithful dead, but to reward
> His faithful, and receive them into bliss,
> Whether in Heav'n or Earth, for then the Earth
> Shall all be Paradise, far happier place
> Than this Eden, and far happier days."
>   So spake th' Archangel Michael, then paused,
> As at the world's great period; and our sire [Adam]
> Replete with joy and wonder thus replied.
>   "O goodness infinite, goodness immense!
> That all this good of evil shall produce,
> And evil turn to good; more wonderful
> Than that which by creation first brought forth
> Light out of darkness! Full of doubt I stand,

Whether I should repent me now of sin
By me done and occasioned, or rejoice
Much more, that much more good thereof shall spring,
To God more glory, more good will to men,
From God, and over wrath grace shall abound."[1]

Milton alludes to an early church hymn called the *Exultet*, probably written by Ambrose (A.D. 339–97), that also reflects on the purpose of the fall. It introduces the well-known Latin phrase *O felix culpa*, which is best translated as "O fortunate fall." The phrase occurs in a line that reads: "O assuredly necessary sin of Adam, which has been blotted out by the death of Christ! O fortunate fault [fall], which has merited such and so great a Redeemer!"[2] This is a strange and unsettling statement. How could the fall of Adam and Eve be considered "fortunate"? That their sin was "necessary"? What was Ambrose saying? Why did Milton echo his sentiments in *Paradise Lost*?

The passage in Milton summarizes the threefold biblical storyline of creation, fall, and redemption. The archangel declares that once God receives "His faithful" into heavenly "bliss," this future "Paradise" will be a "far happier place" than "Eden," with "far happier days." Adam ("sire") responds with "joy and wonder," but why? Shockingly, he rejoices that evil produces this future good, that light has come out of darkness. But the evil and darkness he speaks of is his *own* sin! The fall of Adam and Eve produces this greater good—this "goodness infinite, goodness immense!" —this future paradise that exceeds that of the original.

The thought is so revolutionary that Adam wonders whether it is better to "repent" of his sin or "rejoice" at the "much more good thereof" that "shall spring" from it. The archangel says that God gets glory when his justice is leveled against "th' unfaithful dead." Yet "over wrath grace shall abound." Michael and Adam agree: God gets "more glory" from his

---

1. John Milton, *Paradise Lost*, ed. William Kerrigan, John Rumrich, and Stephen M. Fallon (New York: Random House, 2007), bk. 12, lines 460–78 (408–9).

2. David Lyle Jeffrey, ed., *A Dictionary of Biblical Tradition in English Literature* (Grand Rapids: Eerdmans, 1992), 274.

grace toward sinners than his justice toward them. Yet without Adam's spectacular fall, this glory to God never abounds.

In assessing the problem of evil, it is impossible for us to explore the untold reasons that God may have for particular instances of sin, tragedy, catastrophe, or adversity in this earthly cauldron of pain and sorrow. But we need not despair of having no answer to the broader question of why there is evil in the first place. The panoramic narrative of the Bible tells us that the fall occurred so that the Father would have occasion to put the glory of his grace on full display through the work of the Son's redemption.

When the divine Son took on a human nature to become the world's Savior, he set his person apart as utterly unique in all of human history. Furthermore, the work he achieved to resolve the conflict of evil is infinitely more magnificent than we can imagine. There is no way to measure the radical contrast between the blackness of the cursed cosmos and the refulgent glory of the triune God's work of redemptive grace that shatters the dark grip of evil.

What is important to see is that this glorious grace has no occasion to be displayed unless the colossal conflict of the ages overtook the world. God has hard-wired humans to loathe the hollowness of Eden's curse and to fill our empty souls with something of lasting worth. But only the Christian story can satisfy this longing. God's writing of the fall of mankind into the *rising action* of history's plotline ignites a burning hunger for redemption that can be satiated only by the startling *climax* of the cross and empty tomb. These stupendous events epitomize the grandest story of all. They bring the greatest glory of all to its incomparable divine Author. As a result, they bring the greatest good of all to those who taste of the triune God's glorious grace.

This is why I call this the *greater-glory theodicy*. I believe that it is the theodicy of the Bible, and it warrants further exploration.

THE ARGUMENT FOR THE GREATER-GLORY THEODICY

The greater-glory theodicy is a species of the greater-good defense (see chapter 2). The biblical narrative reveals a wise and sovereign God who has generated a purposeful plan for all things, whether good or evil. He superintends the unfolding of that plan with his invisible hand, meticulously ensuring that *everything* in it takes place. Furthermore, God would not allow any evil to occur unless it served some greater good. He must necessarily have some supremely good and wise intention for *all* the evil that transpires in this fallen world. The question is, what is that overarching intention?

The greater-glory theodicy seeks to provide an answer best demonstrated by the following argument, which rests on three premises. If they are true, then the conclusion (4) follows.

(1) God's ultimate purpose in freely creating the world is to supremely magnify his glory to his image-bearing creatures—human beings.
(2) God's glory is supremely magnified in the atoning work of Christ, which is the sole means of accomplishing redemption for human beings.
(3) Redemption is unnecessary unless human beings have fallen into sin.
(4) Therefore, the fall of humanity is necessary to God's ultimate purpose in creating the world.

Let us take a more detailed look at each of the points in this argument.

Glory Is God's Ultimate Purpose

Why did God create the world? Was he lonely? Did he just need someone to love? Such notions are silly. God has no needs. He has been perfectly self-satisfied in the blessedness of his own Trinitarian being from all eternity. God had nothing to gain from creating anything. He had no obligation to make the heavens, the earth, or us lowly creatures. Thus, when we read in Genesis 1:1 that "in the beginning God created . . . ," we must see this act as proceeding strictly from his sovereign freedom. The psalmist proclaims, "Our God is in the heavens; he does all that he pleases" (Ps. 115:3), and this includes the freedom to create the cosmos and all it contains.

God has manifold purposes in creating the world that are known only to him, but what was his *ultimate* purpose? That question has been posed by every generation of theologians in history, and the uniform answer has been largely undisputed. God created the universe, and particularly the world, to serve as a theater for his glory.

The New England pastor-theologian Jonathan Edwards (1703–58) writes: "The design of the Spirit of God is not to represent God's ultimate end as *manifold*, but as ONE.... For it appears, that all that is ever spoken of in the Scripture as an ultimate end of God's works, is included in that one phrase, *the glory of God*."[3] Both the Westminster Larger and Shorter Catechisms declare that God decrees "for his own glory . . . whatsoever comes to pass."[4]

These theological reflections echo the testimony of Scripture. Paul says: "For from him and through him and to him are all things. To him be glory forever. Amen" (Rom. 11:36). God is the Creator ("from him"), Sustainer ("through him"), and goal ("to him") of "all things." Therefore, in all things "to him be glory forever." In Isaiah's vision of Yahweh in the temple, the seraphim "called to [one] another and said: 'Holy, holy, holy is the LORD of hosts; the whole earth is full of his glory!'" (Isa. 6:3). Likewise, David exclaims: "Be exalted, O God, above the heavens! Let your glory be over all the earth!" (Ps. 108:5).

God displays his glory throughout the universe (Ps. 19:1) so that his creatures will be awed by the wonder of who he is. It is out of the overflow of God's own self-satisfying joy in his intrinsic glory that he has chosen to give his creatures a glimpse of it. While God did not make the world for our uninterrupted happiness, nonetheless it is in his glory that we too find lasting and supernal joy. This explains why the first question of the Westminster Shorter Catechism is "What is the

---

3. Jonathan Edwards, "The End for Which God Created the World," in *God's Passion for His Glory: Living the Vision of Jonathan Edwards*, ed. John Piper (Wheaton, IL: Crossway, 1998), 242.

4. Questions 12 and 7, respectively. See also Westminster Confession of Faith 3.3, 3.5, and 3.7.

chief end of man?" The answer: "Man's chief end is to glorify God, and to enjoy him forever."

Herein notice that the argument is that God has chosen to magnify his glory to the *supreme* degree specifically to his *image-bearing creatures*—the pinnacle of his creation, made on the sixth day: "So God created man in his own image, in the image of God he created him; male and female he created them" (Gen. 1:27). No other creature is crafted in the image of God, tasked with worshiping, serving, and honoring him as his representatives on earth (vv. 28–30). Not even the angels have this exalted role.

David extols the Lord for this privilege:

> When I look at your heavens, the work of your fingers,
>   the moon and the stars, which you have set in place,
> what is man that you are mindful of him,
>   and the son of man that you care for him?
>
> Yet you have made him a little lower than the heavenly beings
>   and crowned him with glory and honor.
> You have given him dominion over the works of your hands;
>   you have put all things under his feet,
> all sheep and oxen,
>   and also the beasts of the field,
> the birds of the heavens, and the fish of the sea,
>   whatever passes along the paths of the seas. (Ps. 8:3–8)

Human beings are the focus of God's greater displays of glory—not animals, not angels. Thus, it follows that humans reside in a unique position by which to behold this greater glory. Their special relationship with the Creator means that they become recipients of his actions in unique ways that no other creature experiences. But the *greatest* glory of God is reserved for the work he does in those humans he chooses to redeem, as we will see. Even the angels long to fully grasp this glorious work of God reserved for the elect few (1 Peter 1:12).

The Center of Supreme Glory

This leads to the next premise in the argument. How do we answer the question, "Where has God supremely magnified his glory?" Certainly, we might think of the glory of the heavens (Ps. 19:1). Anyone who has seen the recent images of the starry host captured by the James Webb Space Telescope cannot help but be awed by the glory of the Creator. What about the beauty that still permeates our fractured planet? Anyone who has hiked down the Grand Canyon to Havasu Falls, or trekked up Mount Everest, or floated along the Amazon River, and then nonchalantly denies the existence of God is begging for that despised moniker—fool (14:1).

We might think of God's miracles: the parting of the Red Sea (Ex. 14:21–22), Jesus' feeding of the five thousand (Matt. 14:15–21), his giving sight to the blind (John 9:1–12), or his raising Lazarus from the dead (John 11:1–46). The fierceness of God's glory is seen in judgment, such as during the global flood (Gen. 7:6–24) or the destruction of Sodom and Gomorrah (Gen. 19:1–29).

But none of these things represents the center of *supreme* glory. That is reserved for one place—the death and resurrection of the Son of God to rescue sinners (Rom. 4:25). When Revelation 5 looks at the vast scope of history's culminating storyline, the focus is on "the Lion of the tribe of Judah" (Rev. 5:5), "the Lamb who was slain" (v. 12), who "purchased for God" a people "from every tribe and tongue and people and nation" (v. 9 NASB).

Everything in the narrative plot of Scripture and history is moving toward redemption of cursed image-bearing sinners, and the bloody cross and empty sepulcher are at the nucleus of that plan. There is a reason why the cross has been the perennial symbol of the Christian faith for two thousand years. The *crucifixion* is literally the *crux* (Latin for "cross") of the matter. Everything in history hinges on this *crucial* event.[5]

Furthermore, the redemption of sinners is at the center of an all-encompassing plan to restore the entirety of the fallen world (Rom.

5. *Crucial* has the same Latin origin as *crux*, meaning a "cross" used to "crucify" criminals.

8:18–25). According to Ephesians 1:3–14, God's plan to save a chosen people is "to the praise of his glorious grace" (Eph. 1:6; cf. vv. 12, 14) and includes the restoration of "all things" by Christ (vv. 10–11; cf. Acts 3:21). In other words, "things in heaven and things on earth" (Eph. 1:10)—the entire cosmos. Thus, the work of redemption is a broad work. It entails the eternal Son's remarkable incarnation and birth by the virgin Mary, his life of perfect obedience to the Father, his trial and crucifixion, his burial and resurrection from the dead, his ascension to his place of former glory and authority at the right hand of the Father, and his eventual return to vanquish all remaining foes and consummate his eternal kingdom for the redeemed in a renewed creation.

Furthermore, this argument for the greater-glory theodicy is true *only* if the atoning work of Christ is the *sole* means of redeeming fallen and alienated people. This is clear from Scripture. There is only one name (Acts 4:12), one Mediator (1 Tim. 2:5), one High Priest (Heb. 9:11–14) capable of executing this rescue plan. Once God in his sovereign freedom determined to redeem a people for himself, then absolutely no other means was available to him. To accomplish the work of redemption, the Son of God *had* to take on human flesh, live a life of perfect obedience, suffer a bloody atoning death, and rise again from the grave to demonstrate victory over sin, death, and the devil (1 Cor. 15:17, 24–26, 54–57).[6] Christ alone is able to reverse the cosmic curse—undoing the damage Adam did—and return the cosmos to paradise.

Redemption Is Unnecessary without the Fall

Without a preexisting conflict spoiling something good and valuable and desirable, the notion of redemption makes no sense. Each of the good and meaningful stories or historical narratives we cherish presupposes a conflict-resolution pattern in its plot. The conflict must drive the movement toward resolution. Consequently, if God's purpose in creating the world is to treat it as a theater to supremely magnify his glory in the manner we

6. John Murray, *Redemption Accomplished and Applied* (Grand Rapids: Eerdmans, 1955), 3–13.

have described, then we must conclude that without the fall, such a plan of redemption would be unnecessary.

God created the world in a state of unsullied beauty, order, perfection, peace, joy, and righteousness. He created Eden, where Adam and Eve and their progeny could bask in the glory of their Creator, enjoying perfect fellowship with him as well as the work of his hands. Then the fall ruined this paradise. But God also created conditions whereby Adam and Eve *would* fall. Otherwise, why the test of obedience? Why place forbidden fruit within easy reach? If there were no possibility of spoiling the good creation, then these things would seem to serve no purpose.

God would not have allowed the serpent to slither into the garden of delights. He could have placed the flaming cherubim to guard the way to the garden *before* the serpent entered instead of *after* Adam and Eve sinned (Gen. 3:24). He could have arrested the first couple with his mighty hand as they raised the alluring fruit to their mouths, much as the angel intervened at the last moment as Abraham was about to slay his son Isaac (22:10–12). God could have created Adam and Eve with unflappable wills such that they could choose *only* good, the same sort of incorruptible wills that all the redeemed will have in the new paradise.

He did none of these things.

Our primordial parents lived in a prefall world where they would willfully and inevitably succumb to sin and temptation. The subsequent curse that God placed on the creation and his creatures, however, formed the opportunity for him to magnify his glory in ways that simply would not have been possible in the unfallen world. How so? Without the fall, God had no opportunity to pour out the unprecedented riches of his grace on ill-deserving rebels. An unfallen world needs no grace. It needs no saving heroics.

The Son of God would have no need to condescend to the plane of this-worldly existence to identify with those imprisoned by their own rebellion and then rescue their sin-wretched souls. He would have no need to don the robes of humanity, to experience the effects of the curse via temptation and suffering. The watching world would not get to witness him overcome evil's lure by his humble and hard-won human obedience, to wrestle with it and disembowel it in his excruciating death, and to demonstrate his victory over it by rising again.

This is supreme glory for a supremely glorious God.

It happened because Eden was designed in the eternal counsel room of the Godhead to become a *fallen-needing-redemption world*. There is no question that God's glory could certainly be magnified in an *unfallen-not-needing-redemption world*, but such glory would be without the cross and empty tomb. The glory that God is unfurling in this present evil world, whose terrain is in disarray, is like the glory of a vermilion sunset irradiating the snow-capped Himalayas that have come into view after the last black clouds of a deadly blizzard have dissipated. The glory of Eden before its spectacular fall is more like the glow of paler hues cast across a less magnificent mountain range—one that never bore up under the assault of any storm. Eden was certainly a "very good" world—a model world whose primal substance will soon be restored—but it has not the grandeur of the fallen but soon-to-be-fully-restored world that is coming.

The severity of this present crisis cries out for "such and so great a Redeemer!"—one who would elicit our deepest worship because of his unbounded love for rebel hearts, his desire to condescend to our lowly estate, to immerse himself into the very muck and grime of the conflict, and to pay the gruesome price required for our ill-deserved rescue. The triune God is *supremely* glorified only in this fallen-needing-redemption world. No other possible world that he could have designed seems poised to exalt him so supremely as this broken one.

Consequently, it is better to see the storyline of Scripture as J-shaped. If it were merely U-shaped (as normally conceived), then the restored paradise rising up from the depths of the fall would appear no more glorious than the paradise of prefall Eden (i.e., the initial creation), and we would have reason to question why the fall should have ever taken place. The greater-glory theodicy argues that the paradise of the new creation will be far better precisely and surprisingly because of the fall. The fall was a grand *Eucatastrophe*—a "good catastrophe," a most fortunate occurrence!

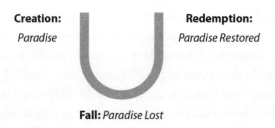

Fig. 6.1. Standard U-Shaped Storyline of Scripture and Good Stories

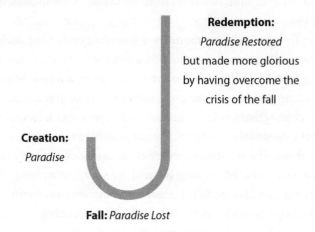

Fig. 6.2. J-Shaped Storyline of the Greater-Glory Theodicy

The Fall Is Necessary

The conclusion is certain. The fall of Adam and Eve was necessary. But note that the fall, in and of itself, is not an event that occurred by some *intrinsic* or *absolute* kind of necessity. That would suggest that God was somehow obligated to make a world that would become corrupted by evil and thereby place his integrity as God in question. He had no obligation to create the world, and once he decided to do so, he was under no obligation to make it a particular way. God was free to act according to his sovereign pleasure (Ps. 115:3).

Furthermore, we have good reason to think that once God decided to create the world, it would be good—in fact, "very good" (Gen. 1:31).

God is perfect goodness, and therefore he could not establish the world in an initial state of corruption. But—and this is important to note—it does not mean that he would never create a world that would *become* corrupted in the course of time, because that is precisely what he did. Nor does it mean that he is morally culpable for Adam's sin. While God decreed the fall to take place for a supremely good and wise purpose, he did not directly cause Adam to sin or implant evil thoughts in his mind. To be sure, there is mystery in how Adam and Eve, created in a state of moral perfection, could fall from that state. Nonetheless, it was all part of God's plan.

The greater-glory theodicy argues that once God decided to make a world that would *supremely* magnify his glory, then no other world is possible. Once displaying his maximal glory to image-bearing creatures became his ultimate purpose, then the whole grace-drenched work of redeeming that world became necessary. No other scenario could achieve that glory-maximizing goal. It is not possible to conceive of a world where God could be glorified more greatly than in such a world as this. And that is what makes the fall necessary. To be sure, it is a *conditional* necessity. In other words, the fall's necessary occurrence is *conditioned* on God's sovereign freedom in creating this fallen-needing-redemption world whereby he has chosen to maximize his glory.[7]

GREATER GLORY PREFIGURED IN THE EXODUS

The historical narrative of Moses and the exodus is a microcosmic reflection of the grander storyline of Scripture. As such, it is the premier story of redemption in the Old Testament and sets the paradigmatic pattern for all lesser biblical stories of redemption (e.g., Noah and the flood, Abraham and the sacrifice of Isaac, David and Goliath, Ruth and

7. See my fuller treatment on the mystery of the fall and its conditional (contingent) necessity in *What about Evil? A Defense of God's Sovereign Glory* (Phillipsburg, NJ: P&R Publishing, 2020), 218-24, 301-6.

Boaz, Esther and Haman).[8] It pulls together the cosmic motifs of creation, sin, and bondage; of divine rulership, presence, glory, judgment, mercy, and deliverance; and of the covenant promises of paradise restored.[9] These redemptive themes help illuminate the greater-glory theodicy. Note that the plotline fits the same pattern that Gustav Freytag later codified in Freytag's Pyramid (see chapter 5).

The Plot of the Exodus

The (1) *exposition* of the story begins in the latter chapters of Genesis when Joseph settles the patriarchal family in "the best of the land"—the land of Goshen in Egypt (Gen. 47:6). As we come to the book of Exodus, everything looks peaceful and promising. Goshen is not unlike Eden before the fall. "The people of Israel were fruitful and increased greatly; they multiplied and grew exceedingly strong, so that the land was filled with them" (Ex. 1:7).[10] But these favorable conditions do not remain that way for long.

In the (2) *rising action*, a new ruler of Egypt feels threatened by the prosperity of the sons of Israel (Ex. 1:8–10). So he enslaves the fledgling foreigners, and this establishes the principal conflict of the story. Furthermore, he orders newly birthed boys to be slaughtered to prevent the Israelites from multiplying (vv. 12, 15–16). Yet the baby Moses is preserved from death (2:1–10). He is divinely destined to be his countrymen's redeemer.[11] But Moses' heroic rise is itself littered with conflict, since he must flee Egypt after killing one of Israel's taskmasters (vv. 11–15). After years in exile, he remains an unlikely and reluctant hero (4:1–17).

Nonetheless, God compels Moses to return to Egypt to confront Pharaoh and demand that he release God's people (Ex. 5:1), who are

8. Northrop Frye, *The Great Code: The Bible and Literature* (New York: Harcourt Books, 1982), 171–72.

9. See L. Michael Morales, *Exodus Old and New: A Biblical Theology of Redemption* (Downers Grove, IL: InterVarsity Press, 2020).

10. Note parallel to Genesis 1:26–30.

11. Note parallel to Herod's plot to kill the baby Redeemer Jesus in Matthew 2:13–18.

"groaning" for deliverance (2:24). But Pharaoh's heart is repeatedly hardened as the tension in the plot gets tighter. God pours plague upon devastating plague on the Egyptians and their fake gods (12:12) through the hands of Moses. Things turn dire for Pharaoh and the Egyptians in the final destructive plague whereby "at midnight the LORD struck down all the firstborn in the land of Egypt, from the firstborn of Pharaoh who sat on his throne to the firstborn of the captive who was in the dungeon, and all the firstborn of the livestock" (v. 29). The terror of the supernatural "destroyer" (v. 23) and the toll of death hits every Egyptian home (v. 30) and finally constrains Pharaoh to let the Israelites go (vv. 31–32). Moses finally leads his people out of Egypt.

But the tension of the plot reaches its epic (3) *climax* when Pharaoh's heart is hardened one last time (Ex. 14:4–5, 8). He races his chariot force to trap the Israelites against the Red Sea, leaving them utterly defenseless and devoid of hope. Deadly retribution is at hand, and now the Israelites are the terrified ones (vv. 10–12). The sudden turning point in the plot comes when Moses exhorts his people: "Fear not, stand firm, and see the salvation of the LORD, which he will work for you today. For the Egyptians whom you see today, you shall never see again. The LORD will fight for you, and you have only to be silent" (vv. 13–14). Moses raises up his staff and stretches out his hand over the sea, and Yahweh miraculously parts the waters for the Israelites' escape (vv. 16, 21).

The (4) *falling action* ensues immediately as the Egyptian army pursues the Israelites into the deadly sea. Yahweh brings them into abject confusion, and before they can realize their error, crashing walls of water quickly consume them, killing every last member of the colossal force (Ex. 14:23–28). Meanwhile, the Israelites escape with nary a scratch as they scurry across the sea bottom, towering walls of water marking their left and right (v. 29).

The (5) *denouement* comes as they sing a song of victory (Ex. 15:1–18) and make their way to Mount Sinai (19:1–2) to receive their national covenant, the law of Moses (vv. 4–6). The Mosaic covenant was designed to prepare them to enter the promised land. This new paradise holds hope for renewing their peace and prosperity (cf. Deut. 27:3) as "a kingdom of priests and a holy nation" (Ex. 19:6).

Of course, we know that this plan is foiled by the Israelites' rebellion. Their failure to keep the stipulations of the Mosaic law, however, sets the stage for the larger redemptive arc of Scripture that the exodus prefigures. Israel's place in that larger story is prime evidence that humans' desperate attempts at redeeming themselves always come to ruin. The world needs a fundamentally different kind of hero and a radically different plan of redemption. The exodus points to that plan.

The Typological Significance of the Exodus

What makes the glory of God shine forth in the greater-glory theodicy is a whole constellation of contrasts, ironies, and dichotomies that encompass both the expected and the unexpected, the conventional and the unconventional, the ordinary and the extraordinary. Once these antithetical realities are placed side by side, the magnification of God's glory in the work of redemption is amplified even more. The exodus prefigures several of these contrasts. The vast and dramatic scale of divine judgment against the Egyptians is the backdrop for the sublimity of the glory found in God's mercy poured out on the Israelites. Their deliverance cannot be appreciated without this backdrop of extreme judgment.

Yahweh establishes the principal goal for his unforgettable deliverance of the Israelites in Exodus 14:4: "I will harden Pharaoh's heart, and he will pursue [the sons of Israel], and I will get glory over Pharaoh and all his host, and the Egyptians shall know that I am the LORD" (cf. Ex. 14:17). Divine "glory" is the singular goal. No one would witness or hear of the devastating judgments and think that this was a run-of-the-mill sort of conflict. Something phenomenal and terrifying has taken place in the most powerful nation on earth. It is otherworldly.

The plagues were undeniably supernatural, indicating that they were summoned from none other than the voice of the almighty Ruler of the universe. This is why the freed people of God would sing: "Who is like you, O LORD, among the gods? Who is like you, majestic in holiness, awesome in glorious deeds, doing wonders?" (Ex. 15:11). Moses declared, "There is no one like the LORD our God" (8:10).

Just to be clear on this matter, in the aftermath of the sixth plague in which all Egyptian men and beasts broke out in boils and painful sores on their bodies, Moses delivered a foreboding message from Yahweh to Pharaoh:

> For this time I will send all my plagues on you yourself, and on your servants and your people, so that you may know that there is none like me in all the earth. For by now I could have put out my hand and struck you and your people with pestilence, and you would have been cut off from the earth. But for this purpose I have raised you up, to show you my power, so that my name may be proclaimed in all the earth. (Ex. 9:14–16)

God, in one fell swoop, could have wiped out the entire nation with pestilence and been done with them. In fact, he could have refrained from hardening Pharaoh's heart from the get-go. God could have ensured that Pharaoh complied peacefully with Moses' initial request, and there would have been no exodus. Just a quiet departure for the promised land. But that was not God's "purpose." God wanted to "show" the magnificence of his "power." His name would "be proclaimed in all the earth." This is why the exodus not only prefigures the broader work of biblical redemption, but has also become an archetypal story of deliverance for the ages. Oppressed peoples everywhere in history long for the sort of mighty rescue from their unbearable hardship and mistreatment by despotic oppressors that the exodus has long typified.

Such rescue is far more glorious when the conflict seems more unrelenting, the villain more intractable, the victims more vulnerable, the hero more invincible, and the victory more mind-blowing. Consider the two polarizing destinies of the oppressed and the oppressor. Egypt has inexplicable terrors crashing down on her unsuspecting head, while Israel rides to freedom on the wings of equally inexplicable supernatural power.

The Author amasses greater glory in such stories of redemption. And yet the exodus is no match for the broader story it typifies in which the true archetypal hero—the Son of God: the true and better Adam, the better Moses (Acts 3:22–23)—comes to bring true and lasting rescue to the vast panorama of God's people. Pointing to *this* story is the real purpose of the exodus.

This is made clear in the tenth and final plague. It comes in the wake of the ninth plague in which "the land of Egypt" was "covered with a darkness so thick you [could] feel it" (Ex. 10:21 NLT). This was no physical kind of harm; it was psychological terror. It was preparing Pharaoh and his people for something even more terrifying: the mysterious angel of death—the "destroyer" (12:23)[12] who would invade the unsuspecting abode of every Egyptian household to claim its firstborn.

But the sons of Israel would be spared. The angel would "pass over" their doors marked by the blood of slaughtered paschal lambs (Ex. 12:21–23). This suggests that the Israelites were not somehow immune from divine judgment just because they were God's chosen people. They too could have been subjects of judgment. Instead, in what must be understood as an unexpected display of mercy, Yahweh diverted his wrath reserved for the guilty to innocent sacrificial lambs. This mercy was denied their Egyptian neighbors, whose piercing screams could be heard all night long as young and old fell limp into the quivering hands of distraught parents.

The Israelites quivered as well. They had every reason to solemnly reflect on Egypt's unrelenting judgment while they got overflowing mercy. They possessed no moral or spiritual beauty to attract such favor. John Bunyan urges believers to never take the mercy that God lavishes on them for granted: "Be often thinking of the cries and roarings of the damned in hell."[13] But for the grace of God, there go we all.

The thought drives a holy fear into our souls and causes us to appreciate the undeserved glories of heaven as never before. Out of the black dread of judgment emerges the brilliant grace of God toward wretches—a supernal grace that supremely magnifies his glory. His marvelous hand draws us

---

12. See also 2 Sam. 24:16; Isa. 37:36.

13. John Bunyan, *The Works of John Bunyan* (1854; repr., Carlisle, PA: Banner of Truth, 1991), 2:543.

forth "from the pit of destruction, out of the miry bog" (Ps. 40:2), and sets our feet on the rock of his "great salvation" (Heb. 2:3).

Consider the deeper spiritual truths here. First, Passover signals that while God's people are being delivered from their external enemies, the more important deliverance is that of being rescued from their own internal enemy—wicked hearts that are never immune from divine judgment.

Second, Israel's perpetual celebration of Passover became a typological pointer to the coming Redeemer, who ironically rescues God's people not by conventional heroics and extraordinary displays of power, but by abject humility and weakness. He offers himself as the Paschal Lamb (1 Cor. 5:7) who diverts divine judgment from guilty sinners to his pure and innocent self, shedding his precious blood and plastering it all over the doors of the souls of those for whom his death atones. Thus, it is no mistake that God providentially ordered Jesus' crucifixion some fifteen hundred years later to coincide with the slaughter of the paschal lambs in the temple during Passover.[14]

The Exodus and God's Supreme Glory in Romans 9

If there is one place in Scripture that offers us a more explicit basis for the greater-glory theodicy, then it must be found in Romans 9, where Paul picks up the themes of the exodus to make much of the glory of God in redemption. He begins by pointing out God's sovereign freedom in election whereby he "hated" (rejected) Esau and "loved" (chose) the scoundrel Jacob (Rom. 9:12–13). Paul can hear the hue and cry, "That's not fair!" Is not this preferential treatment "injustice on God's part?" (v. 14). It is not a matter of justice or fairness, however, but of God's unrestrained prerogative in choosing to extend mercy to some but not others (vv. 15–16).

Paul explains by recalling the events of the exodus: "For the Scripture says to Pharaoh, 'For this very purpose I have raised you up, that I might show my power in you, and that my name might be proclaimed in all

---

14. Harold W. Hoehner, *Chronological Aspects of the Life of Christ* (Grand Rapids: Zondervan, 1977), 76–93.

the earth.' So then he has mercy on whomever he wills, and he hardens whomever he wills" (Rom. 9:17–18; cf. Ex. 9:16). Israel gets the warm, velvety robes of mercy. Pharaoh gets a stone-cold heart.

Again, a hue and cry rises forth from offended quarters: "Why does he still find fault? For who can resist his will?" (Rom. 9:19). Doesn't this take away human responsibility and make God a moral monster? Paul responds by striking a fatal blow to our human pride, our self-centeredness, our woeful lack of God-centeredness. Referencing Jeremiah 18:1–11, Paul says: "But who are you, O man, to answer back to God? Will what is molded say to its molder, 'Why have you made me like this?' Has the potter no right over the clay, to make out of the same lump one vessel for honorable use and another for dishonorable use?" (Rom. 9:20–21).

(Crickets . . .)

Understanding why God chooses to dispense mercy to some but not others is inscrutable. We are in no position to judge his freedom, his goodness, his just righteousness, or his unfathomable wisdom. When standing before the mysterious glories of the transcendent God, we will cover our mouths and fall on our knees to say with Job, "I have uttered what I did not understand, things too wonderful for me, which I did not know" (Job 42:3).

Now Paul comes to the *crux* of the matter (remember that word?). In Romans 9:22–23, he writes, "What if God, desiring to show his wrath and to make known his power, has endured with much patience vessels of wrath prepared for destruction, in order to make known the riches of his glory for vessels of mercy, which he has prepared beforehand for glory . . . ?" These may be the most important words that Paul ever uttered.[15] The apostle draws a stark contrast between God's mighty judgment and his rich and tender mercy. It is not unlike the difference between a raging inferno in the depths of a volcano like Krakatoa and the refreshing spring water of the French Alps that sparkles with tranquility while trickling out in Évian-les-Bains.

---

15. Thomas R. Schreiner, *Romans*, 2nd ed., Baker Exegetical Commentary on the New Testament (Grand Rapids: Baker, 2018), 507.

Consider the severity, immensity, and supernatural terror that God inflicted on Egypt. It was not short-lived. Wave upon wave of holy judgment fell on these recalcitrant oppressors, eliciting no repentance and stretching his "patience" quite thin. God could have dispensed with the nation by a snap of his fingers. Instead, the prolonged and fierce series of judgments on a stronger, vaster nation served to highlight his miraculous mercy to the helpless little Israelites—sheepherding rabble of no consequence. A quicker and quieter form of judgment would not have allowed the sons of Israel to appreciate the glory of their rescue in quite the same way.

Paul's point bears emphasizing. The effusive favor that God showers on the undeserving elect few ("vessels of mercy") in light of his judgment heaped on the deserving majority ("vessels of wrath") is designed "to make known the riches of his glory" (Rom. 9:22–23). When the Red Sea split wide open, God provided a far more glorious exit path for the sons of Israel from the ferocious Egyptian army than they could imagine. As the massive waves consumed countless horses, iron, and men, less than a spear's throw ahead, the panicked little tribe escaped unscathed on dry sand. A lesser deliverance would have elicited far less praise for the Deliverer.

This prefigures the even more remarkable salvation of Christ. The mountains of water that should have been crashing down on "vessels of mercy" crushed Christ in their stead. He became, as it were, a "vessel of wrath" in our place, bearing the full brunt of God's fierce judgment (Rom. 5:8–11). Furthermore, salvation unto the "kingdom of heaven" is a rare pearl of inestimable value (Matt. 13:45–46), and only a few get to partake of this treasure, while the vast majority are left to stray down the broad highway to destruction (7:13–14). The scarcity of the privilege is another facet of redemption that evokes awestruck praise from the elect few.

Isaac Watts captures the glory of what the sinless Savior did to rescue us from the watery grave that should have been our destiny:

> Alas! and did my Savior bleed,
> And did my Sovereign die!
> Would he devote that sacred head
> For such a worm as I!

Was it for crimes that I had done
He groaned upon the tree!
Amazing pity! Grace unknown!
And love beyond degree![16]

This is the greater-glory theodicy. It is the theodicy of Scripture.

STUDY QUESTIONS

1. Why is it strange and unsettling to refer to the fall of Adam and Eve as "fortunate"?
2. Why does the author call his theodicy the *greater-glory theodicy*?
3. For what ultimate purpose did God create human beings?
4. What are some of the remarkable ways in which God has glorified himself, according to the Bible? How has God glorified himself supremely above all these other ways?
5. Could God have chosen to redeem fallen sinners in more than one way? Why or why not?
6. Why has the author described the storyline of redemption as J-shaped instead of U-shaped?
7. Was the fall of humanity into sin a necessary part of God's plan? What does the author mean when he says that the fall was a "*conditional necessity*"?
8. In what ways does the story of the exodus mirror the broader story of redemption in the Bible?
9. In what way does the Passover mirror the work of Christ on the cross?
10. Read Romans 9:9–24. How does the author use this passage to defend the greater-glory theodicy?

16. Isaac Watts, "Alas! and Did My Savior Bleed" (1707).

7

THE GRAND HERO OF HISTORY

In the history of great heroes, few compare with the protagonists in classical Greek mythology.[1] One thinks of Odysseus, the principal character of Homer's epic poem *Odyssey*. Odysseus' unflappable courage and combat prowess were indispensable in defeating the Trojans. The demigod Perseus cleverly killed the snake-haired Medusa, who had turned all previous would-be assassins to stone as they unwisely gazed upon her beauty. Theseus, the revered Athenian hero, ventured into the dizzying Cretan Labyrinth to slay the great bull-headed creature Minotaur. In doing so, he saved thirteen of the yearly sacrificial victims sent by the tyrannical King Minos of Crete to be devoured by the man-eating beast.

These are but a few of the famed Greek heroes, but the greatest of them all is Hercules, who has served as an archetypal hero for all succeeding ages. The hulking demigod has forever forged the notion of *herculean* strength. Nothing in the air, sea, or land could overcome his brute force. His mastery of muscle was first on display as an infant when he seized two snakes slithering their way into his crib. He wrung their necks as they

---

1. See Edith Hamilton, *Mythology* (Boston: Little, Brown and Company, 1942); Stephen Fry, *Heroes: The Greek Myths Reimagined* (San Francisco: Chronicle Books, 2020).

tried to coil around his body. One of his greatest battles was waged against the nine-headed monster Hydra. If one of its heads was cut off, two more would grow in its place. After several failed attempts, Hercules managed to systematically cut each of the heads off while his nephew Iolaus came behind quickly with a burning torch to sear the necks, preventing the heads from growing back.

Hercules freed the great Titan Prometheus, who had been inescapably chained to a mammoth rock by Zeus, king of the gods. His crime? Bringing forth the mortal race of men. As further punishment, Zeus sent an eagle to eat away at the immortal god's liver, which regenerated every day. Hercules slew the eagle and released Prometheus from his bondage. The intrepid hero helped another great Titan: Atlas, the strongest of all gods and men. Atlas was also punished by Zeus, consigned to use his *titanic* strength to uphold the heavens on his shoulders so that they wouldn't crash into the earth. Hercules was perhaps the only mortal who himself could bear such weight. He did so briefly as a favor to Atlas in exchange for the condemned god's assistance on one of Hercules' great adventures.

In this world of incurable darkness, the Greeks are not the only ones to clamor for bright-eyed saviors who can offer us hope and salvation. Every civilization in history has sought them out. But since real-world heroes and heroines are so rare, we beleaguered humans tend to forge imaginary ones in our epic poems, our myths and fairy tales, our fictional narratives.

Yet we have a hard time imagining the perfect hero, so we always return to tainted and stumbling saviors—people like us. The gods and heroes of Greek mythology are model representatives. They invariably suffer from limited powers. There is always some Achilles' heel that trips them up. They exhibit as many vices as virtues. All too easily, they succumb to moodiness, jealousy, deception, and cruel vengeance.

But there is one hero who is not like this. In fact, he is unlike any conception of a hero that we have ever produced in our most fertile imaginations. Yet he is the only flawless Savior, the only true hero worthy of worship, the only real-world hero capable of remedying the crisis in which we find ourselves. The apostle Peter made an audacious claim, dismissing all the famed gods and mortal icons of the Greco-Roman pantheon, when he put forth "the name of Jesus Christ of Nazareth" (Acts 4:10) as this sole Redeemer of the world. He boldly declared, "There is salvation in no one else, for there is no other name under heaven given among men by which we must be saved" (v. 12).

When we consider the Son of God as the exclusive Rescuer of mankind who defeats moral evil and reverses the cosmic curse, we must be prepared to have all conceptions of the heroic in our minds strategically blown and reconfigured to gain some small glimpse of the wonder of this grand hero of history.

Paul Helm muses, "It is tempting to think of God as a Herculean figure." Many envision God as being "able to outlift and out-throw and outrun all his opponents. Such a theology would be one of physical and metaphysical power; whatever his enemies can do God can do it better or more efficiently than they."[2] It is true that the triune God has vast reserves of power in his tiniest finger to wipe out the entire cosmos, and one day he will do so.

But God employed a different kind of power once the second person of the Trinity entered our lowly habitat, was wrapped in swaddling cloths, and was laid in a manger (Luke 2:12). This power is unexpected and strangely subversive. It undermines our profile of the stereotypical savior. The Son of God defeats evil by embracing the counterintuitive power of weakness, vulnerability, suffering, and ultimately death.

This is why the most remarkable miracle of all is not God's speaking the creation into existence out of nothing, but rather the infinite Creator's taking upon himself all the finite features of the lowly creatures he made in order to bring about their redemption. We need to explore the miracle contained in the extraordinary polarities and ironies marking the person and work of the one who is both fully God and fully man. Furthermore, we need to see how these seemingly incongruous attributes of the God-man are necessary for the defeat of evil and the reversal of the Edenic curse. Nothing demonstrates the validity of the greater-glory theodicy quite like

2. Paul Helm, *The Providence of God* (Downers Grove, IL: InterVarsity Press, 1994), 224.

the utterly unique Son of God, who shines a searing light on the triune God's greatest display of glory—his incomparable work of redemption.

THE MYSTERIOUS AND MARVELOUS INCARNATION

The incarnation sets Christianity apart from all other religions and ideologies. John of Damascus (A.D. 676–749) speaks of this curious paradox: "He who was of the Father, yet without mother, was born of woman without a father's co-operation."[3] Born into this world of a virgin, this is Immanuel—"God with us" (Matt. 1:23). The transcendent One becomes the immanent One, drawing near to us, dwelling among his creatures as one of them. In this marvelous mystery, the second person of the Trinity assumes a human nature without surrendering anything of his eternal divine nature. The two natures are conjoined in one person in what seems to be an utterly incongruous coexistence between the infinite and the finite.

But this is no half-God, half-man. Each nature retains its full essence. There is no commingling. There is no obliteration of the Creator-creature distinction. Consequently, we cannot escape the strangeness of this tension that theologians call the *hypostatic union*. It is like Death Valley in July being conjoined to the frozen tundra of the North Pole and occupying the same location at the same time.

The incarnation is not a contradiction; rather, it is a deep paradox or mystery, such as the doctrine of the Trinity (one God subsisting as three persons) or the compatibility of absolute divine sovereignty on the one hand with human freedom and responsibility on the other. Without the mystery of the incarnation, there would be no salvation, no remedy to the conflict of the ages. We would be lost, alone, and hopeless in a black eddy of sheer misery and terror.

3. John of Damascus, "The Orthodox Faith," in *Fathers of the Church: Saint John of Damascus: Writings*, trans. Frederic H. Chase Jr. (Washington, DC: Catholic University of America Press, 1958), 4.14.

Consider the remarkable dichotomies of the incarnation. In his condescension as man, Jesus took on the lowly features that essentially mark all human beings living in a postfall world except for the stain of sin (Heb. 4:15). At least thirteen significant points of contrast coexist between the divinity and humanity of the one person of Christ during his earthly mission to procure salvation for lost sinners (see Phil. 2:6–11).[4] Before his resurrection and ascension, the preincarnate glory that Jesus possessed became veiled. Just as the moon veils the glory of the sun during an eclipse, so also Jesus' human nature veiled the glory of his divine nature so that he could achieve his rescue mission—as a man for the race of men. Yet as we will see, both natures are necessary if redemption is to be achieved.

Creator and created. The Son of God is the agent by which everything that exists has come into existence (John 1:3). The eternal uncreated Word spoke, and the sun, the moon, and the stars and planets appeared; skies and oceans and mountains were formed; birds and sea creatures and mammals filled the earth. He created mankind. Every man, woman, and child finds his or her existence rooted in him. The Son of God made the woman—his mother, Mary—and the womb by which, strangely, she bore him when the Word became flesh and dwelt among us as one who now assumes a created nature like ours (John 1:14).

Infinite and finite. As God, the Son is the unbounded and great I am (Ex. 3:14; John 8:58). He is Being itself. The fullness of his being is infinite, and no mortal can comprehend it: "Can you find out the deep things of God? Can you find out the limit of the Almighty?" (Job 11:7). And yet the infinite One took on the finite. He condescended to the tight confines of the mortal creatures he made, bearing all their creaturely limitations.

Independent and dependent. As God, the Son is wholly independent. He is self-sufficient, without a single want or need. He requires no human, no spirit, no substance, no outside force to sustain him (Isa. 40:13–14). But when he took on a human nature for the sake of his earthly ministry,

---

4. After Jesus rose from the dead and ascended to heaven in full glory, not all of these distinctions are retained.

he suddenly became dependent, not relying on his divine powers but subjecting himself to creaturely limitations. He was hungry and needed food (Matt. 4:2). He was thirsty and needed drink (John 4:7). The one who "does not faint or grow weary" (Isa. 40:28) needed rest (Mark 4:38). He lived and acted primarily in and through his humanity while depending on the Spirit of God (Luke 4:1, 14).

Sustainer and sustained. The Creator of all things is also the Sustainer of all things (Col. 1:16–17). Never once has the Son of God suspended his control of the laws that govern heaven and earth, that allow men to live and breathe (Acts 17:25, 28). Yet the one who "upholds the universe by the word of his power" (Heb. 1:3) came and subjected himself to the very powers by which he sustains every molecule (Mark 4:37–38). Jesus is simultaneously Author and actor. He is both the transcendent Writer of the story of the world and one of the actors subject to the Writer's absolute dictation of all things.[5] In fact, he is the principal actor in the story.

Immutable and mutable. Because the everlasting God is marked by unyielding perfection, he cannot change (Mal. 3:6). There is "no variation or shifting shadow" (James 1:17 NASB) in the essence of his being, his mind, his will, or his actions. He is not subject to outside forces that alter him or what he does. In the fullness of his divinity, Jesus Christ is steadfastly immutable, "the same yesterday and today and forever" (Heb. 13:8). Yet in his humanity, Jesus subjected himself to outside forces, yielding to the mutable conditions of his fragile, vacillating creatures.

Invisible and visible. God is spirit (John 4:24), having no material substance. He is invisible (Col. 1:15). But when God became a man, he became visible, acquiring a material body. He became flesh (John 1:14) so that people heard and saw the Word of Life and touched him as he dwelt among us (1 John 1:1).

Omnipresent and spatially located. The invisible God is not confined to the construct of spatial reality. He transcends all measurable

---

5. Gavin Ortlund, *Theological Retrieval for Evangelicals: Why We Need Our Past to Have a Future* (Wheaton, IL: Crossway, 2019), 89–115.

extensions of space, meaning that he is present everywhere (Ps. 139:7–10; Jer. 23:23–24). And then the omnipresent God suddenly confined himself to spatial location when he took on the finite characteristics of a fleshly body (John 16:28).

Timeless and temporal. The God who transcends space also transcends the created construct of time. He is timelessly eternal (1 Tim. 1:17), the God who is "from everlasting to everlasting" (Ps. 90:2). Jesus said, "I am the Alpha and the Omega, the first and the last, the beginning and the end" (Rev. 22:13), meaning that he transcends and encompasses the whole scope of history and eternity. And yet "when the fullness of time had come, God sent forth his Son, born of woman" (Gal. 4:4). The God who does not grow old grew as a boy into a man, living in the era of the first-century Roman Empire (Luke 2:40).

Omnipotent and weak. God commands the universe with his perfect and unbounded power (see Job 38–41). But when the Son of God became a man, "the thunder of his power" that no one can "understand" (Job 26:14) came to coexist with abject weakness. The God who determines the times and places where all men dwell (Acts 17:26) could find no place to lay his head (Matt. 8:20). Again, the same one who "upholds the universe by the word of his power" (Heb. 1:3) had to grow stronger (Luke 2:40) and was so weak that he needed another to bear his cross (Matt. 27:32).

Omniscient and growing in knowledge. As God, Jesus Christ is the one "in whom are hidden all the treasures of wisdom and knowledge" (Col. 2:3). His divinity sees all things and knows all things. "No creature is hidden from his sight" (Heb. 4:13). And yet the one whose divine "understanding is beyond measure" (Ps. 147:5)—in fact, it is "unsearchable" (Isa. 40:28)—had to learn and grow in knowledge and increase "in wisdom" (Luke 2:52) through the exercise of his human mind.

Untemptable and temptable. The unwavering righteousness of God means that he cannot be touched with evil. Because he is the source of all that is right and good and true, no sin can penetrate his holy essence. He is "of purer eyes than to see evil and cannot look at wrong" (Hab. 1:13). He cannot entertain a single unholy thought. Consequently, God cannot be tempted by evil, nor can he tempt others (James 1:13). Nonetheless, to complete his redemptive mission, the incarnate Son of God had to be made like us (Heb. 2:14, 17) and had to suffer temptation just like us (v. 18). But his battle was far greater, surpassing the most severe test that our fragile wills could handle. Fortunately, even in his human weakness, he persevered and extinguished every fiery dart of the evil one without ever succumbing to a single sin (4:15).

Impassible and passible. Because God is perfect and immutable and cannot be adversely affected by any outside force, this also means that he is impassible (Ps. 18:2). The doctrine of impassibility means primarily that God is unable to suffer pain or loss. He cannot endure even an infinitesimal loss to his unbounded blessedness and joy. Yet he became a passible man, "a man of sorrows and acquainted with grief" (Isa. 53:3). In fact, the Son of God bore an unbearable weight of suffering that no creature can comprehend.

Immortal and mortal. Since God is uncreated, self-existing, eternally perfect, immutable, and impassible, it is not possible for him to die, for he "has life in himself" (John 5:26). He is immortal. And yet the immortal One, "who lives forever and ever" (Rev. 4:9), took on a mortal existence. Jesus came to die a brutal, pitiable death (John 19:16–18). Melito of Sardis (d. A.D. 180) declares the strangest of enigmas: "He who hung the earth is hanging; he who fixed the heavens has been fixed; he who fastened the universe has been fastened to a tree; the Sovereign has been insulted; God has been murdered."[6] Of course, this does not mean that the divine nature was snuffed out—that would be impossible. Rather, it means that the divine Son was murdered via his humanity.

---

6. *Peri Pascha*, 96.711–15, quoted by Paul L. Gavrilyuk, "God's Impassible Suffering in the Flesh: The Promise of Paradoxical Christology," in *Divine Impassibility and the Mystery of Human Suffering,* ed. James F. Keating and Thomas Joseph White (Grand Rapids: Eerdmans, 2009), 128–29.

Divinity (no aspect surrendered)	Humanity (assumed in his person)
The uncreated Creator (John 1:3)	Takes on a created nature (John 1:14)
The infinite (unbounded) Being	Takes on a finite (bounded) existence
The independent One, in need of nothing and no one (Isa. 40:13–14)	Takes on a dependent nature, relying in his humanity on the Spirit (Luke 4:14)
The Sustainer of the universe (Col. 1:17; Heb. 1:3)	Becomes subject to its divinely directed laws (Mark 4:37–38)
The immutable (unchangeable) God (Mal. 3:6)	Yields to the mutable conditions of his fragile, vacillating creatures.
The invisible God (Col. 1:15) who is an incorporeal spirit (John 4:24)	Becomes visible, acquiring a corporeal body and living among us (John 1:14)
The omnipresent Being who is not confined to space (Ps. 139:7–8)	Becomes spatially located (John 16:28)
The timelessly eternal One (1 Tim. 1:17)	Comes to live in the temporal realm (Gal. 4:4)
The omnipotent One who possesses all power (Job 26:14)	Coexists with weakness (Matt. 8:20; 27:32)
The omniscient One who is the source of all knowledge and wisdom (Col. 2:3)	Takes on a human mind that learns and grows in knowledge and wisdom (Luke 2:52)
The perfectly righteous One who is utterly untemptable (James 1:13)	Becomes subject to and perseveres under every possible temptation (Heb. 4:15)
The impassible God who cannot suffer (Ps. 18:2)	Becomes passible, "a man of sorrows and acquainted with grief" (Isa. 53:3)
The immortal One "who lives forever and ever" (Rev. 4:9)	Becomes mortal, dying a brutal, pitiable death (John 19:16–18)

Fig. 7.1. The Incomparable Divine-Human Savior

WHY THE INCARNATION?

Why must the grand hero of history possess these seemingly incompatible sets of attributes? Why must the God of all supremacy clothed in breathtaking majesty take on the crude garments of humanity? Because apart from the divine-human Savior, there is no rescue, no redemption, no atonement for sin, no forgiveness, no reconciliation with God, no defeat of evil, no reversal of the curse, no peace on earth. God must become like one of us and must unite us to the person and saving work of Christ in order to eradicate the effects of evil and the curse *in* us and of all the cursed evil *around* us. There are at least four reasons why we need a Savior who is both fully human and fully divine.[7]

A Human Sacrifice, but Divinely Perfect, Rich, and Powerful

We needed a man to offer himself as an acceptable atoning sacrifice for sin (Heb. 10:9). Only human blood can pay the price for human sin (v. 4). It had to be shed and splattered all over the cross. God, in his immaterial being, "has no circulatory system: no heart, no arteries, no veins, and no blood. For God to shed blood, He had to become man."[8] But we needed one who is God to ensure that the sacrifice was perfect, unblemished, blameless, free of the curse of sin (Heb. 2:17; 1 Peter 1:18–19).

If sinners are ever to be reconciled to a holy God, we need one who became like us, to be crushed under all manner of pain and suffering (Isa. 53:3–4), and to bear the punishment that our trespasses deserved (v. 5). Likewise, we needed one with divine riches to pay the high cost that our sin has incurred. Only one who is God could endure the full and terrible weight of sin and crush it to pieces (Heb. 12:2). Only one encompassed with divine fortitude could embrace the cup of divine wrath against sin and drink it down to the very dregs (Matt. 26:39).

7. In what follows, I am summarizing and supplementing Francis Turretin, *Institutes of Elenctic Theology*, ed. John T. Dennison Jr., trans. George Musgrave Giger, 3 vols. (Phillipsburg, NJ: P&R Publishing, 1992–97), 2:302–3.

8. Robert Gromacki, *The Virgin Birth: A Biblical Study of the Deity of Jesus Christ*, rev. ed. (Grand Rapids: Kregel, 2002), 160.

An Obedient Human, but Divinely Impeccable

To be fully justified in God's sight, sinners needed a new human representative to be tested with obedience (Matt. 5:17) where our father Adam failed, but one with a divine nature to facilitate impeccable adherence to the moral demands of the divine will (Rom. 5:18–19).

The Son needed to obey the will of his heavenly Father in his humanity, but not for himself. His deity is already clothed in absolute righteousness. God in himself requires no test of obedience. Rather, Jesus' human obedience earned a second robe of righteousness so that he could remove the filthy rags of wretched sinners and refit each one with these royal robes.[9] Sinners who have trusted Christ to clothe them in his perfect righteousness may stand confidently before the throne of God in bright and clean attire (Rev. 19:8), unconditionally accepted as his own—no longer his enemies, but friends.

A Temptable Human, but an Untemptable God

In the Son's test of obedience, we needed a man to be tempted as we are, but one with a divine nature who is free from the lure and power of sin so as to overcome all temptation (Heb. 4:15). The Son's temptable human will was conjoined to his untemptable divine will (James 1:13), rendering his testing as the second Adam incapable of succumbing to the lure of sin. Jesus was truly impeccable. Consequently, at every point where Adam collapsed, Jesus rose up and succeeded, ensuring victory for the justified sinner.

A Mortal Human, but an Immortal God

We needed a man to die a brutal death of retribution on our behalf as demanded by God's just condemnation of our sin (Isa. 53:4–9). The divine nature cannot die. Only humans suffer under the curse of death; therefore, the Son had to be born of a woman (Gal. 4:4). But we need one who is God marked with immortal power to destroy death in and through

9. John Bunyan, *Pilgrim's Progress*, updated ed. (Abbotsford, WI: Aneko Press, 2014), pt. 2, the Third Stage, 238–40.

the Son's dying and rising again (1 Cor. 15:20–26). The Son's divine work, extending from a dark Friday afternoon till Easter morning, ensures that death's ugly head will never breathe its eternally fatal flames into the faces of the redeemed (vv. 50–57).

Jesus is the one and only hero who overcame death and destroys that enemy forever. Likewise, those who are united to him in his death, burial, and resurrection are freed from death and sin forever (Rom. 6:1–11). The Holy Spirit must join us to Christ so that all the blessings of redemption become ours. John Calvin exhorts, "We must understand that as long as Christ remains outside of us, and we separated from him, all that he has suffered and done for the salvation of the human race remains useless and of no value for us."[10]

As you can see, the problem of evil is no trivial matter. The fall introduced a quagmire of epic proportions whereby rebellious creatures have dishonored their holy Creator, maligning his righteous majesty as God and becoming alienated from his blessed presence. The whole created order is so intractably hampered by the curse that no solution to evil's problem can be found in this worldly plane of existence.

Consequently, the crisis could be solved only by God himself, yet *only* by entering the cursed order of creation *as a man* to bridge the chasm between Creator and alienated creatures: to pay the costly price of forgiveness, to pour out his undeserved favor on rebels, to undo the damage they have done, and to restore *shalom* ("peace") in the cosmos. The Son in neither his divinity alone nor his humanity alone could do this. Only the Son as both fully God and fully man can save us.

This is heroics beyond herculean, beyond any earthly exemplar that we might uphold. It is strange and perfect. While it required the God-man to immerse himself in our ugliness and befoulment, it is a salvation that is mysteriously pure and beautiful. It is sublime. The gravity of what the promised Messiah came to do is like the weight of heaven and earth

---

10. John Calvin, *Institutes of the Christian Religion*, ed. John T. McNeill, trans. Ford Lewis Battles, Library of Christian Classics 20–21 (Philadelphia: Westminster, 1960), 3.1.1.

coursing through the veins of those who have been transformed from reprehensible sinners to regal saints. The glory of it outshines ten thousand suns and transports grateful souls of the redeemed to celestial realms unimagined.

> Man of Sorrows! what a name
> For the Son of God, who came
> Ruined sinners to reclaim:
> Hallelujah! what a Savior!
>
> Bearing shame and scoffing rude,
> In my place condemned he stood,
> Sealed my pardon with his blood:
> Hallelujah! what a Savior!
>
> Guilty, vile, and helpless we;
> Spotless Lamb of God was he;
> Full atonement! can it be?
> Hallelujah! what a Savior![11]

THE SUFFERING SERVANT

When facing villains or overcoming the crisis that threatens peace, most heroes summon great courage or exert brute force in pursuit of victory. Some outwit their opponents. Underdogs muster strength that they didn't know they possessed. The vigilant ones reach down deep for an iron will or discover secret wisdom for their quest from nether regions hitherto unexplored in the recesses of their minds. And sometimes they stumble to the finish, overcoming the conflict by sheer coincidence. Now, this is all stuff of conventional heroics. But when we consider the grand hero of history, we are not dealing with the conventional. Jesus defeats

11. Philip P. Bliss, "Man of Sorrows! What a Name" (1875).

evil in the most unusual way—by succumbing to all its feral wickedness, heaving it upon his faltering shoulders, absorbing the darkness of it, and thrusting himself into the pits of evil's great end—death and hell itself.

Satan was convinced that killing the Son of God would defeat the divine plan of redemption, using pawns such as the traitor Judas (Luke 22:3–4). But the crucifixion of Jesus did no such thing. Satan is the most self-deceived creature in the universe. Ironically, the devil and all his minions—human and demonic—were actually the pawns of God. The early church father Athanasius (A.D. 296–373) asserts, "A marvelous and mighty paradox has ... occurred, for the death which they thought to inflict on Him as dishonor and disgrace has become the glorious monument to death's defeat."[12] The scandal of his dubious arrest, illegal trial, sad mocking, public shaming, torturous beating, and gruesome crucifixion all helped ensure that the innocent Messiah—the Suffering Servant of Isaiah's prophecies—would gain glorious victory over sin, corruption, decay, ugliness, injustice, war, sickness, disease, catastrophe, and ultimately death.

No greater burden for overcoming evil has rested with anyone in history or fiction. What Jesus Christ was tasked to do is unthinkable for anyone else. Isaiah tells us that God's messianic Servant caused men to be "astonished." His appearance at the peak of his suffering was so "marred" that he no longer looked human (Isa. 52:14). In Isaiah 53, the prophet tells us, "He was despised and rejected by men, a man of sorrows and acquainted with grief; and as one from whom men hide their faces he was despised, and we [his Jewish kinsmen] esteemed him not" (53:3). He was treated as a lamb "led to the slaughter" (v. 7). Though he was completely innocent (v. 9), "by oppression and judgment he was taken away" and "cut off out of the land of the living" (v. 8).

But the irony is that he was actually "smitten by God" (Isa. 53:4), but not for his own sin, for "he had done no violence, and there was no deceit in his mouth" (v. 9). Nonetheless, "it was the will of the LORD to crush him; he has put him to grief" (v. 10).

---

12. Athanasius, *On the Incarnation* (Crestwood, NY: St. Vladimir's Seminary Press, 2000), § 24.

Why?

To bear the griefs of the redeemed, to carry their sorrows (Isa. 53:4). "He was pierced" by the will of God "for our transgressions; he was crushed for our iniquities; upon him was the chastisement that brought us peace, and with his wounds we are healed" (v. 5). He did this for his sheep (cf. John 10:11) even as we all (Jew and Gentile alike) "have gone astray," each turning his own way from the Shepherd of our souls (Isa. 53:6).

Yet Yahweh, the ever merciful One, "laid on him the iniquity of us all" (Isa. 53:6) so that we might be "accounted righteous" (v. 11) in him (cf. 2 Cor. 5:21). The Lamb of God (John 1:29) was willingly "stricken for the transgression" of all of God's people (Isa. 53:8), interceding on their behalf (v. 12), so that in the end the hand of the Messiah would "prosper" (v. 10). Though he was crushed, alienated, forsaken of his Father, and damned with pungent curses equal to an eternity in the fires of hell, nonetheless, "Out of the anguish of his soul he shall see" his victory "and be satisfied" (v. 11).

Only such a suffering hero as this is the conquering hero par excellence and worthy of the name to whom "every knee should bow, in heaven and on earth and under the earth," confessing that he "is Lord, to the glory of God the Father" (Phil. 2:10–11). In fact, this incarnate suffering, this condescension, this abject humility, and this obedient subjugation to the slaughter of crucifixion (vv. 7–8) is precisely why the Father *supremely* exalted the name of Jesus above every other name (v. 9). It is *this* that brings God "glory" (v. 11). And we are not speaking of just any sort of glory, but unique, unprecedented glory—glory that is *supreme*— cosmos-shattering glory.

Let us not miss how profound this is, since we have already noted that God in his divine essence cannot suffer pain or loss because this would threaten his intrinsic joy as the God who is forever completely self-satisfied in the blessedness and excellency of his immutable perfections. God as he is in himself—that is, his intrinsic nature apart from his providential actions in creation—is immutably and perfectly glorious. Nothing can add to or detract from that internal glory. But when he as Creator chooses to display his glory in varying degrees within the creation (1 Cor. 15:40–41), and especially to us, his image-bearing creatures, then nothing could supremely magnify this external glory more than the sort of suffering and death that the Son of God was subject to.

Just how profound was this suffering?

THE UNFATHOMABLE SUFFERING OF CHRIST

The greatest mysteries of the gospel and the Christian faith are bound up in the unfathomable suffering of Christ and the inscrutable breach it created in the Father-Son relationship. Jesus did not merely suffer at the hands of evil men (Acts 2:22–23). This was divine wrath ordered by the Father's hand. Strangely, the cross is the preeminent location where unbridled wrath *and* mercy embrace one another. It featured the greatest outpouring of divine displeasure and unmitigated judgment, ironically resting on the holy and beloved Son, while simultaneously it featured the greatest outpouring of mercy to debased sinners. The pure and innocent One is inescapably nailed to the cross and punished on behalf of the guilty, who are set free (Rom. 5:8–11).

Punishing the guilty is justice. Punishing the lone innocent One for the guilty is grace. This does not mean that justice is swept under the cosmic rug of divine disregard. Rather, it means that the sinless God-man absorbs the full weight of justice that the guilty deserve while they get the grace of unmitigated pardon that they don't deserve. The obligatory demands of God's justice do not fail to be satisfied when he chooses in his sovereign freedom to dispense this effusive grace. Jesus takes care of the justice of God so that grace may be freely poured out on sinners.

Paul declares in 2 Corinthians 8:9: "For you know the grace of our Lord Jesus Christ, that though he was rich" in his preincarnate divine glory, "yet for your sake he became poor"—condescending to our humble estate and dying a disgraceful death—"so that you," the redeemed, "by his poverty might become rich"—that is, restored to all the benefits of being untainted human beings, at peace with God, and at home in a new and better paradise. And God alone gets glory for this remarkable grace—supreme glory.

The Father's glorious grace came at a severe price, however, one that he was willing to set forth and one that the Son was glad to pay. That payment involved suffering the moment Christ was born and laid in a lowly manger. Yet it was not until Jesus entered the garden of Gethsemane that his affliction became acute, taking on its full redemptive character. As he anticipated the climax of his suffering, Matthew tells us, "he began to be sorrowful and troubled" (Matt. 26:37). This is an understated translation. The term "sorrowful" indicates deep sadness, and "troubled" means exhibiting "bewilderment, anxiety and near-panic."[13] Mark's Gospel is even stronger. He says that Jesus was "greatly distressed" (Mark 14:33), indicating "a profound disarray, expressed physically before a terrifying event: a shuddering horror."[14]

Donald Macleod asks us to imagine "the feeling we experience in the presence of the unearthly, the uncanny and the utterly eerie. In Gethsemane Jesus knew that he was face to face with the unconditionally holy, that absolutely overwhelming might that condones nothing, cannot look on impurity and cannot be diverted from its purpose."[15] Jesus was not afraid of armed guards, unjust law courts, or powerful magistrates. He did not fear physical torture. He was trembling in the face of a preternatural force that no mortal could wield.

When facing the impending "cup" (Luke 22:42) of the wrath of his holy Father all alone *as a man*, he felt the sheer terror of this daunting prospect. Jesus desires in his human will for the cup to be "removed." He casts his plea before the throne, praying earnestly as none before or after, "Not my will, but yours, be done." Jesus teeters on the point of no return. "For a moment the whole salvation of the world, the whole of God's determinate counsel, hangs in the balance, suspended on the free, unconstrained decision of this man. There is dread here and bewilderment and awe and self-doubt, and fear."[16]

13. Donald Macleod, *Christ Crucified: Understanding the Atonement* (Downers Grove, IL: InterVarsity Press, 2014), 27.
14. Raymond E. Brown, *The Death of the Messiah*, 2 vols. (Garden City, NY: Doubleday, 1994), 1:153.
15. Macleod, *Christ Crucified*, 28.
16. Macleod, 29.

The trauma was so severe that in his prayerful striving, "his sweat became like great drops of blood falling down to the ground" (Luke 22:44). This bloody sweat appears to be a rare instance of *hematidrosis*.[17] It occurs in circumstances "associated with a severe anxiety reaction triggered by *fear*."[18] It includes shortness of breath, sensations of choking, strong heart palpitations, muscular tension, weakness, tightening of the chest, and trembling.[19] But Jesus' suffering has only just begun.

As the Messiah passes through his humiliating trial (Matt. 26:47–68) and shameful treatment by Praetorian guard members (27:27–31) after having been whipped within an inch of his life (v. 26), he is laid bare upon the rough-hewn cross, whose sharp fibers scrape across his raw flesh. Iron spikes are pounded through his trembling wrists and ankles. But this pain is a pale reflection of his greater mental anguish. Soon a threatening noontime darkness creeps over the city of Jerusalem and an unearthly silence descends on his quivering form.

Now comes the most incomprehensible suffering in human history, descending on the blood-red head of the Son of God—the apex of his redemptive distress. In that moment, Jesus pierces the silence with an unearthly cry, repeating the forlorn prophetic words of David from Psalm 22:1:

My God, my God, why have you forsaken me? (cf. Matt. 27:46)

This was a cry of divine abandonment, of God-forsakenness—the cry of dereliction. This does not indicate a rupture in the unity of the triune Godhead. Nonetheless, it did mean that the Father's face was turned from his beloved Son as he suffered alone—*in his humanity*. The Father offered no words of paternal comfort or commendation. Rather, the full magnitude of his displeasure was poised to crush the

17. Frederick T. Zugibe, *The Crucifixion of Jesus: A Forensic Inquiry* (New York: M. Evans and Company, 2005), 8–15.
18. Zugibe, 9.
19. Zugibe, 11–12.

Son. He would not rescue the Rescuer from his predicament. This is not cosmic child abuse. If the Father dared to spare his Son this ignoble treatment (Rom. 8:32), then there would be no rescue for others. At this moment, Christ's "agony was so compacted—so infinite—as to be well-nigh unsustainable. . . . The whole entail of sin (pains and agonies it would have taken the world eternity to endure) were all poured out on him in one horrific moment."[20]

As darkness overwhelmed Calvary, Jesus was thrust into outer darkness (Matt. 8:12; 22:13; 25:30). He was the antitype of the scapegoat condemned on the Day of Atonement described in Leviticus 16, sent to die in the wilderness, away from the blessedness of Yahweh's presence in the encampment of Israel. Likewise, the human soul of Messiah was struck from the presence of God and transported "beyond the cosmos, the realm of order and beauty, sinking instead into a black hole which no light could penetrate and from which, in itself, nothing benign or meaningful could ever emanate."[21] In this place, Jesus bore the weight of the unbearable. He completely eradicated the sins of the redeemed, satisfying every last demand of God's just wrath against them. These guilty ones are here declared innocent. They are freed from their bondage.

And this explains why the Son of Man embraced this mysterious hour whereby he would be glorified (John 12:23). Martin Luther said that it was the moment when the innocent Christ was regarded as "the greatest thief, murderer, adulterer, robber, desecrator, blasphemer, etc., there has ever been anywhere in the world."[22] The Father had to turn his righteous visage from this obscene mass of sin.[23] Yet somehow the transcendent God of the universe in the mystery of all mysteries makes this death his

20. Donald Macleod, *The Person of Christ* (Downers Grove, IL: InterVarsity Press, 1998), 176.

21. Macleod, 177.

22. Martin Luther, *Lectures on Galatians, 1535: Chapters 1–4*, vol. 26 of *Luther's Works*, ed. Jaroslav Pelikan and Walter A. Hansen, trans. Jaroslav Pelikan (St. Louis: Concordia, 1963), 277.

23. R. C. Sproul, *The Truth of the Cross* (Orlando, FL: Reformation Trust, 2007), 134.

own without the divine nature's directly experiencing it.[24] Throughout the whole phenomenal ordeal, God and redeemed sinners participate together in the filthy, bloody mess of a God-forsaken *cross* (Gal. 2:20), ironically resulting in God-exalting *glory*.

Two cries reverberated across the heavens and earth from the mount of crucifixion. One was dark and forlorn. The other was bright and victorious. The first cry of dereliction seems to spell the loss of everything, leaving the crisis to loom on in a tragic forever. The second cry dispelled all such dispiriting thoughts when Christ—battered and bleeding and on the brink of his last breath—carried his voice like thunder and bellowed out the singular most triumphant word ever uttered—*Tetelestai!* (John 19:30): "It is finished." Only the divine-human Savior could declare success in this *cruci-centric* plan of redemption that the professing wisdom of the world regards as foolishness (1 Cor. 1:18–21).

But the heavenly host thought otherwise. They bellowed out their own chorus of triumph: "Worthy is the Lamb who was slain, to receive power and wealth and wisdom and might and honor and glory and blessing!" (Rev. 5:12). This is a fitting *doxology* (literally, "a word of glory") for the grand hero of history. It focuses its attention on God's supreme glory, a glory that is forever connected with "the Lamb who was slain." Here in the cross of a crucified and risen Christ we behold ineffable light shining forth out of unspeakable darkness, crushing that darkness forever (Gen. 3:15).

STUDY QUESTIONS

1. When you were growing up, did you have any heroes? What made them so special to you?
2. Consider the polar differences that the author mentions between the divine and human natures of Christ. How does the existence of these polar differences affect your view of the person of Christ?

24. Gavrilyuk, "God's Impassible Suffering," 146–47.

3. Why did the Son of God have to take on a human nature in addition to his divine nature? The author lists four reasons why. What are those reasons?
4. What is your response to the remarkable requirements that God had to meet for sinners to be redeemed?
5. How would you describe the heroics of most heroes whom people tend to uphold? How do they differ from the heroics of Christ in the salvation of sinners?
6. Read the description of Christ and his redemptive work in Isaiah 53. What is most striking about this passage?
7. Where is God's glory most supremely magnified?
8. How are the demands of God's justice satisfied when he saves sinners by his grace?
9. How do we make sense of Jesus' cry of dereliction (abandonment/ forsakenness) on the cross recorded in Matthew 27:46?
10. Read 1 Corinthians 1:18–21. Why does the world regard a crucified Savior as foolishness?

8

THE REST OF THE STORY

In 1516, Thomas More (1478–1535) coined the term *utopia* in a small book he wrote by that title. *Utopia* means "no place," by which he meant a "good place," a far better place that people imagine than where they live now. More's dream was nothing new. Throughout history, societies everywhere have envisioned some sort of utopia. Hesiod (eighth century B.C.) spoke of the Golden Age. Plato (fourth century B.C.) envisioned the perfect society in *The Republic*, and his younger contemporary Aristotle had his competing vision in book 7 of *Politics*. Hinduism, Buddhism, Confucianism, Taoism, Shintoism, and Islam all have their versions of utopia. In 1620, disaffected Puritans came to the New World, landing on the shores of Plymouth, seeking to establish a better life. Ten years later, John Winthrop (1588–1649) came with more Puritans to form their ideal Christian society in the Massachusetts Bay Colony, imagining it as a City on a Hill. The whole American Experiment was an exercise in utopianism.

But the darkness that encompassed the world in the twentieth century and its two world wars gave rise to dystopian fears that remain unabated today. These fears were poignantly expressed in Aldous Huxley's novel *Brave New World* (1932) and George Orwell's *Nineteen Eighty-Four* (1949). Many twentieth-century utopian visions turned out to be dystopian hellscapes. Karl Marx (1818–83) and Vladimir Lenin

(1870–1924) had their ideal society enshrined in Communism, and Adolf Hitler (1889–1945) forged his perfect Aryan world in Germany's National Socialist movement (Nazism). Mao Zedong (1893–1976) borrowed from Marx and Lenin to build his Maoist utopia for China. Altogether these sterling(!) examples have been responsible for unimaginable mass murder and mayhem.[1]

Despite the appalling record of atrocities in these recent blueprints for better societies, many global elitists think that better versions of utopia are just on the horizon. For example, the World Economic Forum, which has beguiled many of the world's most powerful political and corporate leaders, has proposed the Great Reset, promising a global society marked by unprecedented peace and prosperity by utilizing cleverly repackaged Marxist ideas. The fact is, utopian dreams never die. Why is that? No doubt because a fundamental intuition in the human soul tells us that the world is not the way that it is supposed to be. We live in a perpetual state of disenchantment, longing for the days of unspoiled Eden. Our discontent confirms the crisis of the fall and leads us to idealistic notions of a better world.

Sadly, the world's utopian dreams almost always end up as dystopian nightmares, as Huxley and Orwell understood all too well. Nonetheless, these desperate impulses are hard-wired into our shattered souls, and the irony is that though we constantly suppress the truth of the Christian faith (Rom. 1:18–23), yet our visions for a better world indistinctly mimic the very mother lode of true utopianism as sourced in Christianity's story of paradise lost and restored. No vision of the good life can match the plan mapped out in Scripture's grand narrative whereby the grand hero of history reverses the damage wrought in the world and makes it right again.

The Bible portrays Christ's work of redemption as all-encompassing. He is not merely the Savior of an elect number of miserable sinners out of the miry muck from which they were imprisoned (Ps. 40:2), but also

---

1. Lewis M. Simons has calculated that around 90,829,000 people have died as a result of these utopian visions for society. See "Genocide Unearthed," *National Geographic*, January 2006, 28–35.

the Rescuer of creation itself and the Judge of all remaining evil. He is the cosmic Redeemer who is poised to restore "all things" (Eph. 1:10; cf. Acts 3:21) to their proper place in the created order.

This work entails both conventional and unconventional displays of power. It includes a constellation of the expected and the unexpected, the usual and the unusual, the ordinary and the extraordinary. Christ defeats evil in two ways: through his incarnate condescension, suffering, and death, and then through his resurrection, ascension, and return to earth as the glorified Lord of all. He is poised to establish his worldwide kingdom by both a cross and a crown. He will soon come to judge the vast host of rebellious and unrepentant creatures, human and angelic, and to restore the entire cosmos, bringing "all things" under his wise and benevolent rule.

The full scope of Christ's heroic actions provides further testimony to the claims of the greater-glory theodicy that the fundamental design of God in decreeing the fall of mankind and its curse on the created order is to supremely magnify his glory through this panoramic work of redemption. The grandeur of the triune God is enhanced when we juxtapose the Messiah's improbable and inglorious path to the cross alongside his resplendent honor as the risen and reigning Lord. We must canvass the broad trajectory of Jesus Christ's mission so that, as the infamous news commentator Paul Harvey used to say, "Now you know *the rest of the story.*"

THE LION AND THE LAMB

As we have already seen, the person of Christ dismantles our conventional expectations of the archetypal hero. On the one hand, we expect that if Jesus is truly the Son of God, then he is nothing less than the eternal agent and Sustainer of creation (Col. 1:16–17), the immutable (Heb. 13:8) and invincible Lord of the universe (Eph. 1:20–22). On the other hand, we must be surprised that he cast aside his preincarnate glory to take on the lowly mantle of humanity, that the "King of the ages, immortal, invisible, the only God" (1 Tim. 1:17) would choose to be made flesh and to suffer the most excruciating affliction and injury that this grim world has ever foisted upon another (Phil. 2:6–8). But if God would bring defeat to death and evil for the redeemed, then ironically it was necessary for him to die. Yet this is not the complete picture of his work to reverse the curse.

We have no reason to expect that his gracious salvation extends to all (Matt. 7:13–14) or that his atoning sacrifice dispenses with his broad justice elsewhere. He absorbed the judgment that rested on those he rescues from sin and condemnation (Rom. 8:1–2), but the unrepentant have no warrant to expect the same mercy. Seven hundred years before a group of shepherds outside Bethlehem received a startling announcement from heavenly visitors about a newborn babe, Isaiah prophesied these words concerning that little one lying in a manger:

> For to us a child is born,
> to us a son is given;
> and the government shall be upon his shoulder,
> and his name shall be called
> Wonderful Counselor, Mighty God,
> Everlasting Father, Prince of Peace.
> Of the increase of his government and of peace
> there will be no end,
> on the throne of David and over his kingdom,
> to establish it and to uphold it
> with justice and with righteousness
> from this time forth and forevermore.
> The zeal of the LORD of hosts will do this. (Isa. 9:6–7)

While Isaiah 53 predicted a Suffering Servant—a Lamb sent to slaughter for the transgression of God's people—Isaiah 9 predicted a lionlike figure who will rule the world as a mighty King. Revelation 5 throws these two disparate images of Christ as Lamb and Lion together. When no one was found who could open the scroll sealed with seven seals, the prophet John began to weep. But one of the heavenly elders in John's vision came to him and said, "Weep no more; behold, the Lion of the tribe of Judah, the Root of David, has conquered, so that he can open the scroll and its seven seals" (Rev. 5:5). Here the messianic hero is pictured as a conquering Lion. Yet ironically, in the next verse he is depicted as "a Lamb standing, as though it had been slain" (v. 6). By his blood, this slain Lamb "ransomed people for God from every tribe and language and people and nation" (v. 9). A chapter later, the whole world will be cowering in fear before the "wrath" of this same Lamb (6:16).

God defeats evil by both unconventional and conventional means. Christianity is unique among the world's religions in positing the idea that the problem of human evil is resolved by an atonement for sin offered on behalf of repentant sinners, yet one made by the sacrifice of the incarnate God himself. Saving mercy and just wrath, however, are not mutually exclusive actions. A righteous and loving God dispenses both. God displays unconventional and unexpected power over evil in the Son's death. This is the power of grace. Yet he also displays conventional and expected power via just punishment for crimes committed by the persistently impenitent. A day of reckoning is on the horizon in which the Messiah will triumph over all his enemies. In fact, even his atoning sacrifice is pictured in the New Testament as being made by One triumphing in battle over dark forces.

CHRIST THE VICTOR

The saving work of Christ was described by Gustaf Aulén as *Christus Victor*, a term he used in a book of that title in 1931.[2] This metaphor of Christ the Victor encompasses both his humiliation and his exaltation, alluding to the raw power he displays in the full panorama of his redemptive mission. Aulén puts it this way: "Christ—Christus Victor—fights against and triumphs over the evil powers of the world, the 'tyrants' under which mankind is in bondage and suffering, and in Him God reconciles the world to Himself."[3] The grand hero of history gains victory over sin and

2. Gustaf Aulén, *Christus Victor: An Historical Study of the Three Main Types of the Idea of Atonement*, trans. A. G. Herbert (New York: Macmillan, 1969).
3. Aulén, 4.

death through the cross and empty tomb, but also through his supreme lordship and exaltation at the right hand of the Father (Eph. 1:19–21; Phil. 2:9–11), and his final triumph over the forces of evil at his second coming (1 Cor. 15:24–26).

The core and defining component of Christ's redemptive mission is his substitutionary atoning sacrifice on the cross that required the shedding of his blood for the remission of sin (Heb. 9:12). His sacrifice was the judicial infliction of capital punishment for crimes of others (Rom. 5:6–10). Likewise, it served as a ransom that redeems enslaved souls from their oppressive conditions (Matt. 20:28). Consequently, the Messiah gains victory over the enemy—the whole complex of evil forces arrayed against the Judge of the universe and the cursed world. Penal substitution serves as the central motif of the atonement of Christ—the means by which the Lion-Lamb secures victory.

The J-shaped story of redemption follows a carefully scripted narrative. The disobedience of our primordial parents in the unsullied environs of Eden brought about humanity's enslavement to sin (John 8:34). As a result, "the whole world" now "lies in the power of the evil one" (1 John 5:19). But this dire situation was already anticipated and countered by the prophecy in Genesis 3:15 whereby the messianic Seed of Eve is predestined to crush the head of the evil one.

Failure happened in the garden of Eden, and success is mounted in another garden—the garden of Gethsemane, where the Messiah takes hold of the cup of divine wrath against human rebellion and begins to swallow every last bit of its caustic contents. The terrible conflict emerged at one tree—the tree of the knowledge of good and evil (Gen. 2:9)—and was overcome by the cursed tree (Gal. 3:13) to which the Seed of Eve was nailed. The Messiah's tender heel was crushed by those nails.

But the irony of all ironies occurred when this act of crushing resulted in a decisive blow to the wily serpent's head. Satan was defeated as the Messiah's death gave birth to victory. We the redeemed can let the trumpets blare all along the cosmic thoroughfares, for God "has delivered us from the domain of darkness and transferred us to the kingdom of his beloved Son, in whom we have redemption, the forgiveness of sins"

(Col. 1:13–14). According to Romans 16:20, this means that Christ's victory also belongs to us as we anticipate that "the God of peace will soon crush Satan under [our] feet" as we make our way through the gates of the new Jerusalem in the Messiah's future reign. For "the grace of our Lord Jesus Christ" will never cease to be with us, the trophies of his grand conquest.

Paul reinforces how victory was won for the believer in Colossians 2:13–15:

> And you, who were dead in your trespasses and the uncircumcision of your flesh, God made alive together with him, having forgiven us all our trespasses, by canceling the record of debt that stood against us with its legal demands. This he set aside, nailing it to the cross. He disarmed the rulers and authorities and put them to open shame, by triumphing over them in him.

Victory for the believer is achieved over satanic "rulers and authorities" by one surefire method—Christ's canceling our sin-laden debt, "nailing it to the cross" once and for all. Christ's defeat of *human sin* necessarily entails the defeat of *satanic powers*. The villain of Eden must be deposed even as his coenemy sin must be removed from reigning in the hearts of the redeemed.

In John 12:31, Jesus declares that "the ruler of this world [will] be cast out." But how? When Christ allowed himself to be "lifted up from the earth" on a cross (vv. 32–33). This is a strange "lifting up." On the one hand, it speaks of being lifted up to the naked shame of public crucifixion. Yet on the other hand, it was that moment when the Father would uniquely glorify the Son (v. 28) before the entire world. D. A. Carson explains, "When Jesus was glorified, 'lifted up' to heaven by means of the cross, enthroned, then too was Satan dethroned."[4] The apostle John elsewhere states, "The reason the Son of God appeared was to destroy the works of

4. D. A. Carson, *The Gospel according to John* (Grand Rapids: Eerdmans, 1990), 443.

the devil" (1 John 3:8). In one fell swoop, Jesus deposes the ruler of this world and establishes his own rightful claim as the supreme King while bleeding on a cursed cross of wood.

Hebrews 2:14–15 draws a further connection between the power of Satan and the power of death. Both are defeated on behalf of believers through the grand paradox of deadly power resting in the death of Christ: "Since therefore the children share in flesh and blood, [Jesus] himself likewise partook of the same things, that through death he might destroy the one who has the power of death, that is, the devil, and deliver all those who through fear of death were subject to lifelong slavery." Sinclair Ferguson shows how this brings hope to the beleaguered believer:

> Our deepest fear, the fear of death, is a mother phobia which gives birth to all the phobias of life. . . . The angst of man, and many of the spiritual neuroses of our day, must therefore be analyzed in these terms as aspects and symptoms of bondage to Satan, or as aspects of his malevolent efforts to hinder Christian believers and to rob them of their joy in Christ. . . . Christ is not offered to us in the gospel as a panacea for our fears. But he is a deliverer from that bondage to Satan which engenders the fear of death and gives rise to all manner of other fears.[5]

THE RISEN KING OF THE UNIVERSE

This explains why the symbol of the Christian faith for the last two thousand years has been a cross, but it should not be a crucifix. There is a vital difference. A crucifix still has a body affixed to it. A cross is empty. Why? Because the tomb is empty as well. The death of Christ means nothing if his pale, bloody corpse remains on the cross or in the grave to

---

5. Sinclair B. Ferguson, "Christus Victor et Propitiator: The Death of Christ, Substitute and Conqueror," in *For the Fame of God's Name: Essays in Honor of John Piper*, ed. Sam Storms and Justin Taylor (Wheaton, IL: Crossway, 2010), 187.

undergo decay. John MacArthur observes that without the resurrection, the death of Jesus "becomes the heroic death of a noble martyr, the pathetic death of a madman, or the execution of a fraud."[6] If the believer is ever to be assured that Christ's defeat of sin, death, and the devil is real, then the *empty cross* must be followed by an *empty tomb*. Hence, three days, and out of that cold, dark cave of death there must emerge warm rays of new life. "Only the resurrection transforms the cross from a symbol of despair to a symbol of hope."[7]

This is a matter of great historical significance. Christianity is not confined to the realm of religious ideas as the vast array of other religions are. It is preeminently connected to actual events in time, space, and history. As B. B. Warfield said, "[Its historical] facts are its doctrines."[8] Furthermore, the Bible, unlike most of the world's other religious books, is self-consciously written as history. It records the key events around which it stakes its truth claims, with attention given to verifiable details of key personalities, culture, geography, climate, politics, and local demographics. Even its incidental reports of eyewitness testimony go far beyond what characterized other ancient historical writing. This is especially true in the four Gospels and the Acts of the Apostles, since their authors were concerned about the critical life and work of Jesus Christ and the testimony of how he transformed lives in the early church.[9]

This explains why Paul, the former skeptic and persecutor of Christians, became adamant about the central fact of the resurrection. He writes in 1 Corinthians 15 that "if Christ has not been raised, then our preaching

6. John MacArthur, *Acts 1–12*, MacArthur New Testament Commentary (Chicago: Moody, 1994), 64.

7. MacArthur, 64.

8. Benjamin B. Warfield, *Critical Reviews*, vol. 10 of *The Works of Benjamin B. Warfield* (Grand Rapids: Baker, 2000), 479.

9. See, for example, Peter J. Williams, *Can We Trust the Gospels?* (Wheaton, IL: Crossway, 2018); Larry W. Hurtado, *Destroyer of the Gods: Early Christian Distinctiveness in the Roman World* (Waco, TX: Baylor University Press, 2017); Michael J. Kruger, *Christianity at the Crossroads: How the Second Century Shaped the Future of the Church* (Downers Grove, IL: IVP Academic, 2018).

is in vain and your faith is in vain" (1 Cor. 15:14). In the first century, Christianity was—and remains to this day—shockingly unprecedented in the history of religions whereby the pivotal moment that brings resolution to the human predicament is that a man (and no ordinary man at that) would die and then rise again bodily from the grave, *never* to die again. Death is the enemy of every human being, and Christ came to utterly destroy that enemy (vv. 24–25, 54–57).

The literal truth of the bodily resurrection of Christ has an indissoluble connection to its spiritual implications. Paul tells the Corinthian believers that if they have placed their faith in a Christ whose body is still buried in the bowels of the earth, then such faith "is futile and you are still in your sins." Furthermore, he says that "those also who have fallen asleep in Christ have perished. If in Christ we have hope in this life only, we are of all people most to be pitied" (1 Cor. 15:17–19). The whole Christian faith stakes its existence on the fact of the resurrection. No resurrection, no redemption. No redemption means no hope, no future, no end to natural and moral evil, no eternal life, no restored paradise.

Thus, the resurrection of Christ is necessary to the broader work of redemption. Without it, the company of saints, formerly alien malefactors, whom the Father gave to the Son could not be adopted as children of God.[10] Furthermore, just as Christ was delivered over by the hand of the Father to be crucified for our transgressions, our justification is not complete unless he was raised from the dead and serves as our perpetual Intercessor (Rom. 4:25; 8:33–34).

The resurrection is also the ground of our new life in Christ that both sanctifies us (Rom. 6:1–14) and becomes the guarantee of our future glorification. Long ago, one asked, "Can anything good come out of Nazareth?" (John 1:46). Well, because the man from Nazareth rose again, all who put their hope in him are assured that they will one day experience the same exit from the grave, receiving immortal bodies fit to reign with him in his eternal kingdom.[11]

---

10. See John 6:37–40; 17:2; Rom. 1:3–6; 8:23.
11. See 1 Cor. 15:42–43, 50–57; Phil. 3:20–21; 2 Tim. 2:11–12; 1 John 3:2.

It is hard to assess just how remarkable and incomprehensible the symbiotic relationship between the cross and the empty tomb truly is. The convergence of these two polar events highlights the strange dichotomies of God's redemptive work, giving evidence of its unhindered splendor. Together they ignite an otherworldly force analogous to the energy that is released from a tiny atom split in two during nuclear fission —the kind that produced the bombs that ended World War II. But even this is an insufficient illustration. No analogy can compare to these one-of-a-kind moments in space and time resulting in an explosion of divine glory and grace.

Consider the wide contrast.

The cross transported the Son of God into the blackest, most brooding moment in history whereby the cosmos seemed to totter on the slimmest edge of survival. Therein the infinite Son entered abject human humiliation and the horror of God-forsakenness. He displayed the enigmatic strength of brokenness as his person quivered violently with mental anguish and damnation unknown to any mortal being. What can we say about this inscrutable moment? Indeed, "the foolishness of God is wiser than men, and the weakness of God is stronger than men" (1 Cor. 1:25).

> Well might the sun in darkness hide,
> And shut his glories in,
> When Christ, the mighty Maker, died
> For man the creature's sin.[12]

But that moment is contrasted by a different kind of power displayed three days later—one boasting an extraordinary and supernatural caliber. While the cross was shrouded in pitch darkness, the empty tomb discharged a light of infinite brightness. As life surged once again through the body of the Son while being lifted off the cold shelf of his sepulcher, all the chains of death disintegrated and disappeared into thin air. Along with it, all guilt, all shame, all judgment, all alienation and internal warfare, all

---

12. Isaac Watts, "Alas! and Did My Savior Bleed" (1707).

the forces of darkness—of death and hell and evil itself—were rendered lifeless on behalf of the redeemed.

> Crown him the Lord of life,
> Triumphant o'er the grave,
> Who rose victorious from the strife
> For those he came to save.
> His glories now we sing,
> Who died and reigns on high:
> He died, eternal life to bring,
> And lives that death may die.[13]

In these two polarizing and momentous events full of mystery and wonder, God has chosen to enter the darkness of the fall and burst forth from it with the brightest rays of his glory. It justifies his predetermined decree of all the malevolence that has descended on this poor planet, starting with Eve's succumbing to the serpent's wicked invitation. Thus, the greater-glory theodicy finds vindication and fortifies the believer to stand firm, unashamed of the risen Lamb of God and his gospel. When challenges concerning evil come hurtling in from every direction by skeptics and scoffers, we will not be moved.

When sin enslaves us, we have a Redeemer. When evil overcomes us, we have one who overcame. When temptation and pain and suffering threaten to undo us, we know one who entered its deepest portals and came forth victorious—for us! This is God's eternal promise, fulfilled through the death and resurrection of his Son, that "we who have fled for refuge" to the inner sanctum of God's mercy "might have strong encouragement to hold fast to the hope set before us. We have this as a sure and steadfast anchor of the soul, a hope that enters into the inner place behind the curtain, where Jesus has gone as a forerunner on our behalf" (Heb. 6:18–20). Jesus, our Great High Priest, has succeeded for us where all others have failed.

---

13. Matthew Bridges, "Crown Him with Many Crowns" (1851; alt. Godfrey Thring, 1871).

THE COMING KING OF THE UNIVERSE

Christ is the all-encompassing Redeemer, the Lion-Lamb who rescues sinners, defeats his enemies, and revivifies the whole created order. God brings glory to himself in salvation, judgment, and cosmic-wide restoration. In other words, "all things" are the subject of Christ's redemptive work. God has a divine "plan for the fullness of time, to unite *all things* in [Christ], things in heaven and things on earth" (Eph. 1:10).

The first coming of Christ represents the first stage of this plan. The final stage occurs in what Peter referred to as the "period of restoration of *all things*" (Acts 3:21 NASB). It comes at the end of the ages when "the former things have passed away" and the coming King of the universe begins "making *all things* new" (Rev. 21:4–5; cf. Matt. 19:28).[14] This is the consummation of the great J-shaped storyline of creation, fall, and redemption.

Salvation through Judgment

The salvation of God's people is not complete without judgment.[15] First, it involved judgment resting on Christ in their stead. But second, it involves judgment falling on all other enemies of the Redeemer and his redeemed. This has been the pattern from the beginning. Noah was saved through a cataclysmic flood that wiped out "the wickedness of man," which was so "great in the earth" that it warranted such extreme measures (Gen. 6:5). Lot was saved under similar circumstances when God rained fire and brimstone on Sodom and Gomorrah (19:24). The paradigmatic story of salvation through judgment came when God rescued Israel from her wicked Egyptian captors during the exodus.

The church will experience a similar rescue through judgment. Although God has "delivered" believing sinners "from the domain of

14. Note how Paul, in the great Christ-hymn of Colossians 1:13–20, makes use of the "all things" phrase again to show God's comprehensive blueprint for history, focused on the all-encompassing work of Christ.

15. See James M. Hamilton Jr., *God's Glory in Salvation through Judgment: A Biblical Theology* (Wheaton, IL: Crossway, 2010).

darkness and transferred us to the kingdom of his beloved Son" (Col. 1:13), this doesn't mean the end of hostilities in the present age. We still wage war against the world, the flesh, and the devil (Eph. 2:1–3). Furthermore, Jesus said, "If the world hates you, know that it has hated me before it hated you" (John 15:18). Second Timothy 3:12 indicates that faithful followers of Christ can expect persecution, especially as the end of the age draws near (2 Tim. 3:1–5).

The Thessalonian believers had a taste of such persecution, but Paul seeks to give them hope. Their perseverance is not in vain (2 Thess. 1:4). Rather, it is

> evidence of the righteous judgment of God, that you may be considered worthy of the kingdom of God, for which you are also suffering—since indeed God considers it just to repay with affliction those who afflict you, and to grant relief to you who are afflicted as well as to us, when the Lord Jesus is revealed from heaven with his mighty angels in flaming fire, inflicting vengeance on those who do not know God and on those who do not obey the gospel of our Lord Jesus. They will suffer the punishment of eternal destruction, away from the presence of the Lord and from the glory of his might, when he comes on that day to be glorified in his saints, and to be marveled at among all who have believed, because our testimony to you was believed. (2 Thess. 1:5–10)

Here we have a picture of God's bringing glory to himself through both salvation and judgment. The believer in the present age is not immune from the forces of evil. We experience the tragic deaths of loved ones. We lose our jobs during recessions. Our homes can be decimated by tornadoes when our neighbors' homes survive unscathed. We get angry when our children are bullied in school. We cry out for justice when we are wrongly accused of being the source of some scandal. Sometimes we stand alone, even among other Christians, for the sake of truth and goodness when everyone else says that truth is a lie and that what is good is evil (Isa. 5:20). There have been many days, and more to come, when proclaiming Christ will cost us our jobs, our families, our freedom, and even our lives. But God will not leave us to wallow in the miseries of this wayward world. He will soon vindicate his righteous ones.

Paul's message to the Thessalonians points all believers to "Jesus who delivers us from the wrath to come" (1 Thess. 1:10)—the penultimate wrath that comes upon the whole world leading up to Christ's return. "For God has not destined us for wrath, but to obtain salvation through our Lord Jesus Christ" (5:9). The world will bear God's judgment while we ride to glory on the wings of salvation. The description of future judgment in the book of Revelation is not for the faint of heart. As it unfolds, the Lamb who was slain (Rev. 5:6, 9, 12) is no longer the one who first came "gentle and lowly in heart" (Matt. 11:29). The Lion-Lamb will take the scroll that he alone is worthy to open (Rev. 5:4–5), and when he breaks its seals, unleashing its oracles of doom, there will be no place to hide.

After he breaks open the sixth seal, we read:

> Then the kings of the earth and the great ones and the generals and the rich and the powerful, and everyone, slave and free, hid themselves in the caves and among the rocks of the mountains, calling to the mountains and rocks, "Fall on us and hide us from the face of him who is seated on the throne, and from the wrath of the Lamb, for the great day of their wrath has come, and who can stand?" (Rev. 6:15–17)

The Lamb serves as Warrior-King, breaking his enemies "with a rod of iron" and dashing them "in pieces like a potter's vessel" (Ps. 2:9).

And this is just the beginning of tribulation for a world that has completely abandoned all semblance of goodness. Just as in Noah's day, "every intention of the thoughts" of human hearts will be "only evil continually" (Gen. 6:5). The pain and suffering inflicted on them induces not repentance but blasphemy (Rev. 16:8–11, 21).

Then at the climax of the divine maelstrom, the King returns in full battle regalia. The apostle John unveils a fierce and valiant image of Christ at his second coming to earth:

Then I saw heaven opened, and behold, a white horse! The one sitting on it is called Faithful and True, and in righteousness he judges and makes war. His eyes are like a flame of fire, and on his head are many diadems, and he has a name written that no one knows but himself. He is clothed in a robe dipped in blood, and the name by which he is called is The Word of God. (Rev. 19:11–13)

Again, this is a far cry from the tender and compassionate Jesus who eats with sinners and tax collectors (Mark 2:16), who shows love for prostitutes (Luke 7:36–50), and who gladly receives "the lame, the blind, the crippled, the mute," and all manner of the downtrodden and the outcast dregs of society (Matt. 15:30).

Instead, when the Lord descends from the sky to the Mount of Olives (Zech. 14:4), "from his mouth comes a sharp sword with which to strike down the nations, and he will rule them with a rod of iron" (Rev. 19:15). The reason he comes "clothed in a robe dipped in blood" (v. 13) is that "he will tread the winepress of the fury of the wrath of God the Almighty" (v. 15).

At his first coming, Jesus shed his own blood to save sinners. At his second coming, he will shed the blood of the impenitent rebels who have refused his proffers of mercy, and he will be drenched in it. At that time, "the dragon, that ancient serpent, who is the devil and Satan," will be "seized" (Rev. 20:2) and cast into the abyss for a thousand years as Christ establishes his just and righteous kingdom: his benevolent reign on earth.

The one and only true utopia is consummated.

The Millennial Reign of the King

In the millennial reign of Christ (Rev. 20:4), the restoration of the cosmos begins, marking a decisive reversal of the curse. God's covenant promises to Israel and the nations made through Abraham (Gen. 12:1–3; 15:1–21) find their fulfillment. According to Romans 9–11, it was God's predetermined plan that the Jews would reject their Messiah at his first coming (Rom. 11:7–10) in order that he might open their covenant promises (9:4–5) to the Gentiles (11:11–18). This is also made clear in one of the most important messianic passages of the Old Testament given to the prophet Daniel.

The title "the Son of Man" comes from Daniel 7:13–14, from which Jesus drew his favorite self-designation in the Gospels.[16] Daniel relates:

I saw in the night visions,

and behold, with the clouds of heaven
there came one like a son of man,
and he came to the Ancient of Days
and was presented before him.
And to him was given dominion
and glory and a kingdom,
that all peoples, nations, and languages
should serve him;
his dominion is an everlasting dominion,
which shall not pass away,
and his kingdom one
that shall not be destroyed.

Jesus drew on this prophecy when he predicted his second coming in Matthew 24:30 and Mark 14:62.[17] We must note that this doesn't mean that God has rejected his old covenant people Israel in favor of the Gentiles, as Romans 11:1 indicates. Rather, it means that "a partial hardening has come upon Israel, until the fullness of the Gentiles has come in" to the present nascent form of the kingdom (Rom. 11:25). God's mercies never fail. At the present time, "as regards the gospel, they are enemies" of the church. "But as regards election, they are beloved for the sake of their forefathers. For the gifts and the calling of God are irrevocable" (vv. 28–29).

The gospel must be proclaimed to the whole world until the end of the present age (cf. Matt. 28:18–20). The Gentiles become beneficiaries

16. Jesus refers to himself as "the Son of Man" eighty-one times in the Gospels, whereas he refers to himself as the "Son of God" only a handful of times.
17. Jesus' claim to the divine title "the Son of Man" is what prompted the Sanhedrin to declare blasphemy and order his execution. See Mark 14:61–63.

of the new covenant as the Lamb who was slain is purchasing "people for God from *every* tribe and language and people and nation" (Rev. 5:9), an allusion to Daniel 7:13–14.

Once all the elect of God are secured, both Jews and Gentiles (Rom. 9:23–26), then the "Deliverer" will return. On that day, "all Israel will be saved," and "he will banish ungodliness from Jacob" (11:26). It is the day when the kingdom of God is fully established, with its King moving his reign from his heavenly throne at the right hand of the Father to his earthly throne to make all his enemies a footstool for his feet, as Psalm 110:1 predicts.[18] And he will make *all* the redeemed "a kingdom and priests to our God, and they shall reign on the earth" with him (Rev. 5:10).

With the governments of the world wrested from wicked rulers and now resting on his shoulders (Isa. 9:6), the bodily presence of his beauty and glory and goodness and righteousness will transform everything. Every earthly government since the curse of Eden has fallen woefully short of the magnificence of this future kingdom.

The denouement of the grand conflict of the ages finally unfolds at the end of the millennium, as the prophetic disclosures of Revelation 20 make clear. After one last desperate attempt to cripple the peace and prosperity of the messianic kingdom (Rev. 20:7–9), Satan and all his henchmen will be cast into the lake that burns with fire and brimstone forever and ever (v. 10). Up to this point, since he first appeared in the garden, Satan has been nothing more than a foil in God's hands whereby the tension between good and evil is heightened in order that God might display his mighty power in evil's defeat and bring himself glory in judgment.

At this poignant end for Satan, his demonic hosts, and the human disciples of his evil, every last vestige of malice, of bitterness and hatred, of lies and the craftiness of deceit will meet its end. All wars, tumults, and torrents of blood will cease. Famines and tornadoes and tsunamis and earthquakes will never lay waste to our habitations again. Pain and suffering and the crucible of angst that has scorched all the corners of the

18. This verse is quoted or alluded to twenty-two times in the New Testament, more than any other Old Testament passage.

earth for untold eons will be washed away. For those reveling in the glories of the eternal kingdom, death—the last enemy—will soon dissipate into the mists of the past (1 Cor. 15:25).

Then the great white throne of the living God from whose "presence earth and sky fled away" (Rev. 20:11) will establish final judgment for the unregenerate masses of history. The "dead, great and small" (v. 12), will stand before their Judge and Maker and give account of their deeds (v. 13). The final verdict is grim: "Then Death and Hades were thrown into the lake of fire. This is the second death, the lake of fire. And if anyone's name was not found written in the book of life, he was thrown into the lake of fire" (vv. 14–15).

The first death is separation of the immaterial soul from the physical body. The second death is separation of body and soul from the blessed presence of God forever (2 Thess. 1:9). Jesus' words will ring hard in the ears of the impenitent: "Do not fear those who kill the body but cannot kill the soul. Rather fear him who can destroy both soul and body in hell" (Matt. 10:28). The world must heed this warning before it is too late.

The Restoration of the Cosmos

According to Romans 8, there is a parallel between the redemption of God's elect image-bearing creatures and the redemption of his creation. The curse of Eden shattered the unsullied goodness and beauty of both. Fallen creatures carry the curse of *moral evil*. The entire created order, however, bears the curse of *natural evil*: cosmic decay and corruption, material wear and tear, illness and disease, natural disasters and misfortune of every kind. In order for redemption to be complete, restored sons and daughters of the kingdom need a restored cosmos as their everlasting abode. This is part of Christ's "restoration of all things" (Acts 3:21 NASB), to undo the ugliness, the messiness, and the imperfection that mars the present order of things.

Believers began their process of redemption at the moment of regeneration and conversion. But their final redemption does not occur until their glorification at the return of Christ, when their souls are conformed to the likeness of his sinless character (Rom. 8:29) and their bodies are resurrected in the likeness of his immortal body (1 Cor. 15:20–23, 50–53). The material creation undergoes a similar process of rebirth and glorification that parallels that of the believer. Paul explains:

> For I consider that the sufferings of this present time are not worth comparing with the glory that is to be revealed to us. For the creation waits with eager longing for the revealing of the sons of God. For the creation was subjected to futility, not willingly, but because of him who subjected it, in hope that the creation itself will be set free from its bondage to corruption and obtain the freedom of the glory of the children of God. For we know that the whole creation has been groaning together in the pains of childbirth until now. (Rom. 8:18–22)

When Adam sinned, his disobedience brought a curse on the whole creation. God "subjected" the created order "to futility" (Rom. 8:20). The laws that governed prefall Eden became less hospitable, leading to the "bondage to corruption" (v. 21). The creature and his habitation were made vulnerable. Sweat and toil and death and decay marked the altered cosmos. The *shalom* ("peace") of Eden was shattered.

Consequently, for redemption to be complete, the creation undergoes its own death and rebirth. In 2 Peter 3, the apostle describes how at the culmination of everything that unfolds after Christ returns to consummate his kingdom, "the heavens will dissolve with a horrific noise; the elements will melt with intense heat, and the earth and everything done in it will be laid bare" (2 Peter 3:10).[19] Peter is not describing utter annihilation here, rendering the cosmos nonexistent. Rather, it is a death by fire, just as the world in Noah's day experienced a death by flood. But in this case, the entire universe is brought to dissolution.

Then out of the ashes of the former world, Peter says, according to God's "promise we are waiting for new heavens and a new earth in which righteousness dwells" (2 Peter 3:13). God does not extinguish believers

---

19. My own translation.

at death and start from scratch (i.e., nothing). At our resurrection, we will have the same bodies we had before death, but they will be utterly transformed: perfect, immortal, and free from the curse. Likewise, there is continuity to the creation as well. The new heavens and earth are simply the old heavens and earth reborn.

The creation carries no "hope" (Rom. 8:20) if it faces extinction only to be replaced by an entirely different created order. God will not call forth all things out of nothing as he did in Genesis. Rather, he will reshape, renew, restore, transform the old into the new. According to Romans 8:18–25, the "eager longing" of the creation is the same as that of the believer— resurrection. The perfect ending of the story is to see our resurrected selves fitted to a resurrected creation.

Everything pines for a restoration of the conditions of prefall Eden. But the end of the story is far better than the beginning. Paul asserts, "The sufferings of this present time are not worth comparing with the glory that is to be revealed" (Rom. 8:18). Why? Because without being dragged through the horrific conditions of a fallen world with its moral and natural evil decimating the pristine goodness of Eden, we could never fully appreciate the glory and grace of its redemption.

The price God paid to restore paradise is worth every storehouse of riches it cost him. This is why the storyline of redemption is not *U-shaped* but *J-shaped*. The new heavens and earth will far outstrip the glory of the old precisely because they had to endure the conflict of the present crisis of evil. A Redeemer of incomprehensible worth was required to rescue the world from its curse.

And so we offer all praise to our Savior and triune God:

Come, thou Incarnate Word,
Gird on Thy mighty sword,
Our prayer attend.
Come, and thy people bless,
And give thy Word success;
Spirit of holiness,
On us descend. . . .

To the great One in Three
Eternal praises be,
Hence evermore.
His sovereign majesty
May we in glory see,
And to eternity
Love and adore.[20]

STUDY QUESTIONS

1. Have you ever imagined a utopian world? If so, what would that world look like?
2. What two animals does Scripture compare Christ to? What is the significance of comparing these two images?
3. What are the two ways in which Jesus defeats evil? Why is one unconventional and unexpected while the other is more conventional and expected?
4. What various forces (enemies) does Christ defeat in his work of redemption?
5. Why shouldn't the symbol of the Christian faith be a crucifix?
6. Why are both the cross and resurrection of Christ essential to his work of redemption?
7. What are some examples in Scripture in which God saves his people through acts of judgment on others? How do these examples reflect the bigger story of God's salvation through judgment?
8. What makes the description of Christ in Revelation 19:11–21 so startling? Should we be surprised by this description? Why or why not?
9. How does Romans 8:18–25 indicate that God will resolve the curse of evil for both the "children of God" and the natural "creation"?
10. According to the author, will the present heavens and earth be annihilated (snuffed out of existence)? What is the significance of his argument, considering what Romans 8:18–25 says?

20. From the anonymous hymn "Come, Thou Almighty King" (c. 1740).

9

FINDING HOPE IN THE DARKNESS

William Carey (1761–1834) is considered the father of modern missions.[1] He brought the gospel to India in 1793 and served there until his death forty years later. His battle cry for missions was enshrined in his famous "Deathless Sermon," in which he declared, "Expect great things from God, attempt great things for God." He gave his listeners this exhortation: "The thought of a fellow creature perishing for ever should rouse all our activity and engage all our powers … [and] indefatigable industry, till we can't find a soul that's destitute of Christ in all the world."[2] Carey's passion for souls was marked by great success.

Yet God's providence was not always of the smiling sort for Carey. He faced a constant stream of trials and tribulations. Early on, his missionary partner John Thomas proved to be undependable and lacking good judgment. Thomas underestimated their expenses, mismanaged their funds, and often departed from their gospel focus. In the first few years in India, Carey and his family were often starving and desperate to find

---

1. Timothy George, *Faithful Witness: The Life and Mission of William Carey* (Worcester, PA: Christian History Institute, 1998).

2. Quoted in George, 28.

adequate housing. Disease and illness were constant threats. Carey met with repeated failure in his attempts to communicate the gospel to a people enslaved by dark and superstitious religions. It took seven years before he saw the first conversion to Christ.

Over the years, he dealt with suspicions about his motives and unfair judgments about his work from supporters in England. He battled factions among his colaborers, envious missionaries seeking to undermine his work, and other missionaries who promoted heresy. Many who joined his efforts died prematurely. The source of his greatest trial, however, came from his illiterate and troubled wife, Dorothy. She never consented to William's missionary zeal. She resented leaving all that was dear to her in England to move to a strange and inhospitable country.

Then their five-year-old boy, Peter, died of malaria within the first year of their arrival in India. This was the last straw for Dorothy. She never recovered from his death, descending into ever darker regions of mental instability. She fostered unwaning bitterness toward William. Over the course of the next thirteen years, until she died of a fever, she suffered from uncontrollable fits of rage, several times trying to kill William. Many tried to convince him to admit her to an insane asylum, but he refused. He cared for her in all her dark hours. He wrote in his journal, "This is indeed the valley of the shadow of death to me, except that my soul is much more insensible than John Bunyan's Pilgrim."[3]

But he did not lose heart. On many occasions he confided in his sisters. He wrote, "God does not willingly afflict nor grieve the children of men [alluding to Lam. 3:33], and that some important purpose is always to be answered thereby." Another time he wrote, "Look not only on the dark side, but take a peep on the other side; see what God has wrought, what He has promised to do; reflect on his power, and on this: that He knows all you have to conflict with—the omniscience of God is a sweet theme to a genuine praying Christian."[4] Carey found solace in the truth of Romans 8:28, "And we know that for those who love God all things," even the dark

---

3. Quoted in George, 109.
4. Quoted in George, 159.

and troublesome things, "work together for good, for those who are called according to his purpose."

Indeed, God was faithful. By 1800, seven years after Carey arrived in India, he had established a missionary community north of Calcutta in Serampore. In time, it housed as many as sixty missionary workers. One of Carey's primary tasks involved translating the Bible into forty languages and dialects in the region, making him one of the greatest Bible translators in history alongside Jerome, John Wycliffe, Desiderius Erasmus, Martin Luther, and William Tyndale.[5] The missionaries set up an extensive printing operation for this work. In 1812, a fire spread through their facilities, destroying many years of labor, but they quickly recovered.

In thirty-one years, they printed 212,000 Bibles, tracts, and various books. By 1821, they had baptized fourteen hundred converts. In 1793, there was one missionary sending agency in the world—the one formed to send Carey. By 1834, when Carey died, there were fourteen agencies in England and several others from America and Europe, all inspired by Carey and the Serampore missionaries.

Carey firmly believed in the faithfulness of God. He was convinced that all the natural and moral evil that befell him contributed to God's grander designs in magnifying his glory through the proclamation of the gospel in India. The calamities Carey faced compelled him to be singularly God-centered and God-dependent. If his mission had met no resistance and faced no trouble, it likely would have engendered a prideful man, tempted to seek honor for himself. Instead, Carey was known to be self-effacing despite his achievements. In 1823, he wrote to John Ryland, his colleague in England: "Should you outlive me, and have any influence to prevent it, I earnestly request that no epithets of praise may ever accompany my name, such as 'the faithful servant of God', etc. All such expressions would convey a falsehood. To me belong shame and confusion of face, I can only say, 'Hangs my helpless soul on Thee.'"[6]

5. George, 141.
6. Quoted in S. Pearce Carey, *William Carey* (London: Wakeman Trust, 1993), 247.

The testimony of Carey and myriads of other faithful believers over the course of church history demonstrates that God indeed has a greater purpose for the trials and tribulations that afflict his saints. They are designed to bring him greater glory, while at the same time those difficulties produce in us a greater good.

This leads us to one of the most important questions when assessing any theodicy. To be more specific, what practical value does the greater-glory theodicy have for us as we live in the here and now? What difference does it make? Do its claims compel us to say that living in this shattered world is worth bearing all its razor-sharp fragments of pain? I believe it does. The greater-glory theodicy gives us the kind of confidence Augustine had when he declared: "The Omnipotent God . . . would not allow any evil in his works, unless in his omnipotence and goodness, as the Supreme Good, he is able to bring forth good out of evil. . . . For God judged it better to bring good out of evil than not to permit any evil to exist."[7]

In this chapter, I will set out four practical ways in which the greater-glory theodicy gives the believer hope and reorients how we view the Christian life. I hope the unbeliever who is coming to grips with the crisis of evil can also find hope in what God means for it all. As it turns out, this theodicy does nothing more than sharpen our focus on the central thesis of Scripture—the redeeming gospel of Jesus Christ our Lord. It seeks to bring greater clarity to the truth of redemption by placing us squarely in the center of God's saving work.

The story of creation, fall, and redemption is not only God's story—it is our story. We must embrace this narrative for ourselves and be fully immersed in the thick of it. As we do, we will see how the supreme glory of God is manifested by bringing supreme benefit to our souls—souls in desperate need of the unimaginable good that his grace injects into the evil that envelops us.

---

7. Augustine, *Enchiridion [Handbook] on Faith, Hope and Love,* 3.11, 8.27, http://www.ccel.org/ccel/augustine/enchiridion.

THE REDEEMER TAKES AWAY OUR EVIL

The first and most important consequence of God's redemptive plan for history is how he addresses evil in the hearts of the redeemed. Too often, those who seek an answer to the problem of evil focus their attention on the evil *out there*—the terrible stuff happening *to us* outside the barrier of our own skin. Evil is not merely a problem in the external world, however; it is first and foremost an internal problem. Yes, evil is perpetrated against us as we become its victims. But we are also perpetrators of evil. We are victimizers. Every human being makes his or her own special contribution to the morass of moral degradation that makes the world such an ugly place.

The self-deception of the human soul is endemic to our fallen state (Jer. 17:9). We tend to think more highly of ourselves than we ought. And our self-deception goes hand in hand with self-righteousness. Isaiah pours a lethal dose of sober and startling truth on our moral delusions when he says that even the nicest deeds we perform are like a bloody "menstrual rag" (Isa. 64:6 NET). Not a pleasant image. Yet there is something that makes the problem of internal evil more acute. Personal sin is not something that merely affects others. Our moral evil is, as the late R. C. Sproul often said, *cosmic treason.*

When David abused his power as king and took Bathsheba into his bedchamber and then had her husband, Uriah, unceremoniously murdered, a wide swath of evil descended on many lives (2 Sam. 11). It became a public scandal and sullied David's benevolent kingdom. Yet when he was brought low and moved to contrition and repentance, his mind was primarily focused not on reconciling himself to those he had hurt in the horizontal realm, but on the damage he had created in the vertical realm—his relationship with God.

In Psalm 51, David's humble prayer of confession, he cried out to his Lord, "Against you, you only, have I sinned and done what is evil in your sight" (Ps. 51:4). He recognized that moral evil is ultimately about one thing. It is a personal problem between human beings and the rightful Creator, Possessor, and Judge of their souls.

The problem of evil is a crisis of cosmic proportions, but before any other aspect of the crisis can be solved, God pours his primary energy into the rescue of sinners from their rebellion. This is why clinging to Jesus Christ and his saving grace is where our first line of hope lies. The Suffering Servant of Isaiah 53 "was pierced for" the "transgressions" of the redeemed. "He was crushed for our iniquities; upon him was the chastisement that brought us peace, and with his wounds we are healed. All we like sheep have gone astray; we have turned—every one—to his own way; and the Lord has laid on him the iniquity of us all" (Isa. 53:5–6).

Not a single human soul can see the untold glory that God gains for himself in an evil world until that person has experienced the surprising grace by which God repairs his or her shattered soul through the crucified and risen Christ. Few have understood this more comprehensively than the apostle Paul, who spent a great deal of his preconversion life opposing the work of redemption, arresting Christians, and rejoicing in their unjust execution (Acts 8:1–3). He never tired of telling his testimony:

I thank him who has given me strength, Christ Jesus our Lord, because he judged me faithful, appointing me to his service, though formerly I was a blasphemer, persecutor, and insolent opponent. But I received mercy because I had acted ignorantly in unbelief, and the grace of our Lord overflowed for me with the faith and love that are in Christ Jesus. The saying is trustworthy and deserving of full acceptance, that Christ Jesus came into the world to save sinners, of whom I am the foremost. (1 Tim. 1:12–15)

The endgame of God's salvation of sinners is the maximization of his own glory. Thus, in contemplating his own rescue from evil, Paul humbly declares a few verses later: "To the King of the ages, immortal, invisible, the only God, be honor and glory forever and ever. Amen" (1 Tim. 1:17). Peter the coward, the one who denied his Lord three times while Jesus was in his darkest hour, knew all too well the restorative glory of his Savior's grace. This is why he summons the redeemed to "proclaim the excellencies of him who called you out of darkness into his marvelous light" (1 Peter 2:9).

Paul speaks at the end of Romans 5 of how Adam's disobedience brought ruin to us all, but the obedience of the greater Adam undoes the damage of the lesser Adam's sin (Rom. 5:19). Then Paul makes this curious statement in verse 20: "Now the law came in to increase the trespass." The apostle is saying that the perfection of the moral law of God (represented in the law of Moses) came into a corrupt world like a thousand suns, exposing every dark corner of sin.

The self-deception of cursed creatures prevents them from seeing how many of their sins, like filthy cockroaches, scurry across the floor until the light of moral truth is turned on. But the law does nothing to eradicate sin. Rather, it compels the children of darkness to flee. Their rejection of its unbending standard leads them down a wide path of greater shameful rebellion until their lives are overrun, as it were, with cockroaches.

But then Paul puts forth a marvelous truth at the end of Romans 5:20: "Where sin increased, grace abounded all the more." What does the apostle mean by this? The more that sin and death reigned on the earth, the more that "grace" had an opportunity to "reign through righteousness leading to eternal life through Jesus Christ our Lord" (Rom. 5:21). This is astonishing. Paul is saying that the more that murder, lies, theft, rape, cruelty, carnage, death, and calamity proliferate, the more that God's undeserved mercy is extended to the perpetrators of these evils. Consequently, his glory and grace are unleashed in ways in which they could not be otherwise.

There is something personal to see here. Many people wrestle with the thought of their sins being beyond the grace of God. Surely there is no pardon for the vilest of sinners. Perhaps you've had an abortion and it won't stop haunting you. Maybe you've regularly abused your wife and children in a drunken stupor. Perhaps you've embezzled money from your employer and his business collapsed. Or you've descended so far into the depths of sexual perversion that it would be unfitting to speak of it.

None of this is too much for the metamorphic grace of the infinite God. There is no sin so deep—so dark, so disgusting—that the grace of our Lord cannot descend deeper still. And the wonder is, the deeper his grace must descend to rescue us from the pit, the higher his glory ascends to the heavens, eliciting the praise of angelic hosts (Luke 15:7).

This effusive grace is not a license to indulge in more sin, as Paul says next in Romans 6:1. That would trivialize the high price that God was willing to pay to make his grace a reality. It would turn the gospel into a sham. His grace does not pave the way for more sin, but puts sin to death (Rom. 6:2) so that we might be made "alive to God in Christ Jesus" (v. 11) and every fiber of our being might be transformed into "instruments for righteousness" (v. 13). Furthermore, we have no way of knowing how God in his infinite wisdom will use evil to further greater goods. Earlier, Paul condemns the notion that we should pursue some evil course of action, thinking that good will come from it (3:8).

Others charge that the greater-glory theodicy is nothing more than the ends justifying the means. The thesis whereby God's design to magnify the glory of his grace by ordaining evil is said to be like a father who throws his son into the river to drown, only to jump in afterward and heroically save him. Or like a chemist who secretly devises a deadly virus and sends it out into the populace but then turns around and devises a vaccine that kills the virus so that he can be publicly praised as a medical savior.[8] If the greater-glory theodicy could be reduced to this kind of scenario, then we might have good reason to reject it.

But this misses a vital point. There is greater good for a redeemed sinner than there would be for the hypothetical good person who never fell prey to Adam's curse in the first place and therefore has no need of redemption (cf. Luke 5:31–32). The flood of love, grace, mercy, kindness, and compassion that God pours out on prodigals is made all the more glorious when those poor wretches consider how it compares to having wallowed in the mud, filth, and stench of rebellion's pigsty (15:11–32). The weight of their redemption is far greater than the weight of their corruption that begged for redemption.

The unfallen good person can have no concept of and no appreciation for the wonder of divine grace. Did Adam and Eve experience the glory of

---

8. Alvin Plantinga, "Supralapsarianism, or 'O Felix Culpa,'" in *The Problem of Evil: Selected Readings*, ed. Michael L. Peterson, 2nd ed. (Notre Dame, IN: University of Notre Dame Press, 2017), 382.

God before they fell? No doubt they did. But could they see God's glory as brightly in their unfallen condition when divine grace was unnecessary and unexpressed? I don't think so. It is better to have been lost and scared and suffering in the valley of the shadow of death and afterward stagger into the golden gates of the Celestial City than to have never been lost at all. When the journey is attended by "many dangers, toils, and snares,"[9] it makes the final destination more glorious.

THE REDEEMER TAKES ON OUR SORROWS

The Suffering Servant of Isaiah's prophecy in Isaiah 53 not only bears our sins (Isa. 53:5–6, 11), but bears our sorrows. Jesus was "a man of sorrows and acquainted with grief" (v. 3 NASB). But these sorrows and griefs were not his own. The Son of God has subsisted in a state of perfect blessedness within the Godhead from all eternity, but when he took on flesh and blood, he assumed the sorrows and griefs of those he came to save. Verse 4 declares, "Surely he has borne our griefs and carried our sorrows."

The pain and sorrow that Jesus carried on our behalf results from the personal misery that our own sin produces in addition to all the misery that the sin of the world foists upon us. He experienced the full consequences of the curse on our behalf. Alec Motyer comments on Isaiah's use of "griefs" and "sorrows." They circumscribe "all that mars our lives. We wish for more than we are able to achieve, so that the good life is always eluding us; we long for a truly happy life but are constantly baulked by sorrow in whatever form it may come—disappointment, bereavement, tragedy, whatever. But he makes our burdens his."[10]

As Jesus vicariously embraces our pain and sorrow, he asks us to embrace him and all that is demanded of us as followers of Christ. And yet, ironically, this is not a heavy burden. Our union with Christ—his

---

9. John Newton, "Amazing Grace!" (1779).

10. J. Alec Motyer, *The Prophecy of Isaiah: An Introduction & Commentary* (Downers Grove, IL: IVP Academic, 1993), 430.

taking on all that is wrong with us, and our taking on all that is good and wonderful in him—brings us *shalom* ("peace"). He urges: "Come to me, all who labor and are heavy laden, and I will give you rest. Take my yoke upon you, and learn from me, for I am gentle and lowly in heart, and you will find rest for your souls. For my yoke is easy, and my burden is light" (Matt. 11:28–30). To see the gentleness of Christ, his humble heart, his forgiving compassion, his unbounded loveliness, his divine beauty—this is what most overwhelms sinners and draws them irresistibly to him.

How does Jesus' assumption of pain and sorrow correspond to divine impassibility? Remember, this is the doctrine indicating that God can neither suffer nor be adversely affected by the evil that transpires in the world. Some suggest that we need a God who is a fellow sufferer. The German theologian Jürgen Moltmann has claimed that "were God incapable of suffering in any respect, and therefore in an absolute sense, then he would also be incapable of love."[11] But this misses two vitally important truths about God.

First, we must not deny that the triune God in his divine essence cannot suffer. The divine nature cannot be touched by evil. Nothing can hurt him or tear at his eternal blessedness and joy. He can suffer no loss or injury to his perfections as God. But this does not mean that he is devoid of a deep and abiding love for us or that somehow, because he does not share our suffering in common with us, he is unable to offer us sympathy or compassion. Those who are sick or injured do not need a fellow sick or injured person to help them. They need a physician who has a powerful healing hand.[12]

The suffering poets of the Psalms find their greatest comfort in the God who is an immovable rock, a fortress, a refuge, and a stronghold in times of calamity, when enemies threaten us, and when the world presses hard against our fragile frames.[13] We need a God who transcends the forces that

---

11. Jürgen Moltmann, *The Crucified God: The Cross of Christ as the Foundation and Criticism of Christian Theology*, trans. R. A. Wilson and J. Bowden (New York: Harper & Row, 1974), 230.

12. Joel R. Beeke and Paul M. Smalley, *Reformed Systematic Theology*, vol. 1, *Revelation and God* (Wheaton, IL: Crossway, 2019), 864.

13. See, for example, Pss. 27; 46; 59; 91.

wreak havoc on the world and our personal lives, whose power crushes them and brings peace to our war-torn souls. "If God were of such a nature that he suffered when his creatures suffered, then he would be the most to be pitied. His omniscience and love would taste the bitter poison of every tragedy in history. The majestic God would be dethroned in misery."[14]

Second, we do have a God who has entered our suffering through the incarnation. The impassible God took on a passible human nature that suffers and does so severely. Such anguish was necessary for the defeat of sin, suffering, and death. But the Son of God also became the "man of sorrows" (Isa. 53:3) in order to fully "sympathize with our weaknesses" (Heb. 4:15). Jesus comes to our aid as one who suffered far more than we can imagine. His cry of dereliction and God-forsakenness on the cross (Matt. 27:46) can only hint at the soul-rattling spasms of pain that our dear Savior endured on our behalf. No one knows our pain as he does. And because he conquered pain and death through his own death and triumphant resurrection, he will never abandon us.

Of course, the Christian has no promise that all pain and suffering will be eradicated in this lifetime. As followers of Christ, we will still get sick and be injured. We will still mourn the deaths of loved ones. Calamity will not avoid us just because we belong to the Savior. Enemies will attack us. Satan and his evil minions will dog our every step. Our character will be maligned by vicious opponents. We will bear ill-treatment from friends and family, even fellow Christians. We will be persecuted for our godliness. Our tears will fill a thousand vales. But this leads us to a third important truth.

THE HOPE AND REALITY OF FUTURE GLORY

One of the purposes for prolonged and painful suffering in this life is to increase our longing and to magnify the hope and reality of future glory when our redemption reaches its consummation. One of the persistent commands of the New Testament is for believers to fix their

---

14. Beeke and Smalley, *Revelation and God*, 864–65.

gaze heavenward, looking "for our blessed hope, the appearing of the glory of our great God and Savior Jesus Christ" (Titus 2:13).[15] This is difficult, however, when we are weighed down by all the physical and spiritual impediments of this fallen world.

Paul was no stranger to these realities, as he makes clear in 2 Corinthians 4. He and his missionary companions were "afflicted in every way" (2 Cor. 4:8). They were "persecuted" and "struck down" (v. 9), "always carrying in the body the death of Jesus" (v. 10). He says that we "are always being given over to death for Jesus' sake" (v. 11). Paul endured a ministry of suffering and affliction, not unlike that of William Carey hundreds of years later and that of countless other ordinary believers in history who have sought to be faithful to Christ.

But Paul goes on to say that "we do not lose heart" (2 Cor. 4:16).[16] Why? Because even "though our outer man is decaying, yet our inner man is being renewed day by day." What does he mean? The "outer man" refers to our mortal bodies, our fragile "jars of clay" (v. 7 ESV), our "mortal flesh" (v. 11) that is cursed by the fall. Our bodies are subject to pain and suffering, sweat and toil, disease and decay. The word "decaying" in verse 16 means "wasting away, breaking down, spoiling, moving toward disrepair." A kind of rottenness in our bones becomes more pronounced as we grow older. The moment we are born, the Edenic curse already starts to tighten its grip till we die. Add all the mental anguish that accompanies a *materially* as well as a *morally* corrupted world, and the weight of affliction seems unbearable at times.

But Paul adds the important adversative "yet" (2 Cor. 4:16). When we experience Christ's redemption, simultaneous with the fact that our "outer man" is daily getting worse, "our inner man is being renewed day by day" (v. 16). The "inner man" is "the new self" (Eph. 4:24; Col. 3:10). Every believer is "a new creation" in Christ (2 Cor. 5:17). We have been regenerated, born anew, having acquired a new nature empowered by the

15. See also John 14:1–3; Rom. 8:18–25; 1 Cor. 15:50–57; Phil. 3:17–21; Col. 3:1–4; 1 Thess. 4:13–18; 1 Peter 1:3–9; Rev. 22:20.
16. My discussion of 2 Corinthians 4:16–18 is based on the NASB.

Holy Spirit, who enables us to be "renewed day by day" (4:16) in the pursuit of being "conformed to the image" of Christ (Rom. 8:29). Paul wants to emphasize the contrast. As our outer (physical) man is moving downward, decaying and pitching us toward death, meanwhile, our inner (spiritual) man is moving upward, getting better, stronger, more mature, more sound, more faithful every day.

Thankfully, once our material bodies decay and die, they too will experience a new birth, a grand and instantaneous renewal at the resurrection. This is our final redemption (Rom. 8:23) that catapults us to future glory in which body and soul will be united in perfect immortal harmony, free of sin, free of pain—free of all effects of the curse. This is why we don't lose heart.

But Paul is not finished.

Verse 17 of 2 Corinthians 4 is one of the greatest sources of hope that the Word of God provides the suffering saint. There is a poetic beauty to it, as seen in its superlatives and stark parallelism: "For momentary, light affliction is producing for us an eternal weight of glory far beyond all comparison" (cf. Rom. 8:18). If we strip this verse down to its bare grammatical components, Paul is saying, "Affliction is producing glory." This is remarkable. Affliction in the life of a believer is not an unfortunate coincidence resulting from the unpredictable nature of free will and how things just happen to unfold in the course of time. Rather, God is providentially, purposefully accomplishing something very good, precisely by means of the troublesome afflictions that assault us every day.

But the apostle is saying something more remarkable. "Affliction" participates in a vital cause-effect relationship whereby it is producing the greater good of future "glory" for the believer. Suffering is not an accident. Losing a job, being mistreated by an abusive husband, becoming a paraplegic via a diving accident, experiencing a miscarriage, being imprisoned for preaching Christ, suffering the consequences for your previous life of drug addiction—*nothing* in the life of the believer is wasted. There is no trial, no tribulation, no adverse set of circumstances, no events that might otherwise become the source of your ruin that God does not use to produce something of supreme value—your future glory.

Now consider the contrast Paul draws between the "affliction" that might otherwise cause us despair and the "glory" that, ironically, it produces. First, present "affliction" that seems forever is merely "momentary." It is a sudden blip in the endless universe of time and eternity. By contrast, the future "glory" it produces, which seemingly never comes—*this* is "eternal." It is impossible to measure. Second, present "affliction" is "light," like a feather floating lazily across the sky. But the future "glory" it produces has an incomparably substantial "weight" to it.

Our tendency is to scoff at this point. Really? We simply don't perceive things this way. Paul must force us to look at our lives with a perspective that we rarely, if ever, entertain. Our natural focus is fixated on the ugly here and now, which obscures the beauty of eternity. The result is that we live with a deeply skewed perception of reality.

But there is more irony here.

How can something so vexing as affliction produce something of such supreme goodness and worth? This is like saying that deadly poison produces life-saving medicine. Not only that, but the minuscule nature of this earthly poison produces such an abundance of heavenly soul-saving treasure that we cannot measure its worth. It is like a speck of contaminated dust producing a Mount Everest of solid gold. How can that be? In qualifying the "eternal weight of glory," Paul uses an interesting phrase to describe how glorious this future glory is. It is "far beyond all comparison." The Greek literally means "hyperbole upon hyperbole." This future glory is so excessive that the affliction that produces it cannot possibly be compared to it. It is a super-excessive glory. It is glory upon glory upon glory.

One of the encouraging implications of this passage is that when afflictions in this life are more severe for believers, then by comparison, their experience of future glory will be exponentially greater. Ironically, it makes severe suffering appear even more momentary and light than less severe suffering. Consequently, God's grace and glory are magnified more fully when believers suffer more deeply. And the greater God's glory, the greater our future joy. No doubt, Peter had this in mind when he said, "Rejoice inasmuch as you participate in the sufferings of Christ, so that you may be overjoyed when his glory is revealed" (1 Peter 4:13 NIV).

Paul puts a bow on the package of this treasure in 2 Corinthians 4:18. He wants to be sure that our eyes are properly focused. The things "which are seen" are the visible "temporal" things of this present life of affliction (2 Cor. 4:17) and the daily grind of our "outer man" wasting away (v. 16). The Word of God is charging us to stop being myopic. Don't narrow your vision to the outward things of the here and now—the remnants of the curse. Don't make them more momentous and overwhelming than reality truly dictates. Rather, fix your eyes on "the things which are not seen"—the things that are invisible but "eternal." This is our redemption, our ultimate reality.

> Turn your eyes upon Jesus,
> Look full in his wonderful face;
> And the things of earth will grow strangely dim
> In the light of his glory and grace.[17]

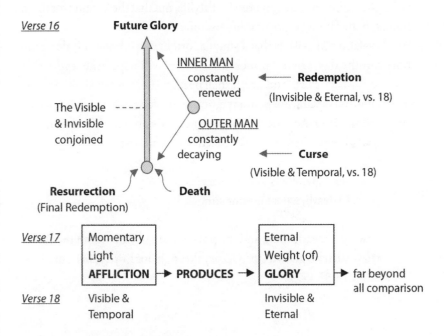

Fig. 9.1. Diagram of 2 Corinthians 4:16–18

17. Helen Howarth Lemmel, "Turn Your Eyes upon Jesus" (1922).

This present darkness will soon be superseded by an effervescent glory that is unspeakable. The Puritan John Flavel (1628–91) noted:

> Naturalists observe, the greatest darkness is a little before the dawning of the morning. It was so with Christ, it may be so with thee. It was but a little while and He had better company than theirs that forsook Him. Act therefore your faith upon this, that the most glorious light usually follows the thickest darkness. The louder your groans are now, the louder your triumphs hereafter will be. The horror of your present, will but add to the lustre of your future state.[18]

We are desperate for relief in the present, and God often grants his children blessed reprieves in the here and now. But Flavel rightly indicates that not all bright tomorrows are reserved for this life, but that the longing for them points to the far more glorious life to come.

Revelation 21 tells us that a singular bright day is hovering along the horizon: the day when our merciful Father "will wipe away every tear from" our weary eyes, "and death shall be no more, neither shall there be mourning, nor crying, nor pain anymore, for the former things have passed away" (Rev. 21:4). And the one "seated on the throne" says, "Behold, I am making all things new" (v. 5). On that day we will sing:

> "O death, where is your victory?
> O death, where is your sting?"

The sting of death is sin, and the power of sin is the law. But thanks be to God, who gives us the victory through our Lord Jesus Christ. (1 Cor. 15:55–57)

---

18. John Flavel, "The Fountain of Life," in *The Works of John Flavel*, vol. 1 (Carlisle, PA: Banner of Truth, 1968), 356.

PRAISING THE GLORY OF REDEMPTIVE GRACE

Finally, the greater-glory theodicy provides a firm foundation for why we worship the triune God. The glory of God's redemptive grace fuels our worship. Adam and Eve walked with God in the cool of the garden. They had unbroken fellowship with their Creator, but he was not yet their Savior, their Redeemer, the one who rescued them from the plight of their own foolish rebellion some days later.

In prefall Eden, there was worship of God. It was undefiled and sustained the sinless couple, but it was not offered from a position of brokenness and contrition. There was less apprehension of the holiness of God, since they had yet to depart from his righteous command. Nor was there an apprehension of the greatest display of his love for his creatures —the pardon for sin flowing freely and undeservedly from his grace.

This answers a serious objection raised against the greater-glory theodicy. Kevin Diller asks: "Would the depths of God's love for creation have been any less if sin and evil had not entered the world? Surely not."[19] But this is simply not true. Grace is a form of divine love that heaps the greatest glory on God's actions in the world, but it is a love that cannot be displayed to those untainted by sin. It is goodness and favor that can be extended only to rebels, to prodigals, to prostitutes, to drug addicts. It goes to the thief, the drunkard, the liar, and the murderer. It brings calm to the vicious and breaks the hardened criminal. It humiliates the pompous and dissolves the pretensions of the self-righteous. It brings relief to the oppressed and brokenhearted. It renders compassion in hues of confounding splendor.

When sinners are laid low, the ugliness of their souls exposed, and they are broken to pieces and moved to contrition and confession before their holy Maker, then the Almighty is most pleased to pitch his tent among them:

19. Kevin Diller, "Are Sin and Evil Necessary for a Really Good World?," in *The Problem of Evil: Selected Readings*, ed. Michael L. Peterson, 2nd ed. (Notre Dame, IN: University of Notre Dame Press, 2017), 397.

For thus says the One who is high and lifted up,
    who inhabits eternity, whose name is Holy:
"I dwell in the high and holy place,
    and also with him who is of a contrite and lowly spirit,
to revive the spirit of the lowly,
    and to revive the heart of the contrite." (Isa. 57:15)

The highest worship that humans can offer is praise to God for his redemptive grace. In the history of the church, no subject has garnered more hymns of praise than the cross of Christ and the redeeming grace that has poured forth from its bloodstained beams. What else would compel Charles Wesley (1707–88) to pen, "O for a thousand tongues to sing my great Redeemer's praise, the glories of my God and King, the triumphs of his grace"?[20] Julia Johnston (1849–1919) had the same urge to adore the King of mercy when she wrote, "Marvelous grace of our loving Lord, grace that exceeds our sin and our guilt."[21] Likewise, only a man who had been rescued from the grip of sin would put forth these magnificent lines:

The love of God is greater far
Than tongue or pen can ever tell;
It goes beyond the highest star,
And reaches to the lowest hell;
The guilty pair, bowed down with care,
God gave His Son to win;
His erring child He reconciled,
And pardoned from his sin.[22]

Of the many moving hymns of praise in church history, few have fueled our urge to sing forth the glories of God's redemptive grace than the most beloved hymn of all—"Amazing Grace." It has been sung more than any

20. Charles Wesley, "O for a Thousand Tongues to Sing" (1739).
21. Julia H. Johnston, "Marvelous Grace of Our Loving Lord" (1910).
22. Frederick M. Lehman, "The Love of God" (1917).

other song. It has been recorded thousands of times, far exceeding any other piece of music, secular or sacred. John Newton penned it in 1772 for his congregation in Olney, England.

Before he was transformed by God's saving grace, Newton was a notorious slave trader, captaining one of the ships of the North Atlantic slave trade. By his own account, he was a drunkard, a blasphemer, a vile and vicious man. He had no conscience for the evil of jamming men, women, and children into the hull of a ship as though it were a floating trash compactor. They were chained, beaten, starved, and nearly suffocated in the toxic stench and stifling heat. Many died in these conditions before reaching their destination, and Newton didn't care.

This horror is what Newton had in mind when he wrote, "Amazing grace!—how sweet the sound—that saved a wretch like me!" Ironically, when Newton originally penned this hymn, it went largely unnoticed in his native Britain. It did not become widely sung until the nineteenth century in America. In God's wonderful and ironic foresight, he saw fit to bring greater good from the slave-trading hymnist's words than many originally imagined. First, the tune to which the hymn has forever been linked appears to have arisen among African-American slaves in the Southern states.[23]

But that is not all. The last verse, as it is commonly sung today, goes like this:

When we've been there ten thousand years,
Bright shining as the sun,
We've no less days to sing God's praise
Than when we've first begun.

Newton did not write this verse. It first appeared in Harriet Beecher Stowe's famous novel decrying the evils of slavery—*Uncle Tom's Cabin* (1852). She pictures the beleaguered slave, Tom, as having a "soul-crisis" in which

23. Jonathan Aitken, *John Newton: From Disgrace to Amazing Grace* (New York: Continuum, 2007), 170–71.

he saw a vision of the "buffeted and bleeding" Christ wearing his crown of thorns whose spikes gradually morphed into "rays of glory." Then, looking up into the stars, Tom began singing the hymn with this last stanza added.[24] The phrase "When we've been there ten thousand years" had already been part of the oral worship tradition of so-called Negro spirituals for half a century before Stowe's novel.[25]

How could slaves elevate a slave trader's hymn to such a glorious status? The visceral nature of the worship associated with slavery in America finds an intimate companion in Newton's hymn. Newton writes from the depths of his soul-wrenching despair at having ever been engaged in the evils of the slave trade. Only grace could remove such despair. The slaves themselves could sing the same hymn from the opposite vantage point—the despair of being oppressed, subjugated, and humiliated by an unspeakable evil.

Grace rescues the oppressed and the oppressor alike. It saves all manner of men regardless of their ethnicity, skin color, or station in life. This is the wonderful design of God. When Jesus saves, "there is neither Jew nor Greek, there is neither slave nor free, there is no male and female, for you are all one in Christ Jesus" (Gal. 3:28). This contributes to why God's grace is so amazing, and why he is most glorified forever in our praises of that grace.

STUDY QUESTIONS

1. What perspective did William Carey maintain that allowed him to press on in his missionary endeavors in India despite great trials and tribulations?
2. What is more consequential—the evil that exists outside or inside us? Why is it important to answer this question in the right way?

24. Harriet Beecher Stowe, *Uncle Tom's Cabin*, Norton Critical Edition, 3rd ed. (New York: W. W. Norton & Company, 2018), 367.

25. Aitken, *John Newton*, 171–72.

3. How did David view his sin, according to Psalm 51:4? What is the importance of his perspective?

4. Would it be better for you to have never sinned at all or for you to be steeped in sin and redeemed by the grace of God? Explain your answer.

5. What is it about Christ that draws sinners irresistibly to him?

6. Why is it important that we believe that the divine nature cannot experience suffering? Why is this good news for us?

7. Why is it also good news for us that the Son of God, in his human nature, did suffer?

8. Read 2 Corinthians 4:16–18. How has the author helped you understand this passage better?

9. What conditions are necessary for God to display his grace? How has this fueled our greatest hymns of praise to God?

10. What makes the story of the hymn "Amazing Grace" so amazing?

10

TRANSFORMING GRACE,
AMAZING GLORY

After Louis Zamperini was converted to Christ at Billy Graham's 1949 Los Angeles Crusade, he was no longer a slave of sin or his past.[1] He too could sing the freedom song, "Amazing grace!—how sweet the sound—that saved a wretch like me!" The grace that Louie experienced that night had a deeply transformative effect. It compelled him to return to Japan—this time with a redemptive mission. "I could not escape the conviction that until I had actually faced the Japanese again and seen the reflection of my supposedly new self in their eyes, I would never know for sure whether or not I had dispelled the past."[2] Louie "longed to look into their eyes and say not only 'I forgive you,' but to tell them of the greatest event of forgiveness the world has ever known when Christ on the Cross, and at the peak of his agony, could say of his executioners, 'Forgive them, Father, for they know not what they do.'"[3]

1. See his story in chapter 1.
2. Louis Zamperini with David Resin, *Devil at My Heels* (New York: HarperCollins, 2003), 252.
3. Zamperini and Resin, 261.

In October 1950, Louie arrived in Tokyo and cautiously stepped off the plane. Most of his captors had been tried for war crimes and sent to Sugamo Prison. He was given special permission by General Douglas MacArthur himself to enter the prison and speak to them. He did not shrink back from recalling the gruesome details of his captivity. Nor did he soft-pedal their evil actions. But then he preached the gospel of Christ's forgiveness to them and extended his arms to embrace each man with his own expressions of forgiveness. Many were dismayed by this act of kindness. Others wanted to know more about his Christian faith.

But Louie's archnemesis, the Bird, the one man he wanted to see most, was not among the prisoners. Louie's seething hatred toward his cruel tormentor had ceased after his conversion. All his intentions for murderous vengeance had dissipated, along with his nightly dreams in which the Bird haunted him. Now all he saw was a lost soul needing the same salvation that he himself had received. But the Bird had disappeared after Japan's surrender, and no one knew whether he was dead or alive.

Nearly fifty years went by, and Zamperini was invited to carry the torch for the 1998 Olympic Games in Nagano, Japan. He was elated. Furthermore, reporters made a surprising discovery. Mutsuhiro Watanabe, the Bird, was alive and well. He had managed to hide away in a remote cabin until a general amnesty for war prisoners was made in 1952. Since that time, he had become a successful life insurance salesman, going quietly unnoticed. A reunion between the two men was being arranged. Watanabe was willing, but his son prevented it.

Louie reflected on what might have happened if they had met:

> I don't think there would be any fuss; we'd just stand there and chat. I'd suggest we have lunch. I'd ask about his family, children, grandchildren, wife. What they're doing. That's all. If he brings up the war, I'd say it's unfortunate that we even had a war.

He wouldn't press him about his war crimes. He wouldn't shove the past in his face. Rather, he would make it a moment to erase the past. "When you forgive, it's like it never happened. True forgiveness is complete and total."[4] Louie's hardened heart had been dissolved in the transforming power of grace.

Of all the practical implications of the greater-glory theodicy, the grace-drenched power of forgiveness is perhaps the most remarkable phenomenon that emerges from the ashes of lives torched by the conflagration of evil. The grace that forgives sinners is a grace that enables those pardoned and cleansed from the scourge of sin to embody that same forgiveness. This unexpected response to evil proves to be one of the greatest apologetics for the truth of the Christian faith. Furthermore, it is often those who are most crushed and stained by evil who experience the grand reversal of grace most profoundly. Where evil abounds, grace abounds (Rom. 5:20–21). And where grace abounds, it ignites a chorus of thanksgiving that "abound[s] to the glory of God" (2 Cor. 4:15 NASB).

FROM JUSTICE TO MERCY

Human beings have reacted to acts of evil in the world in several ways. Many victims of evil recoil in the face of its imminent threats. Fear and self-preservation are powerful motivators. When these are combined with an acute sense of helplessness, it seems that no other course of action is available. Silence. Inaction. Hiding. No one expects the skinny boy with learning disabilities, disheveled hair, and Coke-bottle glasses to defend himself when the hulking, foul-mouthed bully shoves him down onto the floor for being a "stupid little weakling."

In other cases, fear and self-preservation are combined not with helplessness but with cowardice. How many times have we seen videos posted on social media in which the same sort of vulnerable victim is being pummeled by a similar thug in a crowded public venue while capable people stand by motionless, gawking, afraid to interfere with someone else's business. "Outrageous!" we say. But would any of us act any differently if we were in the crowd?

4. Zamperini and Resin, 282.

On the other end of the spectrum, we have vigilante justice. Vengeance. Sometimes with a fury—the kind that drove Louis Zamperini's zeal to kill the Bird before his heart was filled with grace. The American country music singer-songwriter Michael Wilson Hardy (professionally known as HARDY) embodies a rabid machismo in his unsettling song "wait in the truck."

It retells the story of a man who encounters a woman on the side of the road. She has been beaten and bloodied "from head to toe." She climbs into his truck, and they proceed to the "double-wide" where the vile man who did the deed sits unsuspectingly. The driver tells the woman to wait in the truck as the "day of justice" has arrived. He proceeds to bust the door open, and before the woman's abuser can reach his 12-gauge shotgun, her defender has already discharged his pistol. He calmly smokes one of the dead man's cigarettes while he waits for the police. He doesn't mind life in prison.

Reacting to Evil with Justice

The song demonstrates that the first and most fundamental response to evil is the demand for justice. This cry is universal. It requires no special moral fortitude to desire that moral wrongs be redressed with appropriate just retribution. The prophet cries out, "Let justice roll down like waters, and righteousness like an ever-flowing stream" (Amos 5:24). But when justice fails to materialize, many resort to the crooked justice of vigilantism.

The appropriate pursuit of justice, however, is often far more difficult. For William Wilberforce (1759–1833), it was painfully long and toilsome. He sought to abolish the abominable slave trade in Britain, tenaciously slogging along, introducing bills in Parliament for twenty years before his battle saw victory. He fought for another twenty-six years to abolish slavery altogether. The Slavery Abolition Act 1833 was passed three days before he died.

Civil justice seeks to establish peaceful, moral, orderly, and benevolent conditions in the world so that people can flourish. The practice of genuine justice is rooted in the sovereignty, righteousness, and love of God (Pss. 9:7–8; 89:14; Jer. 9:24). First, the Creator's rightful lordship over our lives (Ps. 24:1) means that we as humans owe our allegiance to him in thought, word, and deed (Isa. 45:23). Second, his holy character establishes the foundations for universal, invariant laws of good and evil (Rev. 15:3–4). He is the standard by which all righteousness is measured. Furthermore, he is our Judge and has implanted his moral law in every human heart (Rom. 2:14–15). Third, his unwavering love for what is good (Ps. 33:5) establishes our obligation as his representatives on earth to uphold all that is good and righteous and to punish evil (Prov. 10:29).

We must defend the innocent and charge the guilty, protect the defenseless and pursue evildoers (Prov. 31:8–9; Jer. 22:3). All peoples are to be treated equally in accordance with their actions regardless of ethnicity, biological sex, skin color, economic or social status; otherwise, justice is not served. Contrary to this, the current inroads of critical theory and so-called social justice in our society regarding race, sexuality, gender, economics, and so on constitute an alarming and pernicious evil that threatens peace and spits in the face of biblical justice.[5] This encourages the same old ugly, prejudicial sins that we have tried to erase in the past but that are being cleverly repackaged with a veneer of righteousness, targeting a new set of victims.

The prophet cries out, "Woe to those who call evil good and good evil, who put darkness for light and light for darkness, who put bitter for sweet and sweet for bitter!" (Isa. 5:20; cf. Eccl. 3:16). We must avoid the morass of our current moral confusion, making every effort to pour the salve of compassion (Col. 3:12) upon those traumatized by genuine instances of *actual acts* of racism, prejudice, oppression, and injustice and warn perpetrators that *no* evil deed will go unpunished, no matter how it might be disguised as good (Ps. 1:4–6; Prov. 11:21).

Sometimes extreme measures must be taken to achieve justice, and the path toward that end is not always clear or easy. Nary a shot was fired when Britain abolished slavery. Unfortunately, America endured the bloody Civil War to do the same. The way to peace often requires cutting

---

5. For resources on this issue, see chapter 1, footnote 8.

through a tangled web of truth and error, volatile politics, secret agendas, muddled motives, unforeseen obstacles, and fierce resistance from many diverse quarters.

And sometimes just causes cannot avoid just wars. Biblical justice seeks peace and decries violence. Yet since we live in a world where human depravity, if unchecked, runs with abandon toward unbridled savagery, then true justice cannot sustain a principled and unconditional pacifism. The sword must be wielded (Rom. 13:1–4). But it must be wielded justly, or peace is never established.

As the horrific ordeal of Louis Zamperini makes clear, Imperial Japan did not place a high value on the lives of others. The Japanese army invaded China at the outset of World War II and proceeded to slaughter some ten million Chinese civilians in addition to five million Pacific Islanders. The notorious Rape of Nanking is but one example of countless atrocities that the Japanese committed. Within six weeks, the Imperial Army massacred two hundred thousand people and raped at least twenty thousand women.

> Fathers were forced to rape their daughters, and sons their mothers, as other family members watched. Not only did live burials, castration, the carving of organs, and the roasting of people become routine, but more diabolical tortures were practiced, such as hanging people by their tongues on iron hooks or burying people to their waists and watching them get torn apart by German shepherds.[6]

Many difficult questions surround the dropping of the atomic bombs on Hiroshima and Nagasaki by the United States to end the war with Japan. Some have suggested that pressing unconditional surrender was the wrong tactic, that the Japanese were willing to pursue terms of peace. But this view is not sustained by the facts. An armistice would have kept the Japanese warlords in power and allowed them to continue their course of murder, rape, and pillage. Furthermore, the cultural ethos of the long-entrenched

6. Iris Chang, *The Rape of Nanking* (New York: Penguin Books, 1998), 6.

bushido code meant that the Japanese people, especially its soldiers, were sworn to fight to the bitter end. Surrender was cowardly. The emperor, Hirohito, was regarded as a god. To die for him was the highest honor.[7]

This explains why only tiny handfuls of Japanese soldiers surrendered during the battle for the Pacific. In Saipan, U.S. Marines watched families commit suicide rather than surrender. Parents threw their children off cliffs before casting themselves off.[8] Bushido explains why kamikazes were willing to fly suicide missions as a last-ditch effort to defend the Empire. They managed to sink over thirty U.S. ships and damaged hundreds more.

Two months before the bombing of Hiroshima and Nagasaki, Japanese authorities issued "Operation Decision," the plan to defend the home islands. This involved 2.5 million troops and a civilian militia of 28 million people using muzzle loaders, bamboo spears, and bows and arrows if necessary to fight off the inevitable American invasion.

Everyone knew that such an invasion would cost untold millions of lives. The shock of dropping the bombs was intended to avoid that reality. Tokyo was already reeling when on a single night on March 9–10, 1945, over three hundred B-29s turned the city into an inferno, killing a hundred thousand people. Still no surrender. The atomic bombs "Fat Man" and "Little Boy" were weapons of horrific destruction. Between the two bombs, two hundred thousand people were killed, most of them liquefied in an awesome roar that seemed to unleash hell itself, massive fireballs quickly extending to thirty-eight thousand feet into the sky with temperatures four times that of the sun's core. The first bomb on Hiroshima did not have the intended effect.

The second one on Nagasaki did.

The decision to drop the bombs was not without moral conundrums, even if we agree that it had moral justification—an assessment that cannot be made glibly. War is indeed hell. There is a cruel logic to waging a just war in which casualties to the innocent are at the same time impossibly

7. See Richard B. Frank, *Downfall: The End of the Imperial Japanese Empire* (New York: Penguin Books, 2001).

8. Frank, 29.

painful to accept and yet almost always impossible to avoid. Such weighty decisions will always be attended by regrettable consequences even when every measure is taken to prevent collateral damage.

Unfortunately, the risks of using overwhelming lethal force to extinguish intractable forces of evil are sometimes necessary to stem the tide of greater evil, preventing communities, nations, and the world itself from descending into a totalitarian nightmare. It is one more aspect of a fallen world that should cause us to long for the perfect justice that only Christ will mete out at his return (Isa. 42:1–4).

Perhaps one of the most striking perspectives on the justification for this course of action came during Louis Zamperini's trip to Japan to forgive his captors in 1950. Louis met a survivor of Hiroshima in a burn unit located in a rebuilt hospital destroyed by the blast. The patient revealed the horrific scars that the atomic conflagration had left on his back and declared to the former POW, "I feel honored that this happened to me, to save millions of lives."[9]

No doubt, a tremendous strain is put on the principles of fairness when an innocent man with no choice is placed in this unfortunate position. Yet he was willing to embrace a different kind of principle, one that incidentally reflects what Jesus taught his disciples: "Greater love has no one than this, that someone lay down his life for his friends" (John 15:13). Something sad yet beautiful resonates inside us when a man is willing to bear a small pain (though great to himself) to prevent a larger pain from being inflicted on his countrymen—and more so when he didn't ask for it.

Reacting to Evil with Mercy

This hints at a deeper, more poignant response to evil than justice. It is called *mercy*. While true justice and mercy are rooted in a biblical worldview, reflecting the character and purposes of God, neither is exclusive to the Christian faith. God designed all humans to long for justice. Furthermore, mercy is a virtue that we all appreciate, especially when we are its subjects. Nonetheless, something about some displays of

9. Zamperini and Resin, *Devil at My Heels*, 259.

mercy is uniquely Christian and tangibly highlights the grace wrapped up in the gospel.

At the outset, it should be noted that justice and mercy are not mutually exclusive concepts in Christianity. Justice often means showing compassion for those who suffer injustice. Furthermore, extending merciful pardon to lawbreakers is not a way of disregarding the seriousness of criminal behavior. When God extends saving mercy to sinners, he does not brush the demands of his justice under some cosmic rug. Rather, divine justice is diverted from the pardoned sinner to Christ. Christ bore on the cross the punishment that pardoned sinners deserved, thereby making propitiation for their sins (1 John 4:10). In doing so, he has removed both their guilt and God's just wrath that otherwise rested inescapably on them.

Once again, World War II—the most lethal conflict in history—represents how abysmally low the world can descend into darkness. This is especially true when it comes to the Holocaust. We naturally assume that the destruction of six million Jews could have never come from the hand of God. Now, if we mean that God is somehow morally culpable for the evil that the human architects of the Holocaust perpetrated, then we would be correct. Nonetheless, God's *sovereign will* ordained what his *moral will* despises in order to bring about countless greater goods that we may never fully comprehend. We gain a glimpse of a few of those goods via some surprising and wonderful ironies. Embedded in the malevolent muck of the Final Solution are brilliant diamonds, breathtaking treasures of mercy that reveal the riches of divine glory.

Mercy to Victims

One way in which mercy was displayed during the Holocaust was in the opportunity it provided for many to show extraordinary acts of mercy to its victims. In the south of France was a little-known village called Le Chambon, established by a group of French Protestants known as Huguenots. The Huguenots were no strangers to oppression and violence. They were the victims of the St. Bartholomew's Day massacre in 1572. Within a few weeks, as many as thirty thousand Huguenots were slaughtered in cold blood by Roman Catholic authorities.

Being forever stamped by this identity gave them a unique motive to help those who were similarly mistreated. Under the guidance of the village pastor, André Trocmé, the citizens hid thousands of Jews, eluding the watchful eyes of the local Nazi authorities. Philip Hallie wrote a book on the incident and was deeply moved by the risk that these simple peasant folk took.[10] He was Jewish but not religious. Nonetheless, Hallie had an epiphany of sorts when researching the story, realizing that "there is a mystery to goodness that is even deeper than the mystery of evil."[11]

Where could such risky compassion come from?

Only from those who took seriously a God who is "merciful and gracious, slow to anger, and abounding in steadfast love and faithfulness" (Ex. 34:6). Consequently, such a God calls his people to a "religion that is pure and undefiled . . . : to visit orphans and widows in their affliction" (James 1:27) and to "rescue those who are being taken away to death; [to] hold back those who are stumbling to the slaughter" (Prov. 24:11).

Recipients of Divine Mercy

A second way in which mercy was displayed in the Holocaust came when God provided a special—even a supernatural—grace that enabled Christian victims of the most unspeakable evil to bear up under it with a joy found nowhere else in this cruel world. In some ways, this is a passive reaction to evil because God is the active agent that infuses the believer with this enigmatic joy. Nonetheless, joy as a response to evil is one of the otherworldly commands of Scripture. James exhorts us, "Count it all joy, my brothers, when you meet trials of various kinds, for you know that the testing of your faith produces steadfastness" (James 1:2–3).

When God penetrates the black fog of adversity with his presence, a profound and mysterious joy is the result (Ps. 16:11). Jesus promises all believers that his joy will be made full in them (John 17:13). God does

---

10. Philip Hallie, *Lest Innocent Blood Be Shed: The Story of the Village of Le Chambon and How Goodness Happened There* (New York: HarperCollins, 1994).

11. Os Guinness, *Unspeakable: Facing Up to Evil in an Age of Genocide and Terror* (San Francisco: HarperCollins, 2005), 226.

not always remove us from the storms, but he does promise to infuse his children with an inscrutable calm that bypasses our need to make sense of the chaos surrounding us (Phil. 4:6–7).

The story of Corrie and Betsie ten Boom is a sterling example of this unique display of mercy. Just like the villagers of Le Chambon, the ten Boom family of Haarlem, Netherlands, demonstrated the same kind of rescuing mercy to Jews, many of whom they hid in a secret compartment of their home during the Nazi occupation. Again, they were compelled to do so by their strong desire to honor Christ. But the risk proved too great. They were caught by the Nazis, arrested, and sent to various concentration camps, where most of the family members died. The story is well told by Corrie in her memoir, *The Hiding Place*.[12]

Corrie and her sister Betsie were interned at Ravensbrück, the notorious concentration camp for women. When they arrived, they were immediately stripped naked before SS men and forced into showers. Showers seemed superfluous, since their barracks were constantly filthy, reeking of urine and feces, their straw beds infested with lice. The meager rations caused starvation. They were regularly beaten and overworked. Many women died from the subfreezing temperatures. The two sisters were housed next to the punishment barracks, where the inhuman screams of those tortured were "the sounds of hell itself."[13]

Corrie managed to smuggle a Bible without detection into their barracks. This was the first of God's mercies. She said that having the Bible meant that "we were not poor, but rich. Rich in this new evidence of the care of Him who was God even of Ravensbrück."[14] The reading of the Bible ironically turned their hellish barracks into a small haven:

From morning until lights-out, whenever we were not in ranks for roll call, our Bible was the center of an ever-widening circle of help

---

12. Corrie ten Boom, *The Hiding Place*, 35th anniversary ed. (Grand Rapids: Chosen Books, 2006).

13. Ten Boom, 205.

14. Ten Boom, 204.

and hope. Like waifs clustered around a blazing fire, we gathered about it, holding out our hearts to its warmth and light. The blacker the night around us grew, the brighter and truer and more beautiful burned the word of God. "Who shall separate us from the love of Christ? Shall tribulation, or distress, or persecution, or famine, or nakedness, or peril, or sword? . . . Nay, in all these things we are more than conquerors though him that loved us."[15]

The truth of Paul's words in 2 Corinthians 4:16 came alive to the traumatized women: "We do not lose heart. Though our outer self is wasting away, our inner self is being renewed day by day." Corrie elaborates: "Life in Ravensbrück took place on two separate levels, mutually impossible. One, the observable, external life, grew every day more horrible. The other, the life we lived with God, grew daily better, truth upon truth, glory upon glory."[16] Still, it was difficult to keep this perspective. Later, they moved into more dreadful living quarters, where the biting fleas made life unbearable. Corrie began to fall into despair.

But not Betsie.

After Corrie complained to her sister, their Scripture reading that morning included 1 Thessalonians 5:18: "Give thanks in all circumstances." "All circumstances" included the horrible things, according to Betsie, so she began thanking God for the fleas. Corrie was flabbergasted. She finally conceded to offer paltry thanks "for jammed, crammed, stuffed, packed, suffocating crowds," but definitely not for the fleas![17] That is, until it became clear that the fleas kept the guards out of the barracks, and this meant that they could read the Bible freely. "*All* circumstances" took on new meaning.

Soon Betsie's physical health deteriorated to the point at which she was unable to keep up with the brutal work routine forced on the women. One day a guard whipped her in the face for lagging. Corrie grabbed a shovel to

15. Ten Boom, 206. The reference is to Romans 8:35, 37.
16. Ten Boom, 206.
17. Ten Boom, 210.

attack the guard, and Betsie stopped her. She urged her to keep her focus on Jesus. Corrie marveled at her sister's inner strength. "As her body grew weaker, her faith seemed to grow bolder."[18] As the mortal life in Betsie was slowly draining away, she taught Corrie of the inner reserves of spiritual life and power that could be drawn forth even in the worst of conditions.

Soon Betsie was too weak to do anything, so they laid her on a stretcher to take her to the infirmary. As she lay freezing, barely able to speak, she whispered to Corrie: ". . . must tell people what we have learned here. We must tell them that there is no pit so deep that He is not deeper still. They will listen to us, Corrie, because we have been here."[19] Within minutes of being carried away from Corrie's side, her spirit finally gave up and departed from her emaciated body. Corrie was able to see her one last time.

> For there lay Betsie, her eyes closed as if in sleep, her face full and young. The care lines, the grief lines, the deep hollows of hunger and disease were simply gone. In front of me was the Betsie of Haarlem, happy and at peace. Stronger! Freer! This was the Betsie of heaven, bursting with joy and health.[20]

Saints such as Betsie ten Boom understand something that transcends the worst machinations of evil men, demons and devils, and days of unbearable darkness. Their testimony is a reminder to other believers throughout history of the truths that Paul himself lived and breathed. He urges the troubled Corinthians, "We appeal to you not to receive the grace of God in vain" (2 Cor. 6:1). Grace has transforming power, no matter how dire the circumstances. Paul goes on to say:

> As servants of God we commend ourselves in every way: by great endurance, in afflictions, hardships, calamities, beatings, imprisonments, riots, labors, sleepless nights, hunger; by purity,

18. Ten Boom, 215.
19. Ten Boom, 227.
20. Ten Boom, 229.

knowledge, patience, kindness, the Holy Spirit, genuine love; by truthful speech, and the power of God; with the weapons of righteousness for the right hand and for the left; through honor and dishonor, through slander and praise. We are treated as impostors, and yet are true; as unknown, and yet well known; as dying, and behold, we live; as punished, and yet not killed; as sorrowful, yet always rejoicing; as poor, yet making many rich; as having nothing, yet possessing everything. (2 Cor. 6:4–10)

No earthly salve can soothe the troubled souls of battered men and women like the grace of the living God. It is not that believers possess exclusive ability to tolerate the intolerable. Survival in barbaric conditions is not unusual, believers or not. Rather, what is unusual is to see genuine Christians such as Betsie persevere through extreme trials and do so with a singular suffusion of divine joy filling their souls. This is not just unusual —it is supernatural. It is the same transcendent, supernal joy experienced by the martyr Stephen while stones were breaking his bones and ripping gashes into his body (Acts 7:54–60). It points to a God who extracts effervescent glory from abject blackness.

Mercy to Victimizers

Yet an additional mode of mercy as a response to evil points to the uniqueness of the Christian faith. It is the mercy of forgiveness filling the forgiven and extended to their victimizers. We saw it in Louis Zamperini when he converted to Christ and forgave his Japanese captors. We see it in the testimony of Stephen as he forgave those who stoned him to death (Acts 7:60). Stephen was simply following the example of his Lord's response to his executioners (Luke 23:34). And we are about to see it in Corrie ten Boom after she providentially escaped the horrors of Ravensbrück.

Paul urges believers to "bless those who persecute you; bless and do not curse them" (Rom. 12:14). Seeking justice, even vengeance, is a natural response to evil. But Paul is pointing to an unnatural response, one that reflects Jesus' teaching in Matthew 5. Our Lord indicates that our tendency as human beings is to hate our enemies (Matt. 5:43). On the contrary, "I say to you, Love your enemies and pray for those who persecute you" (v. 44). Scholars have recognized how revolutionary this teaching was in the first-century Jewish and Roman context. It has been revolutionary ever since.

There have always been dark eras and locations where Christianity seems to hang by a thread and believers are threatened with overwhelming trials, injustices, persecutions, and even death. Those dark times appear to be coming for believers today as the moral revolutionaries of our current zeitgeist can no longer tolerate the truth of biblical Christianity. But Peter encourages us, "Even if you should suffer for righteousness' sake, you will be blessed" (1 Peter 3:14).

Blessed for suffering?

How counterintuitive can the apostle be? It stretches our faith beyond the bounds of our cognitive capacities. Peter again exhorts us, "Let those who suffer according to God's will entrust their souls to a faithful Creator while doing good" (1 Peter 4:19). There resides a special grace in our inner man that the Holy Spirit supplies the believer. It blesses us and enables us to extend the same grace to our enemies.

What is the motive behind such proffers of grace and forgiveness? It is knowing that we ourselves are forgiven by God through Christ. The Christian faith extols the notion that God forgives the most foul and incorrigible sinners (Ps. 130:3–4). Paul relates: "Formerly I was a blasphemer, persecutor, and insolent opponent. But I received mercy because I had acted ignorantly in unbelief, and the grace of our Lord overflowed for me with the faith and love that are in Christ Jesus" (1 Tim. 1:13–14). Complete forgiveness and removal of every last one of our sins is the first joy that God pours out from his abundant grace into the hearts of new converts (Ps. 103:11–12).

Thus, to be a Christian is to be forgiven ... *and* to be a forgiver of others. This is why the Lord taught us to pray, "Release us from our debts, as we also have released our debtors" (Matt. 6:12).[21] This grace to forgive

21. My translation. The Greek word normally translated "forgive" in this verse means "to release" something from something else.

came to Corrie ten Boom shortly after the war. In 1947, she was giving her testimony at a church service in Munich, Germany. Afterward, a vaguely familiar man approached her. He was exuberant because he had recently become a believer. He told her that Christ "has washed my sins away!"[22] Then he introduced himself as one of the vile SS guards who had worked at Ravensbrück. Corrie suddenly remembered him as one of the guards who were gawking at the naked women as they were corralled into the showers when they first arrived.

He reached out to shake her hand. She froze. What should she do? "Vengeful thoughts boiled through me. . . . *Lord Jesus*, I prayed, *forgive me and help me to forgive him.*" But nothing changed. There was awkward silence. "I tried to smile, I struggled to raise my hand. I could not. I felt nothing, not the slightest spark of warmth or charity."[23] She wondered how forgiving him would erase what had happened to Betsie.

He wasn't even close to the worst perpetrators of evil at Ravensbrück. Nonetheless, he had been there, and he was a despicable Nazi. Unlike Louis Zamperini, Corrie really struggled in this moment to do what she knew was right. But to harbor bitterness would eat her alive. Failing to forgive the guard would haunt her more than all the harm she had endured in the death camp.

She said that after regathering her thoughts: "I breathed again a silent prayer. *Jesus, I cannot forgive him. Give Your forgiveness.*" It was a halfhearted prayer with little faith to attend it. But it was enough to facilitate a miraculous movement of God's grace. "As I took his hand the most incredible thing happened. From my shoulder along my arm and through my hand, a current seemed to pass from me to him, while into my heart sprang a love for this stranger that almost overwhelmed me."[24] They tightly clasped hands for a long time, the former victimizer joined

22. Ten Boom, *Hiding Place*, 247. See also "Guideposts Classics: Corrie ten Boom on Forgiveness," https://www.guideposts.org/positive-living/guideposts-classics-corrie-ten-boom-forgiveness/.

23. "Corrie ten Boom on Forgiveness."

24. "Corrie ten Boom on Forgiveness."

to one of his victims, sealed together by the unbreakable bonds of Christ-centered unity.

Corrie knew that this was unnatural. Most victims of the Holocaust have never been able to forgive their tormentors. This was a move of the Holy Spirit, of grace-drenched power. She concluded her reflections on this special moment: "So I discovered that it is not on our forgiveness any more than on our goodness that the world's healing hinges, but on His. When He tells us to love our enemies, He gives, along with the command, the love itself."[25]

Corrie ten Boom became a living analogy of the gospel of grace. Forgiving one's enemies is one of the most tangible and remarkable apologetics for the Christian faith. But no such opportunity arises without the emergence of grave injustices in the world, and the infusion of divine grace begetting such gems that bedazzle us with divine glory.

FROM GRACE TO GLORY

This takes us full circle to the greater-glory theodicy and how it can help shape the way that we view the world. Our exploration of the problem of evil has sought to demonstrate that when we search the depths of our being, there is a gnawing sense that the world is askew. Of course, there is plenty of truth, beauty, and goodness in creation and among God's creatures to attract our attention, giving us a glimpse of the way that things are supposed to be.

This is found when joy fills excited parents at their child's first steps. Or when Grandma bakes her scrumptious pumpkin pies for the family at Thanksgiving. You notice it when a gentle breeze sends waves across a yellow field of wheat on a Nebraska summer day while cicadas sing their choruses. Jonas Salk saw glimpses of the good, the true, and the beautiful when he devised a cure for polio. Michelangelo knew the wonder of it when he sculpted the seventeen-foot edifice of David from a massive chunk of

25. "Corrie ten Boom on Forgiveness."

marble. It was heard when Ella Fitzgerald and Louis Armstrong performed "Dream a Little Dream of Me."

But these signs of a better world can't hide the signs of brokenness that surround us as well. The world is fractured. Darkness creeps everywhere. We see it when that first-time mother is excited to give birth and then has a miscarriage. Or when Hurricane Katrina decimated New Orleans. Americans felt the excruciating weight of it when two jetliners crashed into New York's World Trade Towers. It is seen when a mother addicted to fentanyl overdoses, falls into delirium, and dies in front of her small children. It manifests itself when a culture is slowly captivated by sexual degeneracy that only a few years ago everyone saw as morally unacceptable.

Thus, when we see glimpses of good amid the bad, it serves to highlight that deep longing for "kingdom come"—for the ultimate good ending of the story. Furthermore, when the contrast between good and evil is stark and clear, the ache within grows stronger. When all is overcast and murky, the disparities are erased and breed lukewarm indifference. But when the shadows are dark and its edges are crisp, then we know that the sun is shining brightly. It makes us more attuned to the problem as well as the reality of something better. It enhances our longing for wrongs to be made right, for war to give way to peace, for chaos to be transformed to order, for hate to dissolve into love, for wickedness to end and righteousness to reign.

God designed it this way.

In many ways, the world seems to have no light. It is like going down into the bowels of the earth in a cavern that is miles from daylight. Without your headlamp, you can't see your hand two inches from your face. That kind of blackness is eerie. It has a strange weight that you cannot tolerate for long. But God intended us to feel the weight of the world like this. The coldness of it. Its haunting stillness seeping into our bones and disrupting our peace. "That's crazy!" you say.

But we know that God could have easily designed the world to remain unbroken, with no slithering serpent and no tantalizing tree to tempt the inhabitants of the garden. He could have fashioned Adam and Eve with steel wills, like himself—untemptable and forged in perpetual perfection. It's not as though God had no ability to do so. But he didn't.

Why?

Because an *unfallen-not-needing-redemption world* did not serve his purposes. It would have been a fine world, to be sure. Yet only a *fallen-but-being-redeemed world* serves God's remarkable purpose of maximizing his glory to his image-bearing creatures. How does he do so? By piercing the blackness of this cold, dark hovel of a cave we live in with the light of his incarnate Son, divinely born of a virgin, yet stuck in a dirty manger.

The apostle John introduces Christ in his Gospel as "the light" who "shines in the darkness, and the darkness has not overcome it" (John 1:5). We would not know the glory of the light of the snake-crushing, devil-defeating, death-defying, evil-smashing gospel unless God had intentionally purposed a good world to descend into the abyss of darkness (Rom. 8:20)—a darkness that he designed to be penetrated by that brilliant light.

The apostle Paul introduces a variation on this light-darkness metaphor: "For God, who said, 'Let light shine out of darkness,' has shone in our hearts to give the light of the knowledge of the glory of God in the face of Jesus Christ" (2 Cor. 4:6). This image alludes to the creation account, which begins with the earth as a black, watery void (Gen. 1:2–3). Suddenly, out of the darkness a mysterious light bursts forth. The image is counterintuitive. Light doesn't normally emanate *out* of darkness. We think of light shining *into* darkness—like shafts of sunlight pouring into dark caves. In this case, light mysteriously emerges from the depths, illuminating the darkness from within.

Both images speak of the grace of the gospel of redemption suddenly exploding on the scene via the divinely appointed Redeemer, whose heroic work of salvation magnifies the glory of God precisely by means of penetrating the darkness. This glory could not be perceived as clearly and as wonderfully without the presence of the darkness in the first place. And the strange wonder of it all is that Christ defeated evil by entering its dark portals and casting it upon himself to be treated as though he were the villain. He defeated death by dying. And then the grand hero emerged as a Victor from the dead and comes again to lay waste to all remaining evil till, indeed, kingdom come!

Theodore Cuyler was a pastor in Brooklyn, New York, in the late nineteenth century. Two of his children died as infants. A third child died of typhoid fever at age twenty-two. He writes these wonderful words of encouragement to believers assaulted by a cursed world:

> So, to all my fellow-sufferers who are treading their way through the tunnels of trial, I would say: "Tighten your loins with the promises, and keep the strong staff of faith well in hand. Trust God in the dark. We are safer with him in the dark than without him in the sunshine. He will not suffer your foot to stumble. His rod and his staff never break. Why he brought us here we know not now, but we shall know hereafter. At the end of the gloomy passage beams the heavenly light. Then comes the exceeding and eternal weight of glory!"[26]

God's greater glory has shone forth in his Son. That glory will only grow brighter until one day its brightness will fill the whole earth and our entire souls. The last vestiges of darkness will be dispelled forever in the consummation of the Son's kingdom at his imminent return. To that end we cry with the apostle John in Revelation 22: "Amen. Come, Lord Jesus!" (Rev. 22:20). And until that day arrives, the glorious, inspired Word of God ends with this encouragement: "The grace of the Lord Jesus be with all. Amen" (v. 21).

Indeed—Amen!

STUDY QUESTIONS

1. If you were in Louis Zamperini's shoes, would you have had the same determination to seek out your tormentors and offer them forgiveness? Why or why not?

26. Theodore L. Cuyler, *God's Light on Dark Clouds* (repr., Carlisle, PA: Banner of Truth, 2008), 31–32.

2. Why is forgiving others, especially of horrible offenses, one of the greatest apologetics (defenses) for the truth of the Christian faith?

3. Have you ever witnessed examples of vigilante justice? Were you appalled by or secretly approving of such actions?

4. What three attributes of God does the author point to as the biblical basis for civil justice? Why is this important?

5. Do you believe that the United States had justification to drop the atomic bombs on Hiroshima and Nagasaki during World War II? Why or why not?

6. Why is mercy a more powerful response to evil than justice?

7. What is the most impactful part of Corrie ten Boom's story for you? Why?

8. What motivates a Christian to extend forgiveness to his or her enemies?

9. What are some examples in the present world in which we see glimpses of the future glory of God's eternal kingdom?

10. Why is a world yearning for redemption from evil better than a world that needs no redemption?

GLOSSARY

Arminianism. A set of theological beliefs associated with the teachings of Jacob Arminius (1560–1609). Arminianism teaches five basic ideas. First, sin has infected all people, but their wills are made free by God's **prevenient grace**. Second, God elects sinners to salvation on the basis of his **foreknowledge** of their faith in Christ. Third, Christ's death was a universal **atonement** for the sins of all men. Fourth, God's saving grace can be resisted by the **free will** of the sinner. Fifth, Christians can fall away from God's grace and forfeit their salvation. Arminianism's unique beliefs about free will puts it in the category of **free-will theism** and in contrast to **Calvinism**. Arminianism usually embraces the **free-will defense** in response to the **problem of evil**. See **omnipotence** (of God).

atonement. The satisfaction of a holy God's righteous demands against the violation of his moral character and laws so that the sin and guilt of the violator (sinner) may be removed and the sinner reconciled to God. Only the bloody death and resurrection of Christ can serve as an acceptable atoning sacrifice to God for the reconciliation of sinners. **atoning,** adj. See **penal substitution; redemption**.

atoning death. See **atonement**.

atoning sacrifice. See **atonement**.

Calvinism. A set of theological beliefs associated with the teachings of the Protestant Reformer John Calvin (1509–64). Calvinism is often identified by the five points of Calvinism, traditionally represented by the acronym *TULIP*. The *T* stands for *total depravity,* which indicates that humanity is enslaved to sin. The *U* stands for *unconditional election*, which indicates that God chooses people for salvation wholly apart from anything they do. The *L* stands for *limited atonement*, which indicates that Christ's death secured **atonement** only for the elect. The *I* stands for *irresistible grace*, which indicates that God draws chosen sinners to Christ for salvation irresistibly. The *P* stands for *perseverance of the saints*, which indicates that the elect will persevere in their faith until the end. *Calvinism* is broadly synonymous with *Reformed theology* and is contrasted with **Arminianism**. See **compatibilism**; **omnipotence** (of God); **providence** (of God); **sovereign will** (of God).

Christus Victor. A term revived by Gustaf Aulén (1879–1977) that speaks to the victorious aspect of Christ's work of **atonement** and **redemption** whereby he defeats all the forces of **evil**, including sin, Satan and his demonic host, death, and all other curses that came as a result of the **fall** that afflict the **creation**. See **penal substitution**.

climax. The third movement of the plot structure in **Freytag's Pyramid**, which is the critical point, the moment of crisis when the conflict reaches its apex and there appears to be no reasonable way to resolve matters. The climax marks the turning point of the plot. In the case of a **tragedy**, the turning point goes from bad to worse and, in a **comedy**, from bad to good.

comedy. A plot type in classical literature in which a story has a good, happy, or satisfying ending. Comedy is contrasted with **tragedy**. See **Freytag's Pyramid**.

compatibilism. The view of free agency held by most proponents of **Calvinism** that claims that God's sovereignty is compatible with human freedom and **moral responsibility**. There is a dual explanation for every choice that humans make. God meticulously determines human choices, yet every person freely makes his or her own choices. God's **providence** is exercised so that he never coerces people to choose as they do, yet they always choose according to his **sovereign will**. People are free when they voluntarily choose according to their most compelling desires and as long as their choices are made in an unhindered way. While God never hinders one's choices, other factors can hinder people's freedom and thus their moral responsibility. Furthermore, moral and spiritual choices are conditioned on one's base nature, whether good or evil (i.e., regenerate or unregenerate). In this sense, one is either in bondage to his or her sin (unregenerate) nature or freed by a new spiritual (regenerate) nature. The compatibilist view of free agency is contrasted with the views of **free will** held by **Arminianism** and other varieties of **free-will theism**.

contrary choice. One of the ways of describing the view of **free will** held by **Arminianism** and other varieties of **free-will theism**. Contrary choice indicates that people can freely choose between contrary (alternative) possibilities. If a person chooses one course of action (A), freedom of will gives him or her the power to equally choose a contrary (alternative) course of action (not A) in exactly the same set of circumstances.

creation. With respect to the grand storyline of Scripture, the "very good" (pristine) conditions of the world as God ideally intended it before the **fall** of Adam and Eve into sin. The prefall world represented by the garden of Eden was a paradise in which peace (*shalom*) and harmony existed between Creator and creatures (especially God's image-bearing creatures), between image-bearing creatures and themselves (i.e., Adam and Eve), and between God's creatures and the rest of the created order. See **redemption**.

decree(s) (of God). See **sovereign will** (of God).

denouement. The last movement of the plot structure in **Freytag's Pyramid** in which the final unraveling of the action takes place and the conflict is fully resolved—the knot finally untied. In the case of a **comedy**, all is made well; the happily-ever-after can begin. In the case of a **tragedy**, it is the final catastrophe that unfolds, but always with a moral lesson to be learned.

divine foreknowledge. See **foreknowledge** (of God).

divine impassibility. See **impassibility** (of God).

divine providence. See **providence** (of God).

divine sovereignty. See **sovereign will** (of God).

divine transcendence. See **transcendence** (of God).

eternality (of God). See **timeless eternality** (of God).

eucatastrophe. A term coined by J. R. R. Tolkien that means "good catastrophe." It refers to "the sudden happy turn in a story" in which matters otherwise appeared hopeless. Tolkien believed that the highest purpose in a great story comes in the reversal of bad fortunes that then "pierces you with a joy that brings tears."

evil. See **moral evil; natural evil**. See also **gratuitous evil; horrendous evil; problem of evil**.

exposition. The first movement of the plot structure in **Freytag's Pyramid** in which the story is set up, introducing the characters and themes that lead to the emerging conflict.

fall. With respect to the grand storyline of Scripture, the cataclysmic devastation of the "very good" **creation** resulting from the disobedience of God's image-bearing creatures Adam and Eve as they rebelled against their God and Creator. Adam's sin brought about a universal curse on subsequent humanity and the rest of creation, which resulted in the perpetuation of **moral evil** and **natural evil** that now plagues the present world with pain and suffering and causes it to long for **redemption**.

falling action. The fourth movement of the plot structure in **Freytag's Pyramid** in which the conflict moves toward resolution, whether satisfying (**comedy**) or unsatisfying (**tragedy**). In Aristotle's language, it is the "reversal" whereby the knot ("entanglement") starts to be untied.

fatalism. The idea that future events are fixed in such a way that human choices are irrelevant. It claims that what will be will be, and that there is nothing that anyone can do about it. This contrasts with the biblical view of God's **providence**.

foreknowledge (of God). The attribute of God whereby he knows exhaustively and infallibly all past, present, and future events that transpire in history. This presents problems for **Arminianism** (and other varieties of **free-will theism**) and its view of **free will**.

According to Arminianism, one could always make a **contrary choice** to the choice that was made under exactly the same circumstances. If this is the case, then how can God know what his creatures will choose?

free will. The idea that humans, as free moral agents, are designed by God with the capacity for freely making choices, which undergirds their **moral responsibility.** Most proponents of **Calvinism** and **Arminianism** (as well as other varieties of **free-will theism**) agree that some kind of free agency is necessary for moral responsibility. But each branch of theology defines *free agency* differently. The sort of free will that Arminians and other free-will theists hold to indicates that (1) God cannot decisively determine our choices and (2) one could always make a **contrary choice** to the one that was made. Thus, free moral agents have a strong degree of autonomy in their choices. In contrast to this view of free will, most Calvinists hold to **compatibilism.** See **free-will defense; omnipotence** (of God); **prevenient grace.**

free-will defense. A way of addressing the **problem of evil** that claims that God risks the occurrence of **evil** by preserving the valuable good of **free will,** which he bestows on his intelligent free moral agents. The freedom that such free agents possess, and that permits them to choose good, comes with the risk of also choosing evil. Thus, the free-will defense seeks to shift **moral responsibility** for evil from God to such free moral agents. See **Arminianism; free-will theism; greater-good defense; theodicy.**

free-will theism. A theological orientation whose proponents emphasize the importance of God's granting humans significant freedom via a unique view of **free will** that includes the notion of **contrary choice.** They also champion the **free-will defense** in response to the **problem of evil.** Most free-will theists embrace **Arminianism,** but some embrace open theism and Molinism. See **omnipotence** (of God).

Freytag's Pyramid. The elements that frame a commonly used plot structure in storytelling as observed by the nineteenth-century German novelist and playwright Gustav Freytag (1816–95). The plot structure of stories in Freytag's Pyramid is marked by five movements: (1) the **exposition**; (2) the **rising action**; (3) the **climax**; (4) the **falling action**; and (5) the **denouement** of the story. See **comedy**; **tragedy**.

gratuitous evil. Instances of **moral evil** or **natural evil**, which is also usually categorized as **horrendous evil** and which appears to be senseless, that is, without meaning, purpose, or sound reasons for occurring. Such **evil** appears to undermine God's goodness, making him an uncaring and capricious deity.

greater-glory theodicy. A way of addressing the **problem of evil** that claims that God freely chose to create a world that included the crisis of **evil** initiated by the **fall** so that he might supremely magnify his glory through the **redemption** that is achieved by his **incarnate** Son, Jesus Christ. This **theodicy** claims that a fallen-but-being-redeemed world is far better than an unfallen-not-needing-redemption world because such a world brings far greater glory to God. The greater-glory theodicy is a specific version of the **greater-good defense**.

greater-good defense. A way of addressing the **problem of evil** that claims that God brings about greater goods via **evil** that could not otherwise come about without the evils connected to the emergence of those goods. These goods significantly outweigh the evils that they are connected to. Some of God's good and wise reasons for the occurrence of these greater goods can be ascertained, and other reasons cannot. The fact that some reasons remain hidden from us does not soundly argue against their existence. The **greater-glory theodicy** is a specific version of the greater-good defense. See **free-will defense**; **theodicy**.

horrendous evil. **Moral evil** or **natural evil** that is especially horrific, shocking, violent, devastating, or the like, and that causes an unusual amount of pain and suffering. See **gratuitous evil**.

hypostatic union. The union of the fully divine nature to a fully human nature in the one person of the **incarnate** Son of God.

immutability (of God). The attribute of God indicating that the perfections of his essential nature (i.e., who he is in himself) cannot undergo change or alteration. Even though God does not change in his essence and character, he is always acting (i.e., he is not static).

immutable, adj. See **impassibility** (of God).

immutable. See **immutability** (of God).

impassibility (of God). The attribute of God whereby he does not suffer pain or loss. God's impassibility also coincides with his **immutability** as well as his immortality (i.e., the divine nature cannot die or cease to exist).

incarnate. See **incarnation**.

incarnation. The doctrine stating that the second person of the Trinity, God the Son, assumed a human nature in addition to his eternally preexisting divine nature so that he might fully reveal the Godhead to his image-bearing creatures and accomplish the work of **redemption** that God the Father sent him to do. Without the incarnation, the redemption of fallen human beings is not possible. **incarnate**, adj. See **hypostatic union; passibility** (of Christ).

moral culpability. See **moral responsibility**.

moral evil. **Evil** that is objectively unrighteous in nature (i.e., sinful), violating the moral character and standards of God, and that is committed by personal, intelligent, and responsible moral creatures (see **moral responsibility**), and that also causes pain and suffering in the world. Adam's disobedience in the garden of Eden brought about the curse of the **fall** in which he passed on a corrupt sin nature to all his progeny (humanity), who are enslaved to moral evil. In addressing the **problem of evil**, moral evil is contrasted with **natural evil**. See **gratuitous evil; horrendous evil**.

moral responsibility. The culpability that one bears for moral choices to which he or she is obligated. One who does good deserves praise or reward. One who does **evil** deserves blame or punishment. Most proponents of **Calvinism** and **Arminianism** believe that some kind of free agency is necessary for moral responsibility. All Christians believe that God bears no moral responsibility for evil that occurs in the world. See **compatibilism; free will; moral evil**.

moral will (of God). God's revealed, instructive will that is rooted in Scripture whereby he establishes, declares, or commands all that is good, right, wise, and true. See **sovereign will** (of God).

natural evil. **Evil** that consists of some adverse condition in the world that does not necessarily proceed from specific moral choices of intelligent creatures but causes pain and suffering nonetheless. Natural evil came about in the cosmos due to the curse of the **fall**. It generally falls into different categories, such as (1) natural disasters; (2) accidents; (3) illness and disease; (4) physical and mental handicaps; and (5) physical toil. In addressing the **problem of evil**, natural evil is contrasted with **moral evil**. See **gratuitous evil; horrendous evil**.

omnipotence (of God). The attribute of God whereby he possesses all the requisite power to do anything unless it (1) is logically impossible (e.g., God cannot make square circles) and/or (2) contradicts his other attributes (e.g., God cannot sin or act unjustly). **Calvinism** claims that God has unrestricted use of his power, whereas **Arminianism** (and other varieties of **free-will theism**) claims that God restricts the use of his power in order to respect the **free will** of his moral creatures. **omnipotent**, adj.

omnipotent. See **omnipotence** (of God).

passibility (of Christ). An attribute of the human nature of the **incarnate** Son of God whereby he suffered pain and loss during his earthly ministry, which culminated in his crucifixion and death. **passible**, adj.

passible. See **passibility** (of Christ).

penal substitution. The work of Christ whereby his suffering and death served as a voluntary, atoning sacrifice made on behalf of guilty sinners in order to pay the penalty incurred by their sin, which in turn satisfies the demands of God's retributive justice and wrath against those sinners. See **atonement; Christus Victor**.

prevenient grace. A doctrine promoted in **Arminianism** that teaches that mankind is morally depraved as the result of our sin nature inherited from Adam, thus placing our wills in bondage to sin, but that God bestows a unique grace on unbelievers that restores their **free will**, thus allowing them to cooperate with or resist further displays of God's grace, especially his saving grace.

problem of evil. The idea that **evil** poses a problem for belief in the existence of God or in many of the traditional attributes associated with the God of the Bible. The problem of evil is usually expressed in the following trilemma: (1) God is all-powerful; (2) God is all-good; (3) yet evil exists. Since most people believe that premise 3 is a given, then premise 1 or 2 seems to be questionable. A **theodicy** is a Christian response to the problem of evil. See **free-will defense**; **free-will theism**; **greater-glory theodicy**; **greater-good defense**; **moral evil**; **natural evil**.

providence (of God). The exercise of God's power in which he carries out his **sovereign will** in history and in the lives of his creatures. According to **Calvinism**, God ensures that everything he has planned from eternity past will come to pass in meticulous detail in space, time, and history, including all the choices of his intelligent creatures. See **compatibilism**; **transcendent Author** (God as).

redemption. With respect to the grand storyline of Scripture, the God-orchestrated movement within history that brings about the restoration of **creation** due to the universal curse brought about by the **fall**. Only God in his sovereign wisdom, power, and grace can redeem the fallen creatures he has chosen as well as the created order that they inhabit. Furthermore, this remarkable work of redemption can be achieved only by the **incarnation** of the Son of God through his atoning death and resurrection. See **atonement**; **theophany**.

Reformed theology. See **Calvinism**.

rising action. The second movement of the plot structure in **Freytag's Pyramid** in which the conflict builds and the plot thickens. Aristotle saw this as an "entanglement" or the tying of a knot.

sovereign will (of God). The particular aspect of God's will, especially as it is understood in **Calvinism**, whereby he decrees (ordains) all events that transpire in space, time, and history, including all the choices of his intelligent creatures. God's **providence** ensures that everything he has decreed will certainly come to pass. The Westminster Confession of Faith states, "God, from all eternity, did, by the most wise and holy counsel of his own will, freely, and unchangeably ordain whatsoever comes to pass" (WCF 3.1). God's sovereign will is usually contrasted with his **moral will**. See **compatibilism**.

theodicy. A term coined by Gottfried Wilhelm Leibniz (1646–1716) that combines the Greek words for "God" (*theós*) and "justice" (*dikē*). A theodicy seeks to provide an explanation for how an all-good and all-powerful (**omnipotent**) God relates to the **problem of evil** in the world. It attempts to justify the ways of God, including how God is exonerated of **moral responsibility** for **evil**. See **free-will defense; greater-glory theodicy; greater-good defense.**

theophany. A special visible (and sometimes physical) manifestation of the presence of God. Theophanies usually occur in unique and important moments in the history of **redemption** to specially chosen individuals whereby God communicates something important to those individuals.

timeless eternality (of God). The attribute of God indicating that he has no beginning and no end and is not confined to a succession of moments in time, but rather is outside of (or transcends) time as the eternal, infinite God. See **transcendence** (of God).

tragedy. A plot type in classical literature in which a story has a bad, unhappy, or unsatisfying ending. Tragedy is contrasted with **comedy.** See **Freytag's Pyramid.**

transcendence (of God). The attribute of God that indicates his incomprehensible uniqueness as the independent, self-sufficient, exalted Lord of all whereby he is distinctly different from all else. He is utterly holy, meaning that he dwells in unapproachable light (i.e., glory), possessing unique attributes that establish an unbridgeable Creator-creature distinction. God's transcendence is not absolute. He draws near to human beings and makes himself intimately known to them, especially in the **incarnation** of the Son of God. See **timeless eternality** (of God); **transcendent Author** (God as).

transcendent Author (God as). A model of God's **providence** that is based on God's attribute of **transcendence** whereby God's providential actions in the world are likened to that of an author of a virtuous story, though it contains both good and **evil.** Since God is transcendent and therefore distinct from his **creation** (e.g., the Creator-creature distinction) and history, then his ordaining of the events of history means that he bears no **moral responsibility** for the evil they contain, especially since that evil contributes to the overall greater goods (see **greater-good defense**) and virtuous goals that he intends for history.

TULIP. See **Calvinism**.

utopia. A term coined by Thomas More (1478–1535) used in a book by that title. *Utopia* means "no place." More, however, meant it to denote a "good place." Subsequently, *utopia* has come to refer to a place in people's imagination that is marked by perfection, a place where people can live in perfect peace and harmony without threats to their blissful coexistence.

will (of God). See **moral will** (of God); **sovereign will** (of God).

SELECTED BIBLIOGRAPHY

Aitken, Jonathan. *John Newton: From Disgrace to Amazing Grace*. New York: Continuum, 2007.

Bavinck, Herman. *Reformed Dogmatics*. Edited by John Bolt. Translated by John Vriend. 4 vols. Grand Rapids: Baker Academic, 2003–2008.

Beeke, Joel R., and Paul M. Smalley. *Reformed Systematic Theology*. Vol. 1, *Revelation and God*. Wheaton, IL: Crossway, 2019.

———. *Pilgrim's Progress*. Updated ed. Abbotsford, WI: Aneko Press, 2014.

Calvin, John. *Institutes of the Christian Religion*. Edited by John T. McNeill. Translated by Ford Lewis Battles. Library of Christian Classics 20–21. Philadelphia: Westminster, 1960.

Carson, D. A. *The God Who Is There: Finding Your Place in God's Story*. Grand Rapids: Baker, 2010.

———. *How Long, O Lord? Reflections on Suffering and Evil*. 2nd ed. Grand Rapids: Baker Academic, 2006.

Carey, S. Pearce. *William Carey*. London: Wakeman Trust, 1993.

Christensen, Scott. *What about Evil? A Defense of God's Sovereign Glory*. Phillipsburg, NJ: P&R Publishing, 2020.

———. *What about Free Will? Reconciling Our Choices with God's Sovereignty*. Phillipsburg, NJ: P&R Publishing, 2016.

Cuyler, Theodore L. *God's Light on Dark Clouds*. Reprint, Carlisle, PA: Banner of Truth, 2008.

Tada, Joni Eareckson. *Joni: An Unforgettable Story*. Grand Rapids: Zondervan, 2001.

———. *A Place of Healing: Wrestling with the Mysteries of Suffering, Pain, and God's Sovereignty*. Colorado Springs: David C. Cook, 2010.

Edwards, Jonathan. "The End for Which God Created the World." In *God's Passion for His Glory: Living the Vision of Jonathan Edwards*, edited by John Piper, 125–251. Wheaton, IL: Crossway, 1998.

Frame, John M. *The Doctrine of God*. Phillipsburg, NJ: P&R Publishing, 2002.

George, Timothy. *Faithful Witness: The Life and Mission of William Carey*. Worcester, PA: Christian History Institute, 1998.

Godawa, Brian. *Hollywood Worldviews: Watching Films with Wisdom & Discernment*. Updated and expanded ed. Downers Grove, IL: InterVarsity Press, 2009.

Hallie, Philip. *Lest Innocent Blood Be Shed: The Story of the Village of Le Chambon and How Goodness Happened There*. New York: HarperCollins, 1994.

Helm, Paul. *The Providence of God*. Downers Grove, IL: InterVarsity Press, 1994.

Hillenbrand, Laura. *Unbroken: A World War II Story of Survival, Resilience, and Redemption*. New York: Random House, 2010.

Lewis, C.S. *The Problem of Pain*. New York: Macmillan, 1962.

Macleod, Donald. *Christ Crucified: Understanding the Atonement*. Downers Grove, IL: InterVarsity Press, 2014.

———. *The Person of Christ*. Downers Grove, IL: InterVarsity Press, 1998.

Milton, John. *Paradise Lost*. Edited by William Kerrigan, John Rumrich, and Stephen M. Fallon. New York: Random House, 2007.

Murray, John. *Redemption Accomplished and Applied*. Grand Rapids: Eerdmans, 1955.

Orrick, Jim Scott. *Mere Calvinism*. Phillipsburg, NJ: P&R Publishing, 2019.

Pink, A. W. *The Sovereignty of God*. Carlisle, PA: Banner of Truth, 1961.

Pinson, J. Matthew. *40 Questions about Arminianism*. Grand Rapids: Kregel Academic, 2022.

Piper, John. *Providence*. Wheaton, IL: Crossway, 2020.

———. *Spectacular Sins: And Their Global Purpose in the Glory of Christ.* Wheaton, IL: Crossway, 2008.

Plantinga, Alvin. *God, Freedom, and Evil.* Grand Rapids: Eerdmans, 1977.

———. "Supralapsarianism, or 'O Felix Culpa.'" In *The Problem of Evil: Selected Readings,* edited by Michael L. Peterson, 363–89. 2nd ed. Notre Dame, IN: University of Notre Dame Press, 2017.

Ryken, Leland. *Triumphs of the Imagination: Literature in Christian Perspective.* Downers Grove, IL: InterVarsity Press, 1979.

———. *Words of Delight: A Literary Introduction to the Bible.* Grand Rapids: Baker, 1992.

Sproul, R. C. *The Holiness of God.* Carol Stream, IL: Tyndale House, 1998.

———. *The Invisible Hand: Do All Things Really Work for Good?* Phillipsburg, NJ: P&R Publishing, 2003.

Tada, Joni Eareckson. *Joni: An Unforgettable Story.* Grand Rapids: Zondervan, 2001.

ten Boom, Corrie. "Guideposts Classics: Corrie ten Boom on Forgiveness." https://www.guideposts.org/positive-living/guideposts-classics-corrie-ten-boom-forgiveness/.

———. *The Hiding Place.* 35th anniversary ed. Grand Rapids: Chosen Books, 2006.

Tolkien, J. R. R. "On Fairy-Stories." In *The Monsters and the Critics and Other Essays,* edited by Christopher Tolkien, 109–61. London: George Allen & Unwin, 1983.

Vlach, Michael J. *He Will Reign Forever: A Biblical Theology of the Kingdom of God.* Silverton, OR: Lampion Press, 2017.

Wellum, Stephen J. *The Person of Christ: An Introduction.* Wheaton, IL: Crossway, 2021.

Welty, Greg. *Why Is There Evil in the World (and So Much of It)?* Fearn, Scotland: Christian Focus, 2018.

Wiesel, Elie. *Night.* Translated by Marion Wiesel. New York: Hill and Wang, 2006.

Witherington, Ben. "When a Daughter Dies." *Christianity Today,* April 2012, 36–39.

Zamperini, Louis, with David Resin. *Devil at My Heels*. New York: HarperCollins, 2003.

Zaspel, Fred. "Reflections on the Loss of Our Daughter." Credo. November 14, 2013. https://credomag.com/2013/11/reflections-on-the-loss-of-our-daughter-fred-zaspel/.

INDEX OF SCRIPTURE

8:10—117
8:15—75
8:19—75
8:32—75
9:7—75
9:12—74
9:14—77
9:14–16—118
9:16—77, 97, 121
9:34—75
9:35—75
10:1—74
10:20—74
10:21—119
10:27—74–75
11:10—74
12:12—116
12:21–23—119
12:23—116, 119
12:29—116
12:30–32—116
14:4—74, 117
14:4–5—116
14:8—74, 116
14:10–12—116
14:13–14—116
14:16—116
14:17—117
14:21—116
14:21–22—109
14:21–29—27
14:23–28—116
14:29—116
15:1–18—116

15:11—117
19:1–2—116
19:4–6—116
19:6—116
33:20—46
33:22–23—46
34:6—200
34:6–7—57
34:7—58
34:29–30—47
34:34–35—47

Leviticus
10:1–2—27
11:44—44
11:45—44

Deuteronomy
27:3—116
28—97
32:4—58

Judges
9:23—39
13–16—85
16:17—85
16:30—85
17:6—7
21:25—7

1 Samuel
2:6–7—52
2:25—27
16:14—39

19:9—39
26:23—58

2 Samuel
11—173
24:16—119

1 Kings
22:2–23—39
22:28—52
22:34—52

2 Kings
17:20—70

1 Chronicles
28:9—30

2 Chronicles
18:19–22—39
20:6—52

Ezra
10:11—72

Job
1–2—77
1:6–19—55
1:8—38
1:18–19—37
1:21—37
1:21–22—55
1:22—37
2:3—38

INDEX OF SUBJECTS AND NAMES

Smith, Walter Chalmers, 47n7
sorrows, borne by Christ, 177
Sproul, R. C., 27, 173
St. Bartholomew's Day massacre, 199
Steinbeck, John, 56
Stewart, James, 87
storytelling, 27, 82–92, 96–97, 99,
    101–2, 109–10, 115–16
  conflict-resolution in, 84, 89, 110
  plot structure in, 85–86, 89–90,
    92, 112, 123, 167
  plot structure in Bible, 112, 123,
    152, 159, 167
  redemption in, 89
  as U-shaped, 85, 89–90, 92n14,
    112, 123, 167
  universal nature of, 83
Stowe, Harriet Beecher, 187–88
suffering, 1, 4–5, 16, 37, 39, 55, 72,
    134, 141, 149, 158, 160–61,
    179–83, 200
  of believers, 166–67, 178–79,
    182, 205
  God's purpose in, 179
  of Jews, 5, 12, 199
  joy in, 200
Superman, 84

Tada, Joni Eareckson, 58–60
Tale of Two Cities, A (novel), 56
Technique of Drama, The (book), 86
ten Boom, Corrie, 201–4, 206–7, 211
Ten Commandments, The (film), 78
Thanos, 84

theodicy
  criteria of, 33, 40, 67
  definition of, ix–x, 15–16, 20, 33,
    40, 63
theophany, 44, 46
Theseus, 125
Thring, Godfrey, 158n13
Tolkien, J. R. R., 64, 66–67, 79, 84–85
total depravity, doctrine of, 24, 28
Toy Story 3 (film), 85
tragedy (in storytelling), 11, 36, 39,
    85–87, 101, 105, 177, 179
Trocmé, André, 200
Trojans, 125
"Turn Your Eyes upon Jesus"
  (hymn), 183
Turretin, Francis, 134n7
Tyndale, William, 171

Uncle Tom's Cabin (novel), 187–88
unconditional election, doctrine
  of, 24
Uriah the Hittite, 173
utopia, 147–48, 162
Utopia (novel), 147

vigilantism, 194

Walls, Jerry, 57
Walt Disney Company, 7
Warfield, B. B., 155
Washington, George, 82
Watanabe, Mutsuhiro, 2–4, 18–19,
    192, 194

ALSO BY SCOTT CHRISTENSEN

Reconciling the existence of God and evil is a conundrum in Christian theology, and a philosophical approach—rather than a theological one—dominates. Turning to the Bible's grand storyline, Scott Christensen examines how sin, evil, corruption, and death fit into the broad outlines of redemptive history. He argues that God's ultimate end in creation is to magnify his glory to his image bearers, most notably by defeating evil through the atoning work of Christ.

"Christensen's interaction with contemporary literature on this topic is both wide-ranging and charitable, and much profit may be gained in considering how he lays out his case.... Highly recommended."
—**Greg Welty**, Professor of Philosophy, Southeastern Baptist Theological Seminary; author, Why Is There Evil in the World?

"Christensen ... remind[s] us that God's wisdom pervades everything he ordains so that the very existence of evil serves his purpose of maximizing goodness and glorifying himself. Of course, Romans 8:28 and other verses say that this is true. But Christensen shows us how it is true, how even in this fallen world we can begin to grasp something of God's light in the midst of the darkness, indeed especially there. I commend this book to readers who seek a serious and thoughtful treatment of this issue."
—**John M. Frame**, Professor of Systematic Theology and Philosophy Emeritus, Reformed Theological Seminary, Orlando

ALSO BY SCOTT CHRISTENSEN

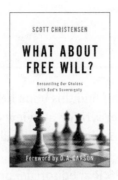

Free will is a complex topic, but the Bible is clear: God's absolute sovereignty exists alongside our free, responsible choices. Only one view, *compatibilism*, fully embraces this truth.

Making a fresh, scriptural case for compatibilism, Scott Christensen explains the issues involved and addresses arguments on both sides. His absorbing pastoral analysis will help you to develop a new appreciation for the role your choices play in God's sovereign plans and to better understand the Bible's views on evil and suffering, prayer, evangelism, sanctification, and more.

"A clear, intelligent, immensely helpful overview of one of the most confusing conundrums in all of theology. . . . Scott Christensen doesn't sidestep the hard questions. The answers he gives are thoughtful, biblical, satisfying, and refreshingly coherent. Lay readers and seasoned theologians alike will treasure this work."
—**John F. MacArthur**, Grace Community Church

Did you find this book helpful?
Consider writing a review online.
We appreciate your feedback!

Or write to P&R at editorial@prpbooks.com
with your comments. We'd love to hear from you.